ROCKHURST COLLEGE LIBRARY

0 0006 0095454 9

P9-CMB-406

DATE

MUTUAL FUNDS
AND OTHER
INSTITUTIONAL INVESTORS

MUTUAL FUNDS
AND OTHER
INSTITUTIONAL INVESTORS
A New Perspective

IRWIN FRIEND

MARSHALL BLUME

JEAN CROCKETT

A Twentieth Century Fund Study

McGRAW-HILL BOOK COMPANY

New York   St. Louis   San Francisco   Dusseldorf   London
Mexico   Panama   Sydney   Toronto

MUTUAL FUNDS AND OTHER INSTITUTIONAL INVESTORS

Copyright © 1970 by The Twentieth Century Fund. All Rights
Reserved. Printed in the United States of America. No part
of this publication may be reproduced, stored in a retrieval
system, or transmitted, in any form or by any means, electronic,
mechanical, photocopying, recording, or otherwise, without
the prior written permission of the publisher. *Library of
Congress Catalog Card Number* 76-128014

07-022456-0

1234567890 MAMM 7543210

HG
4930
F74

7.95

The Twentieth Century Fund is a research foundation which undertakes timely, critical, and analytical studies of major economic, political, and social institutions and issues. Nonprofit and nonpartisan, the Fund was founded in 1919 and endowed by Edward A Filene

BOARD OF TRUSTEES

Adolf A. Berle, *Chairman*

Morris B. Abram
Jonathan B. Bingham
Arthur F. Burns (on leave)
Erwin D. Canham
Hodding Carter III
Evans Clark
Benjamin V. Cohen
J. Kenneth Galbraith
Patricia Roberts Harris
August Heckscher
David E. Lillienthal
Georges-Henri Martin
Lawrence K. Miller
Luis Munoz Marin
Don K. Price, Jr.
James Rowe
Arthur M. Schlesinger
H. Chr. Sonne
Herman W. Steinkraus
Charles P. Taft
David B. Truman

M. J. Rossant, *Director*

90670
ROCKHURST COLLEGE LIBRARY

FOREWORD

THE PAST FEW YEARS have witnessed mounting concern and interest in the growing power of relatively new financial institutions—particularly mutual funds and pension funds. These institutions, which first sparked the cult of common stocks, later attracted public attention to "growth" stocks and created the fashion for instant performance. Innovative and inventive, institutional money managers have ventured into areas where older and more prudent investment men feared to tread, taking positions in the stocks of unseasoned companies, setting up hedge funds, devising new types of securities.

Institutional pools of capital, especially those stressing performance, have had a very definite impact on the traditional structure of the financial community. Institutions have severely strained the machinery of the listed exchanges and brought about changes in the established patterns of buying and selling securities. Their activities have prompted new regulations by the Securities and Exchange Commission, including measures to prevent institutions from gaining access to corporate information that is not available to all investors. Many corporations, fearing possible undue influence on the market price of their shares or on the scope of their operations, favor stricter legislation of the funds. Other institutions, disturbed perhaps by the mediocre results of their own portfolios or awed by the showing of some of the performance funds, have made or talked about making drastic shifts in their own policies.

While Congress, the press, academic journals, and the SEC have all been observing or commenting or criticizing or regulating, virtually no one in recent years has made a comprehensive examination of institutional investment activities. To be sure, the SEC and the New York Stock Exchange have amassed a good deal of data on institutional trading, but research into the longer-term impact of institutional investing on the market and the economy, and analysis, which is essential as a basis for intelligent debate and constructive policy, has been remarkably limited.

Both short-term and long-term questions come under consideration in this new study of institutional investors by Irwin Friend, the Mellon Professor of Finance, and his colleagues, Marshall Blume and Jean Crockett, of the University of Pennsylvania's Wharton School of Finance and Commerce. The study, which in part updates and expands the work on mutual funds conducted by Professor Friend for the SEC in 1962, provides a great deal of fresh and valuable data to scholars, market professionals, lawyers, and regulators. Its analysis of the performance and economic impact of institutional funds may well stimulate more heated debate. Certainly, the study sheds new light on the controversy over mutual fund sales charges, on just how well aggressive institutional managers have performed, and on the effects of institutional purchases on stock and bond prices.

Because The Twentieth Century Fund has a long tradition of sponsoring research on the stock market, its Trustees were pleased to support the work of Professor Friend and his associates. In keeping with another Fund tradition, granting independence to its researchers, the authors of this study are solely responsible for both the facts that they present and their interpretation.

Professor Friend and his colleagues do not pretend to deal with all the many issues raised by institutional investment, but they have made a very useful contribution to our knowledge, as we hope other studies will do. The Fund is grateful to them.

M. J. Rossant, *Director*
The Twentieth Century Fund

PREFACE

THIS STUDY analyzes the implications for the economy as a whole of the increasing importance of institutional investors in the stock market, with particular emphasis on mutual funds. Mutual funds and pension funds carried out the bulk of the new institutional stock investment in recent years and, together with personal trust funds administered by commercial banks, accounted for most institutional stockholdings. However, data for a detailed analysis of the impact of institutional investors on the market and economy are available only for mutual funds. Though the impact of institutional investors on the stock market—a subject which has received widespread attention recently—is analyzed in as much detail as the data permit, it should be noted that our primary interest is not in such market effects per se but in their broader implications for the economy.

The study consists of seven chapters. Chapter 1 discusses the major issues involved in assessing the role played by mutual funds and other institutional investors in the economy, the growing importance of institutional stock investment, the more important findings of past research, and a detailed summary of the new findings of this study. The chapter briefly develops the potential implications of the growth of equity-oriented institutional investment on rates of return to suppliers of funds and the cost of capital to users of funds, on corporate financing and control, on the operational structure of the stock market, on investor welfare, on saving and investment, on economic stability and growth, and most important on the allocational efficiency of investment (discussed at greater length in Chapters 3 and 4). Chapter 2 deals with the trends in institutional and other investment in nonequity assets as well as in stocks and attempts to explain the major changes in the relative yields of the different classes of assets and in the relative importance of these different assets in the portfolios of each of the principal groups of investors.

Chapters 3 to 5, which are closely related in subject matter, analyze in depth the investment performance of mutual funds (Chapter 3), the direct contribution made by the funds to market efficiency (Chapter 4), and the impact of the funds on fluctuations in the market for individual issues (Chapter 5). This material fills in some of the more important gaps in our knowledge of the broad economic impact of institutional investors. These chapters cover not only the investment performance of mutual funds as a whole but also the consistency of performance for groups of funds and for individual funds. They measure the funds' performance in selecting issues which in the long run turn out to be undervalued, assess their ability to predict shorter-term movements in individual issues and in the stock market as a whole, and analyze the degree to which the funds affect individual issues. The extent to which certain funds act as market leaders is also studied. Most of the material presented in these chapters is completely new. They are confined to mutual funds since the necessary data are not available for pension funds, the other major institutional group in the stock market. However, Chapter 6 does present some more limited information bearing on the impact of all institutional investors on trends in market efficiency. The concluding chapter (Chapter 7) considers a number of policy issues pertinent to the regulation of mutual funds and other institutional investors in equity securities.

Much of the material presented in this study represents an updating of the Wharton School *Study of Mutual Funds* (Government Printing Office, Washington, D.C., 1962), the first comprehensive study of the mutual fund industry. (No similar studies have yet been made of pension funds or personal trust funds.) However, several subjects bearing on the economic impact of mutual funds and other institutional investors—notably the changing composition of investor portfolios, the increased importance of institutional stock investors, the effect of mutual funds on market and economic efficiency, and their effect on medium- and longer-term fluctuations in the stock market—are treated in much greater depth. Yet, a number of subjects analyzed in the earlier report are not treated here because of the economic orientation of the present study, inaccessibility of data, and limitations of resources.

Perhaps the most noteworthy omission in view of our extensive coverage of medium- and longer-term impacts of mutual funds on the stock market is the absence of any analysis of the effect of fund activity on very short-term stock market movements. Such an analysis (which was carried out in the earlier Wharton School study) would require access to confidential data. Fortunately, this omission does not seriously hinder an analysis of the impact of mutual funds on the economy as a whole, as distinct from their impact on the day-to-day activity of the stock market. Nevertheless, a number of subjects of considerable interest to the U.S. Securities and Exchange Commission and the financial community (e.g., the impact of block trading on short-term movements in stock prices) are not covered in the present study in view of the absence of the necessary information.

Two other significant omissions from the present study are the absence of up-to-date information on mutual fund control of portfolio companies (companies in the fund portfolios) and on conflicts of interest between fund shareholders and management. These issues and the background data were exhaustively developed in the Wharton School study and were treated again in a more recent SEC report (U.S. Securities and Exchange Commission, *Public Policy Implications of Investment Company Growth*, Government Printing Office, Washington, D.C., 1966). The updating of this information was not feasible without access to confidential data. Again these omissions are not serious for purposes of the present study, both because the available information is not so outdated as the market impact data, which are updated in this study, and because the latter data are much more central to an analysis of the impact of the funds on the economy.

The new information and analysis presented in this study required access to, and processing of, vast amounts of statistical data. Vickers Associates made available to us their invaluable file of quarterly holdings of individual common stocks by individual mutual funds and other investment companies from 1953 to 1968. Other highly useful data on fund activities and on individual stock prices, dividends, and earnings were provided by the U.S. Securities and Exchange Commission and the Standard Statistics Company. We are extremely fortunate to have had the benefit of unusually competent statistical and programming assistance from Stephen Bender, Michael Blum, David Olson, Warren Levy, D. C. Rao, John Shaw, James Wetzler, Paul Weiner, John Wilson, and Mary Wright. Phyllis Hess and Diane Hutson-Wiley did a superb job of controlling the flow of data from original sources to the computer and back again in usable form and in helping us prepare the final manuscript. Gordon Weil and Gnomi Gouldin edited the entire manuscript; Mr. Weil also helped greatly in improving the readability of the summary chapters. We are greatly indebted to all these persons and organizations.

Irwin Friend
Marshall Blume
Jean Crockett

CONTENTS

MUTUAL FUNDS
AND OTHER
INSTITUTIONAL INVESTORS

Chapter One

INSTITUTIONAL INVESTMENT: AN OVERVIEW

THE DRAMATIC GROWTH of institutional investment in equity securities —mostly common stock—has been one of the most publicized and significant economic developments of the past two decades. From an annual rate of $700 million in 1950, institutional purchases of equities ballooned to $12.6 billion in 1968. The preference of money managers for equities has reached such proportions that profound questions are raised about its impact on the investing public, on the stock market, and on the entire economy. How well do the institutional investors fulfill their obligations to the people they represent? Do their trading activities—moving them in and out of specific stocks in massive transactions—contribute to the efficiency of capital markets? How do their investment policies—especially their demand for common stock—affect the growth of the economy?

This study attempts to provide some answers to these questions based on a new and deeper look at the operations of the equity-minded institutions, especially mutual funds.

Role of Mutual Funds and Other Institutional Investors

As students of most elementary economics courses are taught, the common feature of financial institutions is their role as the intermediaries between

1

people who have money to save (and hence to lend to others) and people (or corporations) who need money and must borrow it. Institutions translate savings into investment in productive enterprises.

Because of their size, operating economies, and ability to commit large sums of money for long periods, financial institutions enjoy several advantages. They can usually borrow at lower cost than could individuals, and they can earn higher rates of return for given risk. With the ample resources at their disposal, they can spread the risk inherent in investing far better than most individuals. Some of these benefits are passed on both to the suppliers and to the users of institutional funds. People who place their money in financial institutions in preference to managing it themselves expect to receive a higher return for a given risk. They also benefit from greater investment convenience and liquidity: the ability to turn their investment into cash when necessary. Those who borrow money from the institutions ultimately pay a lower cost for the capital funds they seek than if they obtained the money directly from savers. As a result, investment in the instruments of production becomes more attractive.

Unlike most other financial institutions, mutual funds—and, to a lesser extent, pension funds—specialize in investing in common stocks.[1] Individuals who have extra funds can decide to make direct purchases of stock. But they may find mutual fund shares more attractive, if only because mutual funds can spread their risk over a greater range of securities more easily and efficiently than individual investors. As for pension funds, their equity investments are made with the goal of lowering the amount that employers and employees must contribute while maintaining or even increasing eventual benefits.

Looking at the economy as a whole, the increased demand of institutional investors for common stock should probably lower the cost of raising this kind of capital. This is because there is more money flowing into the market and less need for corporations to pay a high premium in order to induce institutions to buy their shares. At the same time, riskier corporate ventures would probably be stimulated. Of great importance, the increased demand for common stock might raise the average rate of return on the same volume of total investment in productive goods, since on the average riskier ventures are associated with higher rates of return.

Historically, people who have bought common stock have received a big premium for having taken the greater risk of investing their savings in equities instead of fixed-income securities. The closing of this gap between the return on stocks and on bonds might be expected to displace low-risk

---

[1] Mutual funds raise their money by issuing shares that are normally redeemable on short notice at net asset value at the discretion of the shareholder. Pension funds raise money mainly through employer contributions but also through employee contributions; these funds are ultimately paid to employees in the form of retirement pensions.

investment, financed in large degree by bonds, by "riskier" and more profitable investment, financed with equity securities.

From a purely theoretical point of view, it is impossible to determine whether the shift in institutional investment from fixed-interest obligations —like bonds—to purchases of equity securities—common stock—will reduce the cost of capital and hence encourage greater total investment. We do know, however, that business investment (especially corporate) would benefit from this state of affairs more than other kinds of economic investment. In concrete terms, the growth of equity-oriented institutions like today's mutual funds would be more likely to spur investment in plant and equipment than in housing.

The available evidence, admittedly not conclusive, indicates that the real cost of corporate financing has been lower in recent years than at any time earlier in this century. In the bond market, interest rates on all obligations, including the most desirable "high-grade" bonds are, of course, much higher than in the past. But real interest rates—the market rates adjusted for the expected rate of inflation and consequent decline in the dollar's value—have either remained steady or increased only moderately. The evidence also shows that the real rates of return required to raise money through corporate stock issues and through retained earnings, which together account for a higher proportion of total corporate financing than borrowed money, actually seem to have declined markedly in recent years. These trends in rates of return mean that the overall real cost to corporations for raising their needed capital is probably lower now than it has been historically.

Neither theoretical reasoning nor the available evidence indicates, however, whether the growth of institutions investing heavily in common stock has increased total saving and investment in the United States economy.

When institutions shift their investments from fixed-interest obligations to common stocks, it might be expected that corporations would raise more money by issuing stock, greatly increasing new stock issues and soft-peddling the sale of corporate bonds. Actually, no such change has taken place. The volume of new stock issues by corporations—net of their own repurchases and retirements and exclusive of shares issued by mutual funds—has remained relatively small throughout the postwar period and shows no pronounced trend over this period (see Appendix Table 1-3).[2] Even more strikingly, the volume of net new bond issues by nonfinancial corporations grew from $2.5 billion in 1950 to $12.9 billion in 1968, and other corporate debt has also increased substantially.[3]

The reason why corporations did not issue more stock is, in part, the favorable tax treatment of interest they paid on bonds and the corporations'

[2] The tables are placed at the end of the book in the Appendixes.
[3] *Survey of Current Business,* January, 1951, p. 13, and May, 1969, p. 11.

own ability to maintain the desired ratio between their total debt and the market value of their outstanding stock without issuing new stock.[4] The necessary increase in market value was partly achieved by retaining earnings for reinvestment. In addition, the value of the corporate equity base rose simply because the value of the shares outstanding rose in a generally favorable market.

Retained earnings, which are equivalent in effect to the company's issuing more of its own stock, have traditionally constituted the most important source of corporate funds. As a result, they have accounted for the lion's share of total equity financing. When corporations raise their equity funds through retained earnings rather than through new stock issues, the "cost" of equity funds is cut by the amount of the issuance expenses and personal taxes which are avoided. Thus, it comes as no great surprise that the evidence shows that retained earnings have been used as a substitute for new stock offerings.

Yet the virtual absence of any increase at all in net new stock issues in recent years is quite surprising. Perhaps corporate management has been more aware than investors of the much higher historical rate of return on stocks than on bonds (see Chapter 3) but has been less impressed by the need for actually paying such a risk differential between stocks and bonds.

The success of institutional investors as financial intermediaries rests, in part, on their ability to spread the investment risk and thus eliminate any excessive differences between the returns on stocks and on other investments. But once these gaps are eliminated, their success must depend mainly on their efficiency in channeling their money into stocks with the highest rate of return for an equivalent risk. Their contribution to economic efficiency depends to a great extent on their ability to help the equity markets transfer capital into the most profitable investments in productive goods (with due allowance for differences in risk).

The institutional impact on the general level of stock prices may influence not only the market's efficiency in allocating funds but also the level of general economic activity. By affecting the stability of stock prices, the institutions may create expectations which will influence the level of business activity. Excessive speculation and the market's reaction to it can lead to either inflation or deflation in the economy—or both. Such speculative fluctuations in the stock market, unrelated to any change in the actual values of stocks, might unnecessarily increase the cost of funds raised from stock issues and the overall cost to corporations of raising capital. As institutional investors account for more and more stock market activity, they will probably exert an increasing influence on general price movements

[4] See *ibid.* for trend in retained earnings and Appendix Table 1-1 for trend in market value of outstanding equities.

in the market, on the relative prices of different stocks or groups of stock, and on the relative rates of return of all forms of investment.

Mutual funds and other institutional investors in stock may also affect the overall economy through their ownership and potential control of companies whose shares are publicly held. Because institutions are large investors, they may, despite regulatory legislation, accumulate large enough blocks of stocks to exercise a major influence over a corporation's affairs. Much of the public's anxiety about the possible implications of this situation stems from a general dislike of bigness and concentrations of economic power and the fear that institutional investors will ride roughshod over the interests of other shareholders.

The danger to other stockholders which might result from massive institutional ownership of stock in a single corporation takes two forms: First, institutions could have greater access to inside information, because of the size of their investment and their superior resources; with this information, they might be able to act against the interest of other stockholders. Second, institutions usually display their displeasure with management performance by selling their stock rather than by bringing pressure to bear for improvement. Indeed, by acting in this fashion, they have been criticized in many quarters for playing too passive a role as corporate stockholders, because selling out does little to correct or remove inefficient management.[5]

In a sense, these fears are contradictory. Some allege that institutional investors will take advantage of their special position to play too active a role in corporate affairs, while others charge that they do not assume their full responsibilities as shareholders and play too passive a role. There may be little basis for concern about either of these dangers. Institutional investors will probably play at least as active a role as the great number of smaller individual investors whom they displace and who probably did not exercise much control anyway. While it may well be true that institutional investors gain a comparative advantage over smaller investors in acquiring access to corporate information, mutual funds and other members of the institutional fraternity actually enjoy the same kind of advantage that any larger investor has over his smaller co-owner. Presumably, the institutional investor is also subject to the same regulatory safeguards against misuse of insider information as any investor. But the possible need for strengthening these safeguards is discussed later.

The main reason for worrying about increased institutional ownership of corporations is that institutional managers might adversely influence corporate business decisions. If this kind of influence were sufficiently

---

[5] The substantial increase in the turnover of institutional stock portfolios, especially for mutual funds, could be considered as further evidence of their lack of much long-term investment interest in portfolio companies.

widespread, it should be detected by an analysis of the effect of institutional stock investment on economic efficiency. This analysis is a major part of this study.

Finally, the sheer size of stock transactions by institutional investors may conceivably harm both other stockholders in the companies involved and the market in general. Sales of large blocks of stock may severely depress market prices of individual issues and the value of individual holdings. Purchases of large blocks might have the opposite result, with beneficial effects on other stockholders in those companies.

The key issue is whether institutional investors are more likely than small investors to make informed decisions when they buy or sell stock. If there is clear evidence that institutional investors are "wiser" than the rest of the market, then any sharp change in prices which they cause would bring the market price closer to its intrinsic value—a fairer price for future transactions involving the stock. In the process, some individual stockholders might lose their chance to sell their holdings at relatively inflated prices, but there is no valid reason why they should have an opportunity to make such a profit. Their loss would be the gain of new stockholders. But if institutional investors have less insight into intrinsic stock value than the rest of the market, their transactions could make the market less stable, which would be harmful to other stockholders. Thus, a major factor in assessing the impact of institutional sales on general stockholder welfare is the effect of such trading on overall market efficiency, an effect that is analyzed in later chapters.

The large size of institutional stock trades may affect stockholder welfare in still another way. If transactions are large enough, an increasing part of total activity could conceivably be switched from the organized stock exchanges to the over-the-counter market. Such a development would probably be associated with somewhat higher transaction costs for a given volume of activity. There would also be somewhat more erratic short-term fluctuations in stock prices and a reduction in price continuity between transactions. But here again, if middle- and long-term market efficiency are not impaired, the cost is likely to be inconsequential. Moreover, if institutional investment contributes to better market performance in the long run, the economic gains are likely to exceed the economic losses from their activities.

Growth of Institutional Stock Investment

Total institutional stockholdings, including personal trust funds, amounted to at least 34 percent of the total stock outstanding in the United States at the end of 1968, according to the most comprehensive recent data (see

Appendix Table 1-1).[6] The corresponding ratio for shares listed on the New York Stock Exchange—the Big Board—would probably be considerably higher.

Whether stock held in personal trust funds, accounting for 11 percent of outstanding stock, should be considered a part of institutional holdings is questionable. These funds, usually administered by commercial banks on behalf of their beneficial owners, are generally kept separate for investment purposes. Moreover, they are often hemmed in by significant investment restrictions. Yet commercial banks often make the key decisions concerning stock transactions for such accounts and usually exercise voting rights of stock held in such accounts. Virtually no information is available on the stock investment policies for personal trust funds—a gap in knowledge that must soon be filled. Available estimates suggest that for many years the market value of their holdings has represented a slowly increasing share of the value of all stock outstanding.[7]

A more restricted group of institutional investors—private noninsured pension funds and mutual funds—have had the greatest increase in stockholdings, in net stock purchases, and in the volume of stock transactions. They are responsible for most of the overall growth in institutional stock investment (see Appendix Tables 1-2 through 1-4).

The market value of stocks held by these funds rose from $1.1 billion for the pension funds and $1.9 billion for the mutual funds at the end of 1950 to $59.6 billion and $50.9 billion, respectively, at the end of 1968. Their holdings increased far more rapidly than the growth in the market value of all stock outstanding, which went from $150.6 billion to $761.3 billion during the same period, These two groups increased their net stock purchases (purchases less sales) much faster than other groups.

Indeed, for more than a decade pension and mutual funds have made higher net stock purchases than the net amount of stock issued by corporations. This point is graphically illustrated by the events of 1968. In that year, corporate repurchases and retirement of existing stock actually exceeded all new stock issues, but private noninsured pension funds and investment companies (mainly mutual funds) made record net stock purchases of $6.1 billion and $2.9 billion respectively. Other institutional investors—life insurance companies, property and casualty insurance companies, state and local trust funds, and the like—made net purchases of $3.6 billion,

---

[6] These data exclude the holdings of religious organizations and certain other eleemosynary institutions. Shares issued by mutual funds are not included here in the total stock outstanding.

[7] In addition to the data for 1964–1968 in Appendix Table 1-3, see R. W. Goldsmith, R. E. Lipsey, and Morris Mendelson, *Studies in the National Balance Sheet of the United States,* National Bureau of Economic Research, Inc., Princeton, N.J., 1963, vol. II, pp. 120–121 and 314–315.

while foreigners bought a net amount of $2.3 billion. The message inherent in this pattern of purchasing is clear: the remaining sectors of the economy —private individuals for the most part—sold, on balance, the remarkable total of $15.4 billion of stock, exclusive of mutual fund shares. Of particular interest is the behavior of life insurance companies, which hold their assets predominantly in fixed-interest obligations and not in equities, and state and local trust funds, whose total assets have mushroomed. Both have registered a rapid increase in net stock purchases in recent years and have the potential, expecially if investment regulations are eased, for vastly stepping up their rate of equity investment in the future.

Mutual funds have had the money to buy more stock in recent decades, because they have been able to sell more of their own shares. Over any brief period, there may be wide fluctuations in the portion of their new funds that mutual funds channel into the stock market. But the proportion of their assets invested in common stock has always been high, varying from 79.3 percent in 1957 to a high of 86.0 percent in 1967 (Appendix Table 1-5). The even larger increase in stockholding by pension funds reflects both a net inflow of new money and a fairly consistent policy of increasing the proportion of their assets invested in common stock. Their common stock investment rose from 30.2 percent in 1955 to 62.6 percent in 1968 (Appendix Table 1-6). But the proportion of pension fund assets in stock should tend to level off, because they already hold so much stock and because bond yields have become more attractive. Thus, the amount of net stock purchases by both pension and mutual funds will probably depend preponderantly on the inflow of new money. In 1968, net new money inflows into these funds reached new peaks of $8.6 billion for pension funds and $3.0 billion for mutual funds (Appendix Table 1-7). At the same time, the annual rate of inflow as against assets at the beginning of the year was far lower in 1968 than it had been at the start of the 1950s. The dollar rates of inflow have a good chance of increasing moderately over the next few years.[8]

Mutual funds account for a much larger share of stock trading than pension funds (Appendix Table 1-4). Yet they hold about the same dollar amount of stock as the pension funds and in recent years have been accumulating stock at a slower rate. Mutual funds held 6.8 percent of all stock and pension funds 7.8 percent at the end of 1968. But mutual funds accounted for about 12 percent of the value of all trading on the Big Board during the year and 16 percent of all public (non-NYSE member) trading. In contrast, pension funds probably traded only half as much stock in terms of dollar

---

[8] For mutual funds, this statement is based on relating past gross sales of their own shares to personal disposable income, relating redemptions to gross sales and initial assets, and using reasonable projections of income. For pension funds, see Daniel M. Holland, *Private Pension Funds: Projected Growth*, National Bureau of Economic Research, Inc., New York, 1966.

value.[9] In fact, mutual funds may have even been more active in trading in NYSE stock than is apparent from the figures, because they regularly employ other trading channels in buying and selling issues traded on the Big Board.

Mutual funds have had an exceptionally high rate of turnover in their stock portfolio. In 1968, mutual funds had an annual turnover rate of common stock of 46.6 percent, compared with 19.1 percent for the pension funds and 22.3 percent for the Big Board as a whole (Appendix Table 1-8). Trading activity has increased since 1964 for most types of investors, but the mutual funds have outstripped the rest of the pack. Their turnover ratio shot up 150 percent in the 1964–1968 period in contrast to a 50 percent rise in the market as a whole. And mutual funds got started earlier in increasing their turnover than did the pension funds, which did not accelerate their trading until after 1966.

Other institutional investors also boosted their trading activity in recent years more than the rest of the market. Institutions increased their turnover rates further from 1968 to the second quarter of 1969, a time when the overall turnover rate of the Big Board was easing off. The pacesetters in this trend toward more trading were probably the so-called "performance" funds, mutual funds which stress short-term capital gains. Their policy dictates a higher-than-average turnover.

Mutual funds and other institutional investors probably stimulated increases in stock prices during the years of their greatest drive to penetrate the equity market.[10] This conclusion comes from the Wharton study, the only in-depth analysis of the impact of mutual funds on the stock market prior to the present study. The finding is based, in part, on the belief that much of the money flowing into the funds would not have gone into the stock market at all were it not for the growth of the funds and their ability to tap such savings. In addition, institutions have probably been willing to accept a lower rate of return than other investors, because they could di-

---

[9] In estimating the proportion of trading accounted for by mutual funds, the figures for common stock purchases and sales presented in Appendix Table 1-4 were raised by 10 percent for reasons indicated in the note to the table. The allocation between NYSE and other transactions by mutual funds was made on the basis of Investment Company Institute, *Statistical Release No. 48.* The total market value of all transactions on the NYSE (exclusive of U.S. government bonds), which came from the U.S. Securities and Exchange Commission *Statistical Bulletin,* was adjusted downward by 2.5 percent to eliminate the small amount of trading in preferred stock and corporate bonds. The resulting estimate of the relative importance of mutual fund trading on the NYSE is fairly close to an estimate for the first quarter of 1969 by the Exchange on the basis of a survey of member firms (see speech by William C. Freund, "Some Financial Trends in the 1970's," Sept. 26, 1969, mimeographed). The Exchange's estimate for pension funds seems too low, probably because it includes a substantial amount of pension fund transactions in the commercial bank total, which may also be inflated by including a considerable amount of trading in the banks' custodial accounts.

[10] Wharton School of Finance and Commerce, University of Pennsylvania, *Study of Mutual Funds,* Government Printing Office, Washington, D.C., 1962, pp. 21–23.

versify their risk efficiently and this would bolster stock prices. The premise that the funds induced new money to come into the stock market is buttressed by a separate Wharton survey of investors, which found that more than half of a sample group of fund investors in 1962 owned no corporate stock other than mutual funds.[11]

The new findings in this study support the conclusion that the rise in demand for equities by institutional investors over the past two decades has helped push up stock prices. According to the new evidence, pension funds have been a major factor in this development.[12]

Historically, the rates of return needed to attract investment in common stock and the actual return on them have both topped similar rates for fixed-income securities. But institutional stock purchases have reduced this gap, because institutions can diversify their investments and perhaps also because they have better knowledge about what the rate differences actually are and how to take advantage of those differences.

The narrowing of the differences between rates of return of stocks and bonds is highly desirable on economic grounds. But the extent of the long-run impact of institutions on stock prices is not so clear. Other influences at play in the market may have been more significant. The decline in rates of return on common stock in recent years coupled with the rise in bond yields to new highs may already have wiped out the excessive premiums formerly paid for taking the risk of investing in common stock. When institutions invest in common stocks in the future, their success as intermediaries will depend largely on their ability to help the equity markets channel capital into the most profitable investments (taking differing risk into account).

Past Studies of Mutual Funds

Both the Wharton School *Study of Mutual Funds* and, to a lesser extent, two subsequent SEC studies[13] revealed a good deal about the economic performance of mutual funds in the past. (No equivalent studies exist for pension funds or personal trust funds.[14]) These studies also provided many insights into conflicts of interest between mutual fund shareholders and management. While such insights are not a key element in rating the

[11] U.S. Securities and Exchange Commission, *Report of Special Study of Securities Markets*, part 4, Government Printing Office, Washington, D.C., 1963, pp. 273–274.

[12] Pension funds are, of course, the largest institutional net purchasers of stock.

[13] U.S. Securities and Exchange Commission, *Special Study of Securities Markets*, part 4, *op. cit.*, and *Public Policy Implication of Investment Company Growth*, Government Printing Office, Washington, D.C., 1966.

[14] In addition to the data for pension funds analyzed in this study, information is also available on their income and expenditures and insurance coverage but, with unimportant exceptions, not on their investment performance, holdings, and trading in individual securities, or portfolio company control.

economic performance of the funds, they are essential to an appraisal of the "fairness" of fund operations to all who have an interest in them. Conflicts of interest are likely to be more significant for mutual funds, typically managed by an organization distinct from the fund itself and subject to relatively little independent scrutiny, than for pension funds, which are usually managed by a commercial bank under fairly close scrutiny by the organization whose employees are the funds' beneficiaries. For personal trust funds, on the other hand, the extensive interrelationships between the commercial banks which generally administer them and the corporations whose securities are included in their portfolios may result in substantial conflicts of interest at the expense of the fund beneficiaries.[15]

The Wharton study reported that the main problems caused by the growth of mutual funds stemmed from the size of the industry as a whole and not from the size of individual firms, a matter which has been of special interest to Congress. The firm size may be a future problem, because of the potentially great power over the market that could be exercised by a small number of large funds, but size did not appear to be a danger in the early 1960s and did not seem to have caused difficulties then that had not existed earlier.

The two major problems appeared to be, first, the potential conflicts of interest between fund managers and stockholders caused by placing control of fund management in the hands of outside investment advisers and, second, the impact of the industry's growing trading in stocks on stock prices themselves. In fact, only the question of the impact of mutual funds on stock prices is directly relevant to the economic performance of mutual funds. The question of management-shareholder relations is of prime importance for individual investors and thus is of appropriate concern to the SEC and the general public.

How Did the Funds Grow?

Despite the sharp increase in the size of the mutual fund industry and of individual funds between 1952 and 1961, the Wharton study found a decline in the concentration of assets among the largest funds. The proliferation of mutual funds and a big increase in the assets of smaller funds led to this reduced concentration of potential power within the industry. Mutual funds emphasizing common stocks grew more rapidly than the so-called "balanced" funds, which carry a substantial amount of senior securities including corporate bonds, U.S. government issues, and preferred stock in their portfolios. Among the common stock funds, the "growth" funds, which aim at capital gains, showed the most striking rise in total assets. Funds which concentrate on income-producing securities or those with a "mixed"

[15] See *Commercial Banks and Their Trust Activities: Emerging Influence on the American Economy,* vol. 1, Government Printing Office, Washington, D.C., 1968.

policy grew less quickly. Industry sources[16] indicate that the "growth" funds have continued to set the pace in boosting assets through the end of 1968.

The Wharton study also found that individual mutual funds grew faster as sales charges levied on the purchase of new shares went up. Even when funds with no sales charges were excluded, the results were the same. The Wharton study interpreted this situation as illustrating the effect of strong sales inducements on fund growth, especially since there was no evidence that higher sales charges go hand-in-hand with better investment performance. Indeed, the study showed that fund shareholders paying higher sales charges had a less favorable investment experience than those paying less. The faith that mutual fund managers had in sales inducements to promote growth is reflected in the climb in average sales charges between 1950 and 1966.[17] Of the thirty largest funds, fifteen levied a sales "load" of 7.5 percent or less in 1950, and seven charged 8.5 percent or more. In 1966, only seven charged 7.5 percent or less, while eighteen asked for 8.5 percent or more.

The mushrooming growth in plans by which shareholders purchase stock in installments, at least until the mid-1960s, is a further indication of the effect of higher sales charges on fund growth.[18] Big commissions are paid on "front-end load" plans, under which the shareholder pays a large part of the sales charges when he enters the plan. The brakes were applied to the growth of such plans after the mid-1960s, probably as a result, in part, of SEC recommendations that the investment company bill be amended to prohibit the use of such front-end loads in the future.[19] This threat to the plans and the widespread publicity about their disadvantages for investors may have helped to discourage sponsors from putting up the resources needed to sell new plans and investors from entering them.

Mutual fund investors may be growing more sophisticated in their choice of funds by showing increased awareness of the sales charges, or loads, according to the analysis of recent experience in this study. In 1968, for example, the ratio of net sales of mutual fund shares as compared with assets at the beginning of the year (known as the inflow ratio) showed no particular relationship to the size of the sales charges.[20] The slowest growth

[16] Arthur Wiesenberger Services.

[17] U.S. Securities and Exchange Commission, *Public Policy Implications of Investment Company Growth, op. cit.,* p. 208.

[18] See Wharton School, *op. cit.,* p. 6, and Investment Company Institute, *Mutual Fund Fact Book,* 1969, p. 26.

[19] U.S. Securities and Exchange Commission, *Public Policy Implications of Investment Company Growth, op. cit.,* and *Special Study of Securities Markets, op. cit.,* had recommended restrictions on front-end loads even earlier.

[20] The list of funds and the sales charges are those used in the analysis of investment performance in Chap. 3, while the data used to estimate the inflow ratios came from Moody's. The inflow ratios were estimated from the market value of beginning-of-year total assets, end-of-year total assets, and the ratio of beginning- to end-of-year per share assets adjusted for capital changes.

in new investment was for funds with sales charges from 8.0 percent to just under 8.75 percent. Even if the previous performance, risk, and size of the mutual funds are held constant, there is no significant relationship between the inflow ratio and sales charges.[21] This finding for recent years is in sharp contrast with the Wharton study's revelation of a link between high sales charges and high sales growth. Apparently, the appeal of low sales charges now offsets the greater effort made to sell shares with higher loads.

Better performance (higher rates of return for a given risk) did boost sales. And, not surprisingly, the smaller funds grew faster in percentage terms than did the larger ones.

Investment Policy

Mutual funds have always invested most of their assets in stock. Apart from short-run shifts reflecting vacillating attitudes toward the market, they have followed this policy consistently for many years. They have somewhat increased their holdings of common stock while reducing their portfolio of preferred stock. For many years, common stock (mostly of domestic companies) has accounted for more than four-fifths of all their net assets. The rest of these net assets have been in the form of other corporate securities, cash, and similar items. Where there are variations between fund policies in the composition of their portfolios, these differences can be explained by the wide range of investment objectives. For example, balanced funds have had more of their portfolios in senior securities than other funds, though equities were still the majority of their holdings. Smaller funds invest less of their assets in common stock than their bigger brothers even when both groups have the same objective. This may reflect the need of the smaller funds for a minimum amount of cash and similar assets.

Mutual funds have always diversified their investments among many industries. The concentration of their common stock portfolios in a few industries had declined over time.[22] Not at all surprising is the shift in

---

[21] The statistical relationships obtained were

$$F = -3.275 - 0.009S + 3.239\ R_{-1} + 0.279\ \beta - 0.082 \log A \qquad \bar{R}^2 = .29$$
$$\qquad (4.44) \quad (-0.64) \quad (4.75) \qquad (1.20) \qquad (-2.37)$$

$$F = -4.77 + 0.004S + 4.713\ R_{-10} + 0.390\ \beta - 0.119 \log A \qquad \bar{R}^2 = .19$$
$$\qquad (-2.05) \quad (0.28) \quad (2.38) \qquad (1.31) \qquad (-3.32)$$

where F is the inflow ratio in 1968 (related to initial assets), S is the sales charge (as percent of selling price), R_{-1} is 1 plus the rate of return of the fund in 1967 (including captial gains), R_{-10} is 1 plus the annual rate of return for the ten years from 1958 through 1967, β is the beta coefficient with the NYSE price index—a measure of risk—and log A is the natural log of assets (in millions of dollars) at the beginning of 1968. $\bar{R}^2$ is the coefficient of determination adjusted for degrees of freedom.

importance of different industries in the funds' portfolios. Public utilities, including telephone and natural gas, declined from 20.1 percent of the funds' common stock holdings in 1952 to 6.3 percent in 1968. Correspondingly, the position of office equipment, the second largest holding at the end of this period, rose from 1.7 to 9.4 percent. Steel wandered from 2.1 percent in 1952 up to 6.8 percent in 1958 and down to 1.2 percent in 1968, while retail trade moved from 4.8 to 2.2 to 4.0 percent in those years. Oils, the single largest holding in 1968, accounted for 12.8 percent of funds' common stock holdings, somewhat down from earlier years. Financial stocks—banks and insurance and finance companies—accounted for 8.4 percent, also somewhat lower than previously. In comparing the industrial composition of mutual fund common stock holdings with the breakdown of all stock listed on the Big Board in 1968, the funds turn out to hold proportionately less utility stock and more financial stock.[23]

The funds have invested more heavily in the stocks of the larger corporations traded on the New York Stock Exchange than in smaller NYSE issues or issues listed on other exchanges or traded on the over-the-counter markets. But proportionately they held less of the outstanding stock and traded less in these larger issues than in others where a smaller investment represents a bigger share of the total holdings and trading.[24] Stocks listed on the Big Board made up 85 percent of the funds' stock portfolios in 1952 and 81 percent in 1958. In the next ten years, according to estimates made by the Investment Company Institute, this portfolio share remained the same.[25] This stability is surprising in the light of the emphasis by performance-oriented funds on smaller and potentially more volatile issues in recent years. Perhaps it reflects a difference in behavior between the performance funds and the rest of the industry. Another surprising observation in view of the nature of the performance funds is that the "quality" of NYSE stocks held by mutual funds in 1968 seemed about as high as in 1953.[26]

In general, mutual funds carried out a substantial and expanding share of

---

[22] For the 1953–1958 period, see Wharton School, *op. cit.,* pp. 155 and 158; and for 1958–1968, Investment Company Institue, *op. cit.,* p. 35.

[23] See *New York Stock Exchange Fact Book 1969,* p. 23. The NYSE uses a rather different industrial classification from the Investment Company Institute; e.g., what the Investment Company Institute defines as Office Equipment is mainly classified in Electronics, Electrical, by the NYSE, and Natural Gas is combined with Petroleum.

[24] Wharton School, *op. cit.,* pp. 167–169 and 258–262.

[25] *Ibid.,* pp. 183–186 and Investment Company Institute, *op. cit.,* pp. 30 and 32. The ICI results are roughly consistent with an estimate for June 30, 1968, obtained from data on N1Q tapes supplied to us by the SEC.

[26] This conclusion is based on an analysis by Ronald Ofer of the beta coefficients of stock held by mutual funds over the period 1953–1968, showing a moderate rise in risk from the early to late 1950s followed by a corresponding decline to the late 1960s. The beta coefficient, which is a measure of covariability of a stock's return with that of the market, is defined in Chap. 3.

all stock transactions. But their role in specific markets and for individual stocks varied considerably. Recently, they have accounted for a major part of trading activity in many issues.[27] As for their choice of market, the Wharton study indicates that 75 percent of common stock purchases in both 1953 and 1958 were made on the NYSE and 20 percent on the over-the-counter market. In their sales of common stocks, the mutual funds reduced their use of the NYSE; the share of total sales made in that market fell from 84 to 75 percent in the same five-year span. The over-the-counter market and, to a lesser extent, the other exchanges picked up the slack.[28] Unfortunately, more recent and reliable data on market channels employed by funds are unavailable.[29]

Perhaps the most striking change in the funds' investment policy has been the sharp rise in the turnover of their common stock holdings: from 13.1 percent in 1953[30] to 17.6 percent in 1960, 46.6 percent in 1968, and 55.6 percent in the second quarter of 1969. Fluctuating shareholder interest in holding mutual fund shares was not responsible for this policy shift. Redemptions of fund shares as compared with the average assets of mutual funds moved from 5.9 percent in 1953 and 7.8 percent a year later to 6.9 percent in 1967 and 7.9 percent in the following year, hardly indicating a definite trend.[31] In fact, the turnover rate of holdings in mutual funds' own shares was well below the rate for all stocks listed on the Big Board. Apparently, mutual fund shareholders, like small investors generally, are less speculative than others in the market. Higher transaction costs levied on small transactions are probably one key factor in discouraging them from trading more often.[32]

The smallest funds had the highest turnover rate in the five-year period covered by the Wharton study as well as in recent years.[33] Funds managed by advisers affiliated with brokerage firms had high turnover, too, but this may simply reflect their relatively small size. Even among funds of about

[27] Wharton School, *op. cit.*, pp. 262 and 270, and U.S. Securities and Exchange Commission, *Public Policy Implications of Investment Company Growth*, *op. cit.*, pp. 291–292.

[28] Wharton School, *op. cit.*, pp. 184 and 202.

[29] The data available in Investment Company Institute, *op. cit.*, are not useful for projecting trends beyond 1958, since the 1959–1968 estimated breakdown between NYSE and other transactions is based on 1956–1958 information.

[30] The 1953 figure is from Wharton School, *op. cit.*, p. 233, and is computed on a somewhat different basis from the other figures, obtained from Appendix Table 1–8.

[31] Investment Company Institute, *op. cit.*, p. 25.

[32] The trading behavior by small investors generally is assumed to be indicated by the pattern of oddlot transactions. Characteristics of securities owned by different income groups are described in Jean Crockett and Irwin Friend, "Characteristics of Stock Ownership," *Proceedings of the Business and Economic Statistics Section, American Statistical Association*, Washington, D.C., 1963.

[33] See Wharton School, *op. cit.*, pp. 215, 222, and 224–226. The findings for recent years are based on an analysis of 119 funds for each of 1966 and 1967 and 71 funds for 1968. These were the funds that were included among the 136 covered by the investment performance analysis in Chap. 3 and for which turnover was available from the N1R forms submitted to the SEC.

the same size, there was a wide range of turnover policies. In 1966, more than 35 percent of a large group of funds with assets over $10 million had turnover rates below 25 percent, but 29 percent of the group had rates above 50 percent. Two years later, only one-quarter of the group had turnover rates less than 25 percent, while 44 percent of them had a rate above 50 percent. In the latter year, a handful of funds had rates below 10 percent, and 8 percent of the group had a turnover rate above 100 percent.

Institutional Investors and Market Efficiency

No conclusive data are available on the contribution of institutions—except mutual funds—to market efficiency. But we can test if there have been any significant changes in market efficiency over the past decade—a period during which institutional investors grew markedly in importance. To run this test, the ability of the stock market to maintain equivalent rates of return on comparable investments was used as the measure of its efficiency. This ability is required if the market is to facilitate an efficient allocation of economic resources by guiding investment to its most profitable uses. Efficiency itself is measured in terms of medium- and long-run relationships between current prices and later earnings rather than in terms of short-run phenomena.

Despite the greatly increased stock activity by institutional investors, we detect no changes in stock market efficiency from 1958–1960 to 1967–1968. Obviously, in view of the many other changing influences in the market, we cannot conclude from this evidence alone that institutions have had no impact on market efficiency. But their effect has probably not been substantial. Certainly this is supported by the direct evidence for mutual funds.

A useful measure of mutual funds' impact on market efficiency, particularly in the long run, is obtained by analyzing the relationship between their net purchases of individual stocks and later earnings on these issues. To use this purchase-earnings measure, the dollar value of all net purchases of each stock in a year or in a quarter is related to the stock's risk, dividend payout ratio, and the ratio of subsequent earnings to the stock's price at the beginning of the period. For each of the years and quarters selected in the 1954–1968 period, the funds' stock purchases were compared with the ratios of earnings, one to eleven years after purchase, to initial prices. If risk associated with the various stocks as well as dividend payout are held constant, a positive link between stock purchases and this subsequent earnings-to-price ratio (e.g., greater purchases being associated with a higher ratio) would mean that the funds contribute to market efficiency. If this kind of relation did not exist, we could conclude that funds do not contribute to market efficiency.

Mutual funds do not do particularly well or poorly in directing capital into profitable stock investments as determined by this earnings-to-price ratio. Their ability to do so is probably the most relevant single measure of the funds' contribution to the market's efficiency in allocating investment. Yet the funds seem just as likely to invest in a NYSE stock which proves to be overvalued in the light of its later earnings as in an undervalued issue. In fact, funds appear to have bought more stock which in the long run turned out to be overvalued than stock which turned out to be undervalued, though this difference is probably not statistically significant. In one year, 1966, funds tended to buy NYSE stock which then had a relatively favorable earnings record in the next year. But the funds did just the reverse in 1964.

The failure of mutual funds to show any conspicuous ability to choose those stocks which will provide the best subsequent earnings accords with the mixed evidence on their investment performance discussed below. Perhaps the impact of their trading activity on the market rather than their foresight accounted for their somewhat better performance over the past few years compared with the weighted portfolio of Big Board stocks. While the funds do not select stocks with favorable subsequent earnings, except perhaps in the very short run, they may be able to choose stocks whose price-earnings ratios will increase in the long run compared with the market due to a changing evaluation of the risk inherent in those issues. The funds may have an above-average ability to select such stocks, our analysis shows, but apparently not to any significant extent. We have still to explore the further question of the funds' impact on the market, as opposed to their predictive ability.

Investment Performance of Mutual Funds

The usual way of measuring mutual funds' success as financial intermediaries specializing in common stock has been to measure their investment performance, or overall rates of return (capital gains plus dividends), against the market as a whole or at least a major sector of it. Occasionally some, usually inadequate, allowances for differences in risk are made.

The most publicized finding of the Wharton study was that, for the five-year period covered, the average performance by mutual funds was not appreciably better than what would have been achieved by a completely unmanaged portfolio with the same distribution between common stocks and other assets. About half the funds performed better and half worse than such an unmanaged portfolio. When funds were grouped by the number of years in which they topped the average performance, the results appeared completely random.

Much more attention has been focused in recent years on mutual fund performance, in part because of the findings of the Wharton study. Indeed several financial analysts have attributed the cult of investment performance and of performance funds to the public interest in the Wharton results. (These results are updated in Chapter 3.) This study not only carries the earlier analysis through September, 1969, but also uses new stock market data to measure the general market, and the more precise scientific tools to allow for risk that have been developed since the Wharton study.

The earlier analysis of the funds' investment performance also revealed the absence of any significant relationships between performance and turnover rates, sales charges, or management fees. Only a weak link existed between performance and subsequent new investment in the fund. These results implied that fund shareholders did not benefit from high turnover or high management fees and probably suffered from high sales charges (because the performances were rated in terms of the funds' assets rather than as a function of the total investment made by their shareholders). But management clearly benefits from high turnover, sales charges, and management fees. This can mean a conflict of interest between investors and fund managers. (The findings for the 1953–1958 period relating to this potential conflict are reexamined and updated in Chapter 3.)

In this study, mutual fund performance is compared with what could have been achieved by either investing unweighted (equal) amounts or weighted amounts (i.e., weighted in proportion to the value of stock outstanding) in a random sample of all stocks listed on the Big Board. Risk is taken into account by holding it constant in a more satisfactory manner than in most earlier studies. This has been done by keeping constant either the variability of monthly rates of return (closely related to price volatility) or, more often, variations in these rates which parallel movements in the market in general. In evaluating mutual fund performance, the effect of nonequity holdings—like bonds—and of stocks not listed on the Big Board is also given some attention. Most of the analysis covers the period from the beginning of 1960 until mid-1968, but a supplementary analysis extends the coverage to the period from mid-1968 to September, 1969.

Mutual fund investment performance provides more evidence of the funds' ability to provide expert management services to their customers than of their efficiency in helping to channel money into the best investments. A high rate of return on fund shares (appropriately adjusted for risk) may reflect successful forecasting of temporary market fluctuations but may have little to do with underlying, long-run values. This is especially true if the funds' trading affects the stock prices themselves and influences the behavior of other investors. If mutual funds show an above-average investment performance, they might well be contributing to economic efficiency, but we could not be sure of this contribution. However, if they have a below-average performance, the evidence would be stronger that they are contributing to a poor allocation of economic resources. Fund purchases could hardly be expected to drive securities' prices below their long-run values.

The funds' investment performance is, of course, of critical importance to investors, totally apart from its impact on efficiency. Performance is a test of management's investment ability and, after allowing for sales charges, a measure of how investors fared. The funds have usually stressed the potential of professional management for providing the best investment performance.

The overall annual rates of return on investment in 136 mutual funds[34] averaged 10.7 percent for the period January, 1960, through June, 1968 (9.0 percent for the period January, 1960, through March, 1964, and 12.8 percent for the period April, 1964, through June, 1968). Unweighted investment in all stocks listed on the Big Board in the same periods would have yielded 12.4 percent (7.0 percent in the first part and 17.8 percent in the second). Weighted investment in all these stocks would have produced rates of 9.9 percent (9.9 percent in the first part and 9.8 percent in the second). All these rates of return are better than those on random investments in senior securities (short-term government bills, bonds, and preferred stock), which made up about 16 percent of the funds' net assets. But they are lower than rates on random investments in shares traded on the American Stock Exchange and over-the-counter markets, which constituted about 17 percent of fund assets.[35] For the most recent period available—July, 1968, through July, 1969—the average rate of return for the funds was minus 3.8 percent compared with minus 3.3 percent for weighted investments in all stocks listed on the Big Board.[36]

Weighted investment in all NYSE stocks would have therefore resulted in a lower average rate of return than was achieved by mutual funds on their entire portfolio over the 1960–1968 period. (The funds did better in the second half of this period, but not as well in the first half.) In contrast, unweighted investment in all NYSE stocks would have topped mutual fund investments over the entire period. (The funds did better in the first half, but not as well in the second half.) And in the 1968–1969 period, mutual funds generally fared worse than the weighted NYSE results. Even if we adjusted these findings to take into account the percentage of funds' holdings of NYSE stock compared with other stocks and other kinds of securities, the results would probably be about the same.

---

[34] These were essentially all the larger publicly owned funds for which data were available throughout the period covered. The rates of return referred to here are not adjusted for risk.

[35] The overall annual rate of price appreciation on the National Quotation Bureau index of over-the-counter stocks was 15.5 percent for the January, 1960–June, 1968, period compared with 6.7 percent for the NYSE composite price index. For the April, 1964, through June, 1968, period the corresponding rates were 25.4 percent for the American Stock Exchange index, 23.2 percent for the NQB index, and 6.5 percent for the NYSE index. The American Stock Exchange index was not available at the beginning of 1960.

[36] Data are not available for the return on equal investment in each of these stocks over this period.

Not only rates of return but also the associated risks must be considered before we can draw more definite conclusions about the comparative performance of mutual funds and the market as a whole. For this purpose, funds were grouped according to risk. The rates of return over the 1960–1968 period, especially during the last half of this span, were highest for the high-risk funds. But in the 1968–1969 period, these funds had the lowest rates of return.

Much more interesting are the results when funds are compared with random portfolios of the same risk. The higher-risk funds clearly outperformed the weighted NYSE portfolios of the same risk during 1960–1968, especially in the last half of the period. Medium-risk funds also came out somewhat ahead, while low-risk funds did worse. In 1968–1969, the high-risk funds, the only ones for which comparable data on random investments are available, performed less well than the corresponding weighted NYSE portfolio.

All three groups of funds performed worse than unweighted NYSE portfolios during the eight-year period. The performance gap was quite small for the high-risk funds, but fairly large for the others.

Over the past decade, high-risk funds (which include a large proportion of so-called "performance" funds) appeared to have outperformed other funds, even after appropriate allowance is made for differences in return due to risk. In the last year of the decade, however, the reverse was probably true.

A definitive statement on the comparative performance of all funds over the past ten years is more difficult to make. The evidence is reasonably clear that they were surpassed by an unweighted portfolio of NYSE stocks. They probably outperformed a weighted portfolio, but the evidence is not as clear. Both bases of comparison appear in the academic world, but the industry has used only weighted investments in NYSE stocks.[37] If a choice must be made between the two, comparison with the weighted portfolio is probably preferable. Perhaps an even more appropriate basis for comparison is some average of the two measures of random investment performance. This is especially true since the distribution of fund portfolios among different-sized stock issues has tended to fall between the distributions inherent in weighted and unweighted portfolios.

Thus, at present, it is difficult to assess the differences between the funds' investment performances and those that might have been achieved by the various types of random investment in stock traded on the Big Board. The funds' performance compared with a weighted random portfolio appears, however, somewhat better in the 1960s than 1950s—but not in 1968–1969.

---

[37] While the latter is an entirely appropriate basis for comparison if some broad market measures like the NYSE stock price indices are used, the Dow-Jones indices, which are frequently used for comparative purposes, are much less satisfactory.

When funds were classified by fund size, sales charges, management expenses, portfolio turnover, and investment objectives, no consistent relationship was found between these factors and investment performance properly adjusted for risk. To the extent that a relationship exists between performance and sales charges, the funds with the lowest charges, including the "no-load" funds, appear to perform slightly better than the others. The results for the 1960–1968 period show no clear relationship between performance and management expenses, though high-expense funds appear to have an overall edge over the others. (However, in the first half of the period, the low-expense funds performed best, to be succeeded by the intermediate-expense funds in the second half.) Looking at portfolio turnover, there is some evidence that a higher rate of trading activity is linked with better performance in the eight-year period, though the reverse is true in the first four years. In 1968–1969, high management expenses and, to a lesser extent, high turnover seemed to be linked with poor investment performance.[38]

The apparent absence of any consistent relationships between the nonrisk characteristics of mutual funds and their investment performance suggests that, for the industry as a whole, there may be no consistency in the performance of the same fund in successive periods. A more direct test seems to confirm this finding. There is virtually no relation between the average rate of return for a given fund in the 1960–1964 period and its return in 1964–1968, with risk held constant. Of course, some funds may have outperformed the market in more time periods or by larger amounts than could be attributed to chance. But with the available data and statistical procedures, it is impossible to be certain in any specific instance.

Are the riskier funds likely to continue to outperform other funds after appropriate adjustment is made for risk? (This, of course, is different from the question of whether the high-risk funds will continue to have a higher average rate of return than other funds.) The answer depends to a great extent on the relative performance of large and small stock issues, which is mainly responsible for determining the relative success of weighted and unweighted random portfolios. Looking at the 1926–1960 period, the payoff on unweighted portfolios was closer to that of weighted portfolios than in the past decade—and particularly the 1964–1968 period. The speculative psychology of the past few years may have overpriced the riskier and smaller issues or at least may have caused one-shot increases in the ratio between prices and earnings of the smaller and riskier issues. The much

---

[38] The apparent absence of any consistent relationship between mutual fund performance and management expenses or turnover (the latter closely related to commission expenses) may indicate either that fund management is generally able to recoup above-average expenses through somewhat above-average gross portfolio performance or that our tests are not sufficiently powerful to detect the impact of variations in management expenses and commissions on the much larger variation in gross rates of return on portfolios.

more rapid price increases in the 1960–1968 period on the American Stock Exchange and over-the-counter markets and for smaller and riskier NYSE stocks than for larger and higher-quality issues reflect a change in price-earnings ratios applied to various kinds of stocks more than an actual change in their relative earnings. As a result, price-earnings ratios of American Stock Exchange issues and of over-the-counter stocks are now higher than those of issues traded on the Big Board. Thus, the better performance of high-risk funds and of the unweighted random portfolios in the 1964–1968 period may well be a nonrecurring phenomenon.

Some Implications of Mutual Fund Performance

In general, the funds have not matched the performance of the unweighted portfolio of NYSE stock during the 1960–1969 period. But they have matched the performance of the weighted portfolio, and the high-risk funds have even surpassed it, especially in the 1964–1968 period.

Even if this mixed evidence on performance is interpreted as showing that the funds have been no more efficient in their equity investment policy than the stock market generally, the funds have nonetheless served a useful economic function. First, they have provided small investors with a convenient vehicle for spreading risk at a cost that was generally not too high when compared with the alternatives. Second, they raised the average return realized by small investors whose investment alternatives were mainly fixed-interest-bearing assets, like bonds.[39] In addition, the large stock purchases by mutual funds, like those of pension funds and other institutional investors, have helped to narrow the risk differentials between common stock and the formerly much lower rates on other forms of investment.

In view of the present virtual elimination of the high risk premium on common stock, will the intensive selling campaigns of the mutual fund industry and the costs involved in them continue to benefit the economy? This question is especially important if, as the evidence seems to suggest, the funds have been no more efficient in their choice of equity investment than the market in general.

Normally, competition provided by other investment outlets should ensure that the industry's selling efforts do not drive mutual fund stock pur-

---

[39] It is not known how the stocks directly owned by small investors performed in relation to the market as a whole. The only evidence available suggests that in 1960 small investors in publicly owned stock fared fully as well as the rest of the market. (See Irwin Friend and John de Cani, "Stock Market Experience of Different Investor Groups," *Proceedings of the Business and Economic Statistics Section, American Statistical Association,* Washington, D.C., 1966.) However, nothing conclusive can be adduced from evidence for one year.

chases to such uneconomically high levels that common stock would ultimately pay a lower risk premium than is justified by the inherent risk. But the industry's response to competition may well be inadequate, because of the ignorance of purchasers of fund shares and the overwhelming comparative advantage (in knowledge and organization) of the sellers. We shall present later some proposals for making competition more effective.

The performance analysis gave no indication that higher sales charges, management costs, or trading expenses are consistently linked with performance either above or below that of random portfolios. Because no clear payoff results from higher management and trading expenses, a new type of mutual fund with minimal management and trading may be desirable. Such a fund would resemble the fixed or semifixed trusts of former years. These trusts deliberately duplicated the performance of all NYSE stocks or of some other broad range of investments.

This new kind of fund would provide, at a minimal cost, the risk diversification which seems to be the most important continuing service rendered by today's mutual funds. The larger this fund might be, the smaller would be the relative management expenses, and the easier it would be to duplicate the performance of the entire market. Such large funds would become sufficiently well known to the investing public for their shares to be sold at commission rates appreciably lower than the sales loads now charged by mutual funds. Brokerage firms would be obvious sponsors of these new funds, and the same firm might offer several funds, each in a different risk group. Large brokerage firms, which have been reluctant to offer their own funds in view of the possible adverse repercussions that lower-than-average performance would have on their reputation and hence on their other business, would no longer have to suffer from these inhibitions.

Funds which duplicate the performance of the market or some designated part of it will not appeal to those investors who are willing to accept the risks of below-average performance for the chance of better-than-average performance and who believe that professional management will increase their likelihood of success. Although statistical data do not provide us with a clear indication of whether any single fund manager has done better than the market, investors might reasonably prefer, other things being equal, to place their money in those funds which have fairly consistently outperformed the market. For existing types of mutual funds, which charge management fees in return for the expectation of better performance than from a random portfolio, their fees might well be geared to the difference between the fund's and the market's performance (adjusted for risk). This performance gap should be calculated over a long enough period to minimize the probability of overrewarding average or below-average management.

Trading Behavior and Market Impact of Mutual Funds

While the Wharton study provided no dollars-and-cents estimate of the long-run impact of mutual funds on stock prices, it tried to measure the effect of fund purchases on monthly and even daily movements in the stock market as a whole and in specific securities. Some fairly strong indications of short-run effects of fund purchases were found, although the statistical results were not conclusive. Stepped-up purchasing was linked with higher prices, both on a monthly and daily basis. An analysis of thirty of the funds' favorite issues between 1953 and 1958 showed that the funds would usually buy them in two months just before their cyclical rise and would usually sell them in the two months just before a similar downswing. Funds may thus have been partly responsible for the major market movements in these issues, or they may have merely forecast the trends. This might mean that mutual funds have the happy ability to fulfill their own market predictions — that is, to validate their own appraisal of given issues. The Wharton study did not allow a distinction to be made between the actual impact of fund activities and their forecasting ability, but that research gap should be narrowed in this study.

On a day-to-day basis or even on a given day, the Wharton study showed that funds had some ability to stabilize the stock market by acting against the current and immediate past price trends. However, no such relationship exists between their trading and longer-term price movements. When the market reached a turning point, the funds' discretionary behavior — their net stock purchases after the effect of new money has been taken into account — would usually stabilize stock prices at the low points and would do the reverse at the highs.[40] The key points of this analysis, dealing with funds' contributions to economic efficiency and market stability, are updated and greatly refined in Chapters 3 through 5 of this study.

As might be expected, the Wharton study found that the average size of mutual fund transactions in the stock market was much greater than for other investors. No new data are available to update the 1958 figures on the size of fund transactions. But the NYSE has tabulated the volume of transactions involving 10,000 shares or more since the last quarter of 1964. Such

[40] In a much more recent analysis published in Investment Company Institute, *op. cit.,* pp. 33–37, the institute states that mutual funds have "followed a generally consistent pattern [of stabilization] in every major market crisis on record since the end of World War II." The evidence presented, which relates to the major market declines from 1946 to 1966, indicates that the funds tend to buy, on balance, during these periods. To a considerable extent, of course, this simply reflects the investment of new money from sales of their own shares. It is interesting to note that in nine of the time periods of market decline for which complete data were presented, the net money inflow to the mutual funds exceeded their net portfolio purchases, so that for these nine periods the discretionary behavior of the funds might be considered destabilizing.

transactions, in which mutual funds are likely to be involved, rose from 3 percent of NYSE volume at that time to 15 percent in the third quarter of 1969.

Does the funds' short-run trading behavior contribute to the market's short-run efficiency? Can we assess the funds' ability either to predict or cause short-run movements in the general market and in the prices of specific issues? To distinguish between predictive ability and market impact, we look at the rates of return on specific issues bought by mutual funds and later sold after being held for different periods.

An analysis of the relationship during the 1953–1969 period between all funds' quarterly and monthly purchases and sales of common stock and overall price movements on the Big Board during the same period and the preceding and subsequent periods fails to indicate that the funds' trading (with or without an adjustment for the new money they received from the sale of their own shares) leads stock market price movements. In fact, they may well follow monthly market movements. Different results might be obtained for periods of less than a month, but no recent data are available to test this hypothesis.[41] Funds do not seem either to step up or to slow down their purchases when market price levels are particularly high or low in comparison with the following year's average prices. In other words, fund purchases and sales do not appear to be related to subsequent price fluctuations in the general market.

The funds might be able to anticipate or influence short-run price fluctuations of specific stocks compared with market price movements, though they cannot predict or cause monthly or quarterly movements in the market itself. Their total investment performance is, of course, a combination of these two abilities, one relating to the timing of stock purchases generally and the other to their selection of specific issues. Tests of the ties between fund purchases of certain stocks and their relative price behavior in 1958–1959, 1964–1965 and 1966–1967 suggest that fund purchases of a specific NYSE stock in any quarter are associated with an increase in that stock's return compared with the market as a whole in that same quarter. However, this tendency may not be statistically significant. Less evidence exists of any link between purchases and price behavior in the following quarter. If we may conclude from these findings that funds either predict or influence short-term price movements of specific stocks compared with the market, this effect is probably limited to the same quarter.

We looked in greater depth at the link between purchases of specific stocks by the funds and other management investment companies and price changes in these issues for the last quarter of 1967 and the first three months

[41] In Wharton School, *op. cit.*, covering 1953–1958, the correlation between net stock purchases by mutual funds and general stock price movements was somewhat higher on a daily than on a monthly basis.

of 1968. This analysis included both Big Board and American Stock Exchange issues. Investment companies tended to purchase those issues which they had bought in the preceding quarter or which performed well in that quarter or in the quarter of purchase. They tended to sell those issues which they had sold or, to a lesser extent, purchased in the preceding quarter, where they had big initial holdings of these issues or when these stocks performed poorly in the period when the sale was made. Thus the investment companies probably followed market trends in their purchases and, to a much lesser extent, in their sales. But we cannot say whether the investment companies caused the discernible relation between their own purchases and price movements in the same quarter or anticipated these movements or reacted to them.

The predictive ability of mutual funds as distinguished from their market impact for the years 1958–1959, 1964–1965, and 1966–1967 can be examined more satisfactorily through an analysis of the rates of return on specific NYSE issues in relation to the market price over three-, six-, twelve-, eighteen-, and twenty-four-month periods after the date of purchase. The rates of return over these different periods were also computed separately for stocks held by funds from four to six months and those held for seven months or longer. The prices of stocks purchased by mutual funds usually rose in relation to the overall market after the purchase was made and then fell as much as they had risen. This pattern of increase and subsequent decrease took place even more rapidly in 1966–1967 than in the earlier periods. This evidence appears to support the hypothesis that the funds' trading activity affects prices rather than the theory that the funds predict short-term market movements. It also bolsters the belief that their trading activity does not help stabilize the market.[42]

Mutual fund trading has its most marked effect—in first raising and then depressing prices—on the high-risk NYSE stocks, which include some of the smaller, less seasoned companies listed on the Big Board. In view of this effect on NYSE stocks, the funds' trading activity in American Stock Exchange and over-the-counter stocks would presumably have even more impact, these stocks usually being smaller and less seasoned issues than those on the NYSE. But we did not have enough data to test this presumption.

Thus, we conclude that mutual funds have little or no influence in stabilizing stock prices, except possibly in the very short-run.

Portfolio Company Control

The Investment Company Act of 1940 limited the shareholdings by a mutual fund in any one company to an amount not more than 5 percent

---

[42] Destabilizing activities by the funds may reflect in part the fact that a number of fund managers seem to follow the investment behavior of their more successful colleagues. Some evidence in support of this follow-the-leader behavior is provided later in this study.

of the fund's assets and 10 percent of the outstanding voting securities of the company. These limits apply to three-quarters of the fund's total assets.[43] The main reason for these limits was to assure that the fund would have a diversified portfolio. The desire to prevent excessive control of a single company was clearly less important. One-quarter of the fund's assets were exempted from the limits in order to encourage investment in small companies.

If a mutual fund (or other diversified management investment company also covered by the act) owns more than 5 percent of a company's outstanding stock, that firm is defined as an "affiliated person" of the fund. If it qualifies for this classification, most transactions between it and the fund require prior SEC approval.

The Wharton study found that in September, 1958 (the most recent date for which comprehensive data are available), no mutual fund had holdings anywhere near the limits prescribed by the act or by state laws. In only one case in 1958 did a fund or a group of affiliated funds own a majority interest in a portfolio company. Only thirty-nine holdings were large enough (in most cases 10 percent or more of the voting stock) to provide a potential for controlling the company's management. Of these holdings, the bulk were held by medium-size funds. Thirty-one were held by four mutual funds or affiliated groups with assets of $150 million to $300 million. But the largest fund systems did own many large holdings, allowing them some degree of influence on company management short of outright control, which itself was rare. Holdings of 1 percent or more of company voting stock by funds or groups of affiliates rose from 752 at the end of 1952 to 1,503 on September 30, 1958, while holdings of 5 percent or more went from 74 to 183 in the same period.

The Wharton study also revealed that most fund managers demonstrated their approval or disapproval of company management and policies primarily by buying or selling their stocks rather than by attempting to initiate or even participate in a movement for change. But funds, especially the larger ones, have influenced company management simply through the potential effect of the funds' investment decisons on the price of the company's securities. In addition, the fund managers have some influence just because of their continuous personal contact with company management. While this contact serves mainly to provide the funds with valuable investment information, it also enables company executives to get the views of the fund managers.

The Wharton study concluded that neither the extent nor the character of mutual fund influence on portfolio companies as of late 1958 warranted serious concern. The relatively passive stockholder role played by the funds was consistent with their basic objective of optimizing the interests of their

[43] Wharton School, *op. cit.*, pp. 24–27, and U.S. Securities and Exchange Commission, *Public Policy Implications of Investment Company Growth*, *op. cit.*, pp. 294–298 and 307–311.

shareholders. The funds were no more—and probably less—passive than the large number of smaller investors they replaced.

Mutual funds acquired a good deal more large, but not controlling, common stock holdings after 1958, and some played more active stockholder roles, according to the 1966 SEC study of *Public Policy Implications of Investment Company Growth.* But there was no widespread departure from the funds' earlier policy of demonstrating their attitude toward company management by buying or selling shares rather than by trying to change management or its policies. This study also concluded that the relationships between the funds and the companies whose stock they held (except for the special problem of mutual fund holding companies) did not create dangers requiring new legislation.

Could other stockholders be harmed by the funds' greater access to inside information resulting from their larger holdings? Neither the Wharton nor SEC studies considered this question. But the typical fund performance revealed by these earlier studies and our new study suggests that the funds have not benefited much from any inside information they acquired.

Conflicts of Interest

Mutual funds, like other businesses, offer a potential battleground for conflicts of interest between the shareholders and management. But conflicts may be more acute in mutual funds than in business generally. First, the typical fund shareholder is more vulnerable, because he has a smaller investment and lower income and is less well-informed than stockholders as a whole. Second, the unusual structure of the mutual fund industry may limit the usefulness of normal institutional arrangements for safeguarding stockholders' interests. Most funds are controlled by outside investment advisory firms. On some major matters—especially management fees, portfolio turnover, the disposition of commission income generated by this turnover, and inducements offered for selling shares—the interests of the outside adviser in increasing the size of the fund and the amount of management expenses may diverge sharply from the interests of the fund's shareholders, who naturally seek the best possible return on their investment. Thus there can be a clash between the advisers who are seeking profits through fund transactions (for example, from commissions) and investors who are seeking profits from these transactions (for example, from gains in value of fund shares).

According to law, the fund's board of directors and management must try to enhance the shareholders' interests even if in conflict with the adviser's. But practice may not be in line with legal rules. The board normally consists of a majority of directors affiliated with, or directly or indirectly selected by, the adviser. A specified number of unaffiliated directors is required by the Investment Company Act of 1940, but these may include personal friends, relatives, or business associates of the adviser. Fund management, even more than the board of directors, is completely dominated by the adviser.

Do these potential conflicts in fact result in moves by investment advisers and those linked to them that harm shareholders to any significant extent? The 1962 Wharton study and two later SEC probes in 1963 and 1966 attempt to answer this question.[44] The Wharton study found that, in 1960, four out of five funds set their management fees, regardless of the size of the fund, at about 0.5 percent per annum of average net assets. Fees were set in this way even though the adviser's operating expenses were generally lower per dollar of assets managed when he had more funds under his control. And the advisers usually charged mutual funds higher management fees than they charged other clients with the same amount of money to handle. These fees also topped the actual management costs of mutual funds operated without the help of outside advisers.[45] The relatively high rates charged the funds by their advisers did not reflect, moreover, any more extensive or expensive services provided or any better investment performance resulting from the advice. In spite of the high rates charged by many advisers and the below-average performance of many funds, at the time of the Wharton study very few boards of directors, if any, gave serious consideration to changing their advisers or cutting fees on their own.

These findings show that the special structure of the mutual fund industry, involving a close relationship between the outside adviser and management, could weaken the bargaining position of fund shareholders when it comes to setting advisory fees. But this does not mean that shareholders paid higher fees than they would have incurred if they themselves bought the services of some other investment adviser. They simply did not benefit from the lower charges that they might have expected as a result of having pooled their resources in a mutual fund.

The advisory fee rate structure, according to the 1966 SEC study, did not change much between 1960 and 1965. The 0.5 percent fee remained prevalent. Funds with assets topping $100 million on June 30, 1965, and with outside management had an average rate of 0.45 percent, with more of these funds above this rate than below it. The 1965 management expenses of these funds were almost double those of internally managed funds—those without outside advisers—of comparable size. Their charges were also much higher than the fees charged by banks for managing the investments of pension and

---

[44] Wharton School, *op. cit.,* pp. 27–36; U.S. Securities and Exchange Commission, *Special Study of Securities Markets,* part 4, *op. cit.,* pp 144, 148, 192, and 201, and *Public Policy Implications of Investment Company Growth, op. cit.,* pp. 11, 16–17, 23, and 208.

[45] Management fees for the funds with external advisers were also less flexible in relation to size of assets managed than rates charged other clients or than management costs of funds without advisers.

profit-sharing plans. The SEC study attributed the very minor slippages from the traditional flat 0.5 percent fee mainly to the pressures generated by the Wharton study and to shareholder litigation.

The Wharton study pointed out that conflicts of interest can arise between fund shareholders and investment advisers about just how much effort should be devoted to selling shares. Obviously the adviser benefits from continued growth in the fund's size. But the shareholder may get nothing out of this growth unless the management fee rate drops or investment performance improves as a result of greater size. Despite this apparent failure of additional sales to benefit shareholders, the 1966 SEC study found that fund management placed heavy emphasis on selling fund shares. The average sales charge (in percentage terms) rose between 1960 and 1966, and the entire increase went into higher dealer commissions. Fund managers apparently encouraged front-end load plans, at least until the mid-1960s, through their much higher sales charges. These sales charges were especially high for the many investors who paid their charges at the outset but dropped out of the plan before it was completed.[46] The rapid growth in sales under these plans did not appear, to the SEC, to result from any special advantages of the plans, but rather from the massive selling efforts of the plans' sponsors. At the same time, a great many investors seemed ignorant of the plans' costs and of other investment alternatives.[47]

Potential conflicts of interest can also arise between management and shareholders over the way in which the funds hand out their brokerage business. Where management is affiliated with a broker, this broker tends to get a large share of the fund's trading—and the commissions involved. Since investors could obtain valuable services through the judicious use of brokerage, the resort to an affiliated broker without receiving some compensating service to the fund shareholders is open to question.

More often, however, management is not affiliated with a broker. Then, management will typically use its brokerage business as a reward to dealers who sell the fund shares. In 1960, for example, when independent dealers made $100 in fund sales, the larger funds rewarded them with about $1 in brokerage commissions from fund trading, a "reciprocity ratio" of 1 percent.[48] In later years, individual funds paid some dealers as much as an added 5 percent of the dealers' sales of their shares.[49] This compensation must be added to the normal dealer's fee which is part of the sales charge

---

[46] For a sample group of investors purchasing front-end load plans in 1959, one out of every six paid an effective load of 50 percent. U.S. Securities and Exchange Commission, *Special Study of Securities Markets, op. cit.,* part 4, pp. 191–192.

[47] *Ibid.,* pp. 139–146.

[48] Wharton School, *op. cit.,* pp. 32–33.

[49] U.S. Securities and Exchange Commission, *Special Study of Securities Markets, op. cit.,* part 4, pp. 217–218, and *Public Policy Implications of Mutual Company Growth, op. cit.,* pp. 165–166.

borne by the investor. It took the form of either direct brokerage business or credits through "give-up" transactions, in which brokers actually carrying out trading orders are instructed to pay other brokers some fraction of the commissions they receive. For the larger funds, the give-up was usually 60 percent.

The widespread use of brokerage business as a reward for selling fund shares is potentially harmful to fund investors. The desire of fund advisers to use brokerage in this way may lead them not to use the distribution of their brokerage business as a way of obtaining investment advice or other services of greater benefit to the funds than sales of their shares. The pressures to trade stock simply to generate commissions may result in excessive trading and may be at least partly responsible for the skyrocketing turnover of the mutual fund industry's portfolios in the past decade. Fund managers may even refrain from trading in those markets where transaction costs are lowest for the transfer of large blocks of securities. In this connection, the 1966 SEC study found that funds made much less use than did other institutional investors of the "third" market—the over-the-counter market in listed issues, which has no minimum commissions and thus cannot provide give-ups. The SEC study also points out that mutual fund reciprocity and give-up practices may tempt dealers to base their recommendations not on their customers' interests but on the amount of brokerage and give-ups received.

The dangers inherent in the use of brokerage as compensation for selling fund shares may be decreased as the Big Board's commission rates are made more competitive and as volume discounts increase. But, so long as commission rates are not fully competitive in all markets, turnover rates remain high, and fund managers can choose among a variety of markets, the dangers to shareholders will remain.

Both the Wharton study and the two SEC studies concluded that existing mechanisms are inadequate for protecting shareholder and public interests in cases of conflicts with fund advisers. Current safeguards include required reports to shareholders, shareholders' voting rights, the legal obligation to select some independent directors, limitations on transactions by "affiliated persons," and the existence of some (mainly nonprice) competition. In spite of these protective mechanisms, the studies found that there was inadequate competition in the mutual fund industry in management fees, in sales charges, and in doling out brokerage business.

The Wharton study, while refraining from making specific policy recommendations, suggested that more than a mere strengthening of existing mechanisms might be needed to protect fund shareholders more adequately. Several more sweeping methods for handling conflict of interest were examined. The industry might be restructured to require a direct fiduciary relationship between shareholders and controlling managers.

This link could be created by eliminating the outside investment adviser and making management itself responsible for investment decisions. Or the advisers could be required to sell shares themselves in a fund which they managed or controlled. Another reform would be direct regulatory control of selling charges and management fees. But the Wharton study[50] questioned the desirability of any of these proposals. The reduction or elimination of some of the rigid brokerage commission rates was suggested as a more limited but more satisfactory approach.

The SEC, as a result of the Wharton studies and its own work, asked Congress in 1966 to enact three new proposals to correct the most troublesome conflicts of interest in the mutual fund industry. First, all compensation received by any person affiliated with a mutual fund (or other registered investment company) would have to be "reasonable" by certain standards. Second, the maximum sales charge by mutual funds would be 5 percent of their net assets value, with the SEC having the right to change it. Third, future sales of plans involving front-end loads would be prohibited.

These SEC proposals have been considerably modified both by the congressional committees considering the new legislation and by the Commission. In the bill passed by the Senate and under consideration in the House of Representatives during 1969, the first proposal was transformed into an affirmation of the fiduciary responsibility of investment advisers, but the requirement was added that, in any legal adjudication of management fees, appropriate weight should be given to the approval of such fees by directors and shareholders. The 5 percent ceiling on sales charges was eliminated, and instead the National Association of Securities Dealers was given the power to fix "reasonable" sales charges, subject to general SEC review. Finally, the burden of heavy sales charges on investors in the early years of front-end load plans would be eased, but sponsors would still be permitted to sell these plans.

Some Policy Issues

The rapid growth of institutional investment in equities raises three policy issues: First, should any steps be taken to curb this growth in view of its possible distortion of the level and structure of stock prices? Second, should any restrictions be placed on the institutions' trading practices or on their control of portfolio companies? Third, are new measures required to protect shareholders or other beneficiaries from harmful conflicts of interest with institutional managers? Our study provides some answers to these questions in the concluding chapter.

---

[50] *Op. cit.,* pp. 35–36.

Chapter Two

TRENDS IN INSTITUTIONAL
AND PERSONAL INVESTMENT

THE FINANCIAL ASSETS of American investors have grown rapidly in the post-war period. Total financial wealth is estimated to have more than tripled between 1950 and 1967, according to Federal Reserve System data. While estimates of the value of corporate stock are subject to a wide range of uncertainty,[1] both SEC and Federal Reserve System sources suggest that the growth rate for equity securities has been considerably larger than for financial assets generally. The value of stockholdings (including mutual fund shares) increased sixfold over the 1950–1967 period, according to the Federal Reserve *(Flow of Funds)* data, as compared with an increase of 5½ times for mortgages and time deposits in institutions other than commercial banks, a fivefold increase for municipal obligations and time deposits in commercial banks, a fourfold increase for corporate and foreign bonds, and very low growth rates for U.S. government securities, which increased by less than 50 percent, and for demand deposits, which less than doubled. As a result, by 1967 stockholdings accounted for more than a quarter of all financial wealth, as compared with a seventh in 1950.

The growth in stock value, unlike that in other assets, arises only to a

---

[1] In part because an extremely high proportion is held by the household sector, for which accurate records are less readily available than for institutional investors, and in part because price information is very incomplete for over-the-counter stock.

limited degree from new issues. It largely represents a rise in the price of existing issues, reflecting both the growth in earnings on equity—due in large part to the reinvestment of corporate net saving, but also to the inflationary trend in output prices—and the substantial rise in price-earnings ratios that occurred over the postwar period.

Five asset classes—corporate stock, corporate and foreign bonds, municipal obligations, mortgages, and U.S. government securities—which are all predominantly long-term in nature[2]—have accounted for about half of all financial assets since 1950. Time and demand deposits plus currency account for another 16 to 19 percent. Appendix Table 2-1 shows the variation over the postwar period in the relative importance of each of these assets expressed as a proportion of all financial wealth.[3]

In addition to the substantial rise in the share represented by corporate stock, time deposits have risen from 7 to 11 percent of the total and mortgages from 6 to 10 percent. Municipal and corporate bonds have registered modest gains from 2½ to 3½ percent and from 4 to 4½ percent, respectively. Demand deposits plus currency declined sharply (from 12 to 5½ percent), as did U.S. government securities (from 21 to 9 percent).

The exceptionally high growth rate for corporate stock was supported in part by an impressive increase in the wealth of certain institutions with a special preference for stock investment—pension funds, which grew fourteenfold over the 1950–1967 period, and mutual funds, which increased 18½ times—and in part by an increase in the weights attributable to stock in the portfolios of all the major investors in this asset. (Appendix Tables 2-2 through 2-10 examine the composition of the portfolios of selected investor groups over the 1950–1967 period.) For pension funds and life insurance companies the rise in portfolio weights was much more than proportional to the overall rise in the relative importance of stock (from less than 20 to 60 percent for pension funds and from 3½ to 7 percent for life insurance companies). For other insurance companies and for households (including personal trusts and nonprofit institutions) the rise in portfolio weights was less than proportional to the overall increase in the relative importance of stock. For these latter investor groups the change was largely a passive conse-

---

[2]Only in the case of U.S. government securities is there a substantial short-term component, amounting to 30 to 40 percent of the total over the period covered.

[3]The categories included in total financial wealth are monetary reserves; demand deposits (net of interbank deposits) and currency outside banks; time deposits at commercial banks; time deposits at other savings institutions; insurance and pension fund reserves; U.S. government securities (net of holdings by federal trust funds); state and local government obligations; corporate and foreign bonds (net of holdings by nonfinancial business); corporate stock (net of holdings by nonfinancial business); mortgages on residential, commercial, and farm properties; consumer loans; security loans; bank loans not elsewhere classified; other loans; trade credit; equity in noncorporate business; and miscellaneous. Mutual fund shares are included in the totality of corporate stock for present purposes, though they are excluded from this total in other chapters.

quence of the increased price of existing holdings, rather than a result of net purchases. In fact households, in spite of substantial acquisitions of mutual fund shares, sold corporate stock on balance during the 1960s.[4]

Mutual funds, perhaps because the extremely high proportion of their portfolios initially invested in stock left little room for increase, showed the smallest rise in portfolio weight, and none at all since 1954. This is in marked contrast to pension funds, which—in addition to an impact on stock values resulting from the very rapid growth in their total resources—had a further impact arising from a large increase in the portfolio weight which they assigned to stock. Thus, their total influence on stock values over this period presumably was even larger than that of mutual funds. Furthermore, the mutual funds contribute to the supply as well as the demand for stock, since their shares serve to some extent as substitutes for other low-risk shares in household portfolios.

It is of some interest in this connection that, in statistical analysis, the proportion of total financial wealth held by pension funds was found to contribute negatively and very significantly to an explanation of long-run trends in the earnings yield on stock while the proportion held by mutual funds was not statistically significant. There is some indication, however, that the relative growth of mutual funds may influence long-term movements in measures of stock yield that depend primarily on annual capital gains. (The shorter-term stock market effects of the operations of mutual funds, which are more clearly evident, are discussed in Chapters 3 through 5.)

Interrelationship of the Markets for Corporate Stock and Long-term Debt Assets

Corporate stock competes with corporate bonds in the portfolios of pension funds, mutual funds, and life insurance companies; with municipal securities in the portfolios of other insurance companies and households, where the tax advantage of these securities assumes importance; and with U.S. government securities quite generally. There is some competition with mortgages in the portfolios of life insurance companies; but—much more important in terms of the magnitudes involved—there is competition in the portfolios of households with time deposits in savings and loan associations and mutual savings banks, and thus indirectly with mortgages.

The two financial intermediaries, savings and loan associations and mutual funds, have generated their own rapid growth by providing types of

[4]According to the SEC and Investment Company Institute data presented in Appendix Tables 1-3 and 1-7, net new issues of stock (excluding mutual fund shares) amounted to $8½ billion over the seven-year period from the end of 1960 to the end of 1967, while sales less redemptions of mutual fund shares amounted to $13 billion. Households, even after allowing for their absorption of mutual fund shares, disposed on balance of about $17 billion in corporate stock, amounting to about four-fifths of total new issues.

assets which are particularly attractive to households and thus diverting the resources of households in the one case into mortgages and in the other case into corporate stock, to a considerably greater extent than this would otherwise have occurred. Until recently, the savings and loan associations appear to have been the more successful of the two, with time deposits in institutions other than commercial banks rising from 8 to 12 percent of households' portfolios over the 1950–1967 period. While stock rose from 33 to 45 percent of households' financial assets in the same period, this phenomenon does not reflect net purchases but simply a failure (perhaps due in part to inertia) to dispose of stock as rapidly as the value of initial holdings rose. It was associated with some net disposition of stock by households who were disenchanted with the high price-earnings ratios to which the competition of institutional investors, in conjunction with a general reevaluation of risk and of growth prospects, had pushed the market.[5] This is not to deny, of course, that households' net sales would undoubtedly have been much larger except for the inducements afforded by mutual fund shares.

Thus, the markets for the five predominantly long-term asset classes— corporate stock, corporate bonds, municipal bonds, U.S. government securities, and mortgages—are interrelated and cannot be fully understood in isolation from each other. In addition to the five stockholding investor groups which have already been mentioned, the following are important elements in the markets for the four competing assets: commercial banks, savings and loan associations, mutual savings banks, and state and local governments.[6] Appendix Tables 2-11 through 2-15, based on *Flow of Funds* data, show the changes over the 1950–1967 period in the relative importance of the relevant investor groups as holders of corporate stock and of each of the four competing long-term assets.

Corporate stock (including mutual fund shares) continues to be held predominantly by households, though their proportion declined from 91 to 84 percent. The share of pension funds rose from 1 to 6 percent and that of mutual funds from 1½ to 4½ percent.[7] For corporate and foreign bonds, the major holders are life insurance companies and, recently, state and local government trust funds and pension funds, with the share of the first de-

---

[5] It should be noted that institutional investors, because of their greater ability to diversify, presumably require a lower risk premium for stock investment than households, except perhaps for those in the highest wealth brackets.

[6] Mutual savings banks and state and local government trust funds also hold small, but in the latter case rapidly growing, amounts of stock.

[7] SEC data give a similar picture for 1950 but attribute a considerably smaller growth rate to the holdings of the household sector (and thus to total holdings). Using these data, the proportion of stock held by households in 1967 is substantially lower (78 as compared with 83 percent of the total, excluding mutual fund shares), while the proportions held by pension funds and mutual funds are somewhat higher (7 and 6 percent, respectively, as compared with 6½ and 4¾ percent). For mutual funds the SEC data (but not the *Flow of Funds* data) include the estimated assets of nonmembers of the Investment Company Institute.

clining sharply and those of the latter two rising sharply. For municipal securities, the major holders are households and commercial banks. The most notable trends are a decline in the share held by state and local government trust funds (which obtain no tax advantage from these securities) and an increase in the share of non-life insurance companies and, since 1960, of commercial banks.

For U.S. government securities the major holders (outside of the Federal Reserve Banks, which have accounted for a tenth to a sixth of the total) are again households and commercial banks. The proportions held by corporate nonfinancial business, life insurance companies, and mutual savings banks have declined, while relative holdings of state and local governments have risen. For mortgages, the major holders are savings and loan associations, life insurance companies, commercial banks, and mutual savings banks. The share of savings and loan associations rose sharply, while relative holdings of life insurance companies and commercial banks declined moderately.

The attractiveness of stock to investors depends in part on the relative yields of the four competing assets. The relative yield for each of these assets is in turn affected by shifts in the relative supply of the asset (the amount outstanding as a proportion of total financial assets), shifts in investors' tastes for the asset, and shifts (due to growth rate differentials) in the relative importance of those investors specializing in the given asset.

Perhaps the most significant development in the markets for the four long-term debt instruments over the 1950–1967 period was the sharp decline in the relative importance of U.S. government securities (from 21 to 9 percent of all financial assets). This was associated with a precipitate decline in portfolio weights for government securities in the insurance sector and in mutual savings banks, a pronounced switch to stock occurring in the case of pension funds, to mortgages and stock in the case of life insurance companies, to municipals and stock in the case of other insurance companies, and to mortgages in the case of mutual savings banks (see Appendix Tables 2-2 through 2-10.) For households and commercial banks the decline in portfolio weights for governments was more moderate. The switch was to time deposits in institutions other than commercial banks and to stock in the case of households and to mortgages, municipal securities, and short- and intermediate-term loans to business and consumers in the case of commercial banks. The relatively small decline in the importance of U.S. government securities in the portfolios of state and local governments was balanced by an increase in time deposits and in holdings of corporate bonds.

Other notable trends were the increases in the relative supply of mortgages (from 6 to 10 percent of all financial assets) and of municipal securities (from 2½ to 3½ percent of all financial assets). The first was absorbed in part through exceptionally rapid growth in the resources of savings and loan associations and in part by the higher portfolio weights assigned to mortagages by commercial banks, life insurance companies, and mutual savings banks. The increase in relative supply of municipals was accompanied by a decline in the taste of state and local governments for these securities. In response to these two developments there was an increase in the relative holdings of commercial banks and insurance companies other than life.

Asset Yield Relationships

Statistical analysis indicates that the yields on the five long-term asset classes considered here, as well as on the two classes of time deposits, can to a considerable extent be explained by some combination of the relative supply of the given asset, the relative financial wealth of principal holders (the percentage of total financial assets owned by these holders), and investor tastes. Investor tastes are assumed to follow a smooth time trend and also to vary cyclically—with the taste for demand deposits rising in periods of prosperity, as transactions requirements increase, and falling in periods of recession. It was further hypothesized that an asset's attractiveness to investors might be affected by the variance in that asset's yield over the preceding five years. However, such variance measures did not often prove useful in the regressions fitted.[8]

For bonds and mortgages the yield to maturity as ordinarily computed provides a reasonably good measure of the return required by the market on these assets. The yield on corporate stock may be measured in a number of different ways. One alternative which is frequently used is the dividend yield plus the percentage capital gain over some appropriate time period (in the present case, one year). We refer to this as the realized single-period return. While it is reasonable to suppose that the expected value of this variable corresponds closely to the rate of return on equity which is required by the market at a given time, the variable itself is highly erratic, to a considerable extent reflecting purely random fluctuations in stock prices.

A second alternative, the earnings-price ratio, which is much less volatile, proved more susceptible to statistical explanation. Under certain simplifying assumptions, it may be shown that the earnings yield is approximately proportional to the expected value of the realized single-period return, if the risk premium required for equity investment is constant or slowly changing at a constant rate. The factor of proportionality will be less than unity if the risk premium is declining at a steady rate and if the market incorporates the persistent capital gains from this source into its expectations

---

[8] In the relationships explaining portfolio weights for stock which are discussed subsequently, the five-year variance in earnings yield is significant for some investor groups, especially households, but not for others.

for the future, since this will tend to raise current price in relation to current earnings. If, as seems plausible for the postwar period, the required risk premium is declining at a rate which itself decreases fairly rapidly, reflecting the narrowing gap between stock yields and bond yields, then capital gains from this source will decline over time, and the earnings yield may be expected to rise gradually, in relation to the expected value of single-period realized return. In this case the factor of proportionality is an increasing function of time.[9]

Appendix Table 2-16 shows the most satisfactory of the relationships obtained to explain asset yields.[10] The variable used to reflect cyclical variations in investor tastes is the ratio of the money supply to GNP, which measures the overall ease or stringency of credit and tends to influence the general level of yields, while the other explanatory variables have their major impact upon relative yields.[11] As the transaction demand for cash balances rises or falls cyclically, in relation to the money supply, this induces an opposite shift in the demand for other financial assets. In periods of financial ease, when the money supply is high in relation to GNP, the increased demand for income-bearing assets reduces their yield, so that the relationship of yield to the monetary variable is expected to be negative. Since, in the period studied, the ratio of money supply to GNP contains a fairly strong time trend, as well as a cyclical component, it is generally desirable in the statistical analysis to express this variable as a deviation from its trend. This is done in order to avoid attributing to monetary ease or stringency the effects of other taste shifts occurring gradually over time. As a result, the coefficient of time in the relationships presented incorporates all the trend components of taste shifts, whether these are related to increasing monetary stringency, the increasing convenience of holding certain types of assets, changing perceptions as to the risk characteristics of particular assets, or other considerations.

[9] The argument in this paragraph is developed mathematically in Appendix 2: Note.

[10] Annual data are used, and relative supply and relative financial wealth of principal holders are as of the end of the year and are derived from *Flow of Funds* data. Stock and bond yields are from Standard and Poor's *Security Price Index Record*. The stock yield used is the ratio of current year earnings to average price in the current year. Bond yields are annual averages of weekly data representing the mean or median yield to maturity for a sample of bond issues. Yields on time deposits in commercial banks are taken from the *Annual Report* of the Federal Deposit Insurance Corporation. For other time deposits, yields are taken from the *Combined Financial Statements* of the Federal Home Loan Bank Board and refer to savings institutions other than commercial and mutual savings banks. For mortgages, yields are based on secondary market prices for FHA insured mortgages and are taken from Jack Guttentag and Morris Back, *New Series on Residential Mortgage Yields*, National Bureau of Economic Research, Inc., New York, 1970.

[11] Money supply is the sum of currency plus adjusted demand deposits. GNP is in current dollars. The annual ratio is the average of four quarterly ratios based on seasonally adjusted data.

The variable most useful in explaining the earnings yield on stock is the relative financial wealth of pension funds (lagged one year to avoid problems of statistical bias). The effect is negative, since an increase in the relative importance of these funds, which specialize in stock investment and presumably require a lower risk premium than the average stockowning household, favorably influences the demand for stock and therefore tends to depress yield. The pension fund variable remains significant (though erratic in magnitude) in spite of the introduction of a number of additional variables, including several alternative types of time trends. On the other hand, the relative financial wealth of mutual funds (lagged), which might be expected to have similar effects, is never significant. This result is not changed by substituting SEC data on the total assets of mutual funds (or of all investment companies) for the *Flow of Funds* series. The (lagged) relative financial wealth of pension funds and mutual funds combined, the variable used in the first two regressions of Appendix Table 2-16, does not perform quite as well as pension funds alone but is preferred in terms of the underlying logic.

The monetary variable, when combined with the relative wealth variable, is significant or close to significant whether it is expressed as a level or as a deviation from its trend. The correlation obtained is considerably higher (and the regression coefficients quite different) in the former case, but this relationship is not shown in view of the probability of confounding monetary stringency with other effects. Results are worsened when the monetary variable is lagged half a year.

The relative supply of stock does not contribute to the explanation of the earnings yield when the quantity of stock is measured in terms of market value. However, if the quantity of stock is defined independently of its price, in terms of the command over earnings that the outstanding volume of stock represents, then the resulting measure of relative supply is positively related to earnings yield and improves the correlation obtained.[12]

There is some reason to expect a declining trend in stock yields during the postwar period, even apart from the increasing importance of institutional investors. It is reasonable to suppose that the real rates of return required on stock have declined for all types of investors, as the record of continuing postwar prosperity has unfolded and expectations have solidified for a continuing high rate of national economic growth interrupted only briefly by minor recessions. As previously indicated, this decline in the rate at which equity earnings are capitalized leads to capital gains on

---

[12] For this purpose the quantity of stock was measured by normalized earnings (a three-year average of actual earnings) multiplied by a constant price-earnings ratio (specifically, the average ratio over the postwar period).

stock over and above those related to earnings growth. It is further reasonable to suppose that the rate of decline in the required risk premium must taper off as the shift to a new level of expectations is completed and that a lower limit to this risk premium is set by the premium required for corporate bonds (which presumably has also been declining for similar reasons, though to a very much smaller extent).

The decline in risk premiums has, of course, been offset to a considerable extent, particularly in the later years of the postwar period, by the rise in the pure interest rate resulting from increased monetary stringency and the increasing prevalence of inflationary expectations, which require a rise in the nominal interest rate in order for the real interest rate to remain constant. Thus, except for the effects of continuing growth in the relative importance of institutional investment, the required return on stock investment might well have shown an upward trend in the latter part of the postwar period, reversing the earlier downward trend. As previously indicated, the earnings yield may be expected to rise in relation to the required return on equity investment when the rate of decline in the risk premium for stock investment (and the capital gains resulting from this decline) begins to taper off. Thus the argument for a reversal of trend holds more strongly for the earnings yield than for the required return itself.

When a monotonic time trend is included in the earnings yield regression, it is invariably positive and increases the correlation substantially. The apparent effect of the relative financial wealth of pension funds (or pension and mutual funds combined) is also greatly increased, as responsibility for that part of the initial decline in the required return on equity which is in fact due to reduced perceptions of cyclical risk is apparently assigned to this variable.

Turning now to the alternative measure of stock yield, the single-period realized return, the relative financial wealth of mutual funds is occasionally found to have a significantly negative effect but is quite sensitive to the other variables included in the relationship. In this case the change in the ratio of money supply to GNP has a significantly positive effect on yield. This is not inconsistent with the previously observed negative effect of the ratio upon the earnings yield. Under the hypothesis that monetary ease in the current and previous three quarters (by increasing the demand for income-bearing assets) has a favorable effect on stock price, the capital gains component of the single-period realized return will depend on the change in monetary ease from the previous to the current year. The highest correlation was obtained by introducing current and lagged values of the ratio of money supply to GNP as separate variables, rather than by utilizing their difference, but in this case the coefficient of the lagged value is not significant. The values of the monetary ratio in the second quarter of the current and previous year or in the third quarter of the current and previous year also gave relatively good results.[13]

Somewhat more satisfactory results were obtained for interest-bearing assets than for stock yields. The monetary variable, even when expressed as a deviation from its time trend, has a significantly negative effect on U.S. government and corporate bond yields. The relative supply variable is significant in explaining the yields on municipal bonds, corporate bonds, mortgages, and time deposits in savings institutions other than commercial and mutual savings banks. In the case of mortgages the best results are obtained when relative supply is lagged one year.

The relative financial wealth of savings and loan associations contributes significantly to the explanation of mortgage yields (especially when lagged one year), while that of commercial banks is significant or close to significant in regressions explaining yields on both U.S. government and municipal bonds. The strongest influence on time deposit yields is a large and persistent positive time trend, reflecting both the increasing competition for funds among those institutions providing such deposits and, in the case of time deposits in commercial banks, a general tendency for the ceilings on deposit yields to increase over the postwar period. The significantly positive time trends for U.S. government and corporate bond yields appear to be entirely due to increasing monetary stringency, since they disappear when the ratio of money supply to GNP is not measured as a deviation from its trend.

Determinants of Portfolio Weights

Substantial insight into the investment behavior of the various holders of financial assets can be gained from an analysis of the changes over time in the portfolio weights which they assign to particular asset classes. The market impact of these investor groups arises not only from the growth in their total resources but also from shifts in their asset preferences.

---

[13] Typical of the regressions obtained are the following:

$$\text{RSTK} = 13.21 + 499.959 \log \frac{\text{MGNP}}{(\text{MGNP})_{-1}} \quad \bar{R}^2 = .363$$
$$\qquad\qquad\quad (3.0) \qquad\qquad\qquad\qquad DW = 1.88$$

$$\text{RSTK} = -0.59 + 438.395 \log \text{MGNP2} - 411.414 \log (\text{MGNP2})_{-1} \quad \bar{R}^2 = .462$$
$$\qquad\qquad\quad (3.5) \qquad\qquad\qquad\qquad (-3.3) \qquad\qquad\qquad DW = 2.23$$

where RSTK is obtained by adding dividends in the current year to the capital gain from the fourth quarter of the previous year to the fourth quarter of the current year and dividing this sum by stock price in the fourth quarter of the previous year; MGNP is the average of the quarterly ratios of money supply to GNP for the current year and is expressed as a deviation from its time trend; and MGNP2 is the ratio for the second quarter only. The subscript -1 designates the value of the variable in the previous year.

For a single investor or investor group, the sale of one type of security in order to purchase another, with an attendant shift in portfolio weights, is most likely to be motivated by an improvement in the relative yield of the second asset.[14] But such a shift in yield is only a proximate cause of investment behavior and must itself be traced back to (1) a prior increase in the relative supply of the asset, or (2) a prior decrease in the relative attractiveness of the asset to particular holders, or (3) a prior decrease in the relative importance of those classes of holders with special interest in the asset, as a result of differences in the growth rates of the aggregate financial assets of different holders. This last is equivalent to a change in the weighted average of investor tastes which characterizes demand over the market as a whole.

In the aggregate the impact of changing yields on portfolio weights is ambiguous. If the yield on a particular asset rises because new issues have increased the supply, with other considerations constant, then the portfolio weights for that asset must rise for investors generally as the new issues are absorbed. However, if the yield rises because of a decline in investors' taste for the asset, with supply factors constant, then the market value of the asset will fall as holders offer to sell it, while the market value of alternative assets will be bid up, and portfolio weights for the given asset will generally decline. The basic market forces which ultimately govern changes in portfolio weights, as well as in relative yields, are shifts in the relative supply of the various assets, shifts in investor tastes, and differential growth rates of portfolios among holders. For the five long-term asset classes analyzed here, these underlying factors are themselves largely unaffected by the current portfolio decisions of particular investor groups—a highly desirable property from the point of view of avoiding bias in the statistical relationships fitted.[15]

Statistical relationships explaining the portfolio weights of corporate stock for the five major holders are shown in Appendix Table 2-17. Relationships explaining the portfolio weights of other long-term assets for these five investor groups, as well as other holders, are shown in Appendix Tables

---

[14] Other motivations include a change in the holder's taste for one or both of the assets. A favorable shift in tastes might arise from increased information, greater convenience of acquisition, or a more favorable evaluation of the quality of the asset in terms of risk or other relevant characteristics of the subjective probability distribution associated with the future income stream.

[15] The quantity of a given type of long-term asset (when properly defined so as to be independent of its current price) is almost entirely determined by past decisions as to real capital formation and financing methods. A shift in portfolio weights—occasioned, say, by a change in the tastes of some investor group—might affect the asset's current yield, with modest implications for new issues in the current year. However, the impact on the relative supply of the asset would be minimal. In other words the short-run supply curve is approximately vertical, and shifts in demand will have their impact almost exclusively upon price.

When the quantity of stock is defined in terms of market value, rather than command over

2-18 through 2-25.[16] For the four long-term debt assets, portfolio allocations were found to depend strongly on the relative supply of the given asset, while occasionally the relative financial wealth of principal holders also proved useful. For stock, shifts in taste (both long-term and cyclical) were the major factor affecting portfolio weights. The combined relative financial wealth of pension funds and mutual funds, lagged one year, had a significantly positive effect on the portfolio weights of stock for most holders. This variable is closely related to the rising price trend for stocks that has tended to push portfolio weights upward quite generally. In four cases relative supply, lagged one year, was helpful.

Frequently, results were improved by introducing the relative yield of a closely substitutable asset or the relative supply of such an asset. The substitution relationships between particular pairs of assets are much stronger for some investor groups than others, and the last-mentioned variables are helpful in indicating these substitution patterns.

The relative supply of particular assets, the relative financial wealth of particular investor groups, and the relative yield variables all frequently displayed strong time trends. When, in spite of the presence of one or more such variables, a significant time trend persists in the portfolio weight relationships, this suggests a gradual shift in the taste of the particular investor group for the given asset. On this basis it appears that the taste for corporate stock of pension funds and life and perhaps other insurance companies was rising over the period. Such a rise might be attributed to a changing perception of the degree of cyclical risk involved in stock investment, as the record of postwar business stability gradually unfolded, and to increasingly firm expectations of a continued inflationary trend in output prices, raising the prospects of earnings growth from this source. In the case of life insurance companies and pension funds regulatory changes in the permissible extent of stockholdings may also account in part for the rise.

---

earnings or some other concept independent of market price, the relative supply variable must be lagged one period in order to keep it independent of current portfolio decisions, since the latter may affect current price as well as portfolio weights.

The effect of current portfolio decisions on the relative financial wealth of particular investor groups is also expected to be small. To a very minor extent, an unfavorable shift in the tastes for mortgages of some investor group, leading to a rise in current yield, might affect the relative financial wealth of savings and loan associations or mutual savings banks by permitting them to offer higher time deposit yields (in the absence of an effective ceiling of these yields). Of somewhat more serious proportions might be the effect on the relative financial wealth of pension or mutual funds of an increase in stock prices arising from a favorable shift in the demand of some investor group and associated with a general increase in portfolio weights for stock. To avoid the possibility of statistical bias, lagged values of the relative financial wealth of these institutions have been used in relationships explaining yields or portfolio weights for stock.

[16] The relationships obtained for savings and loan associations, which have little flexibility in their investment policies, were not generally satisfactory (due to high autocorrelation of residuals) and are not shown.

There is some indication of an increasing interest in the mortgage market by commercial banks and perhaps by life insurance companies—in the latter case, primarily in properties other than one- to four-family residences. Mixed trends show up in the market for municipal bonds: negative for households, life insurance companies, and state and local governments; positive for other insurance companies and commercial banks, both of which obtain tax advantages from the holding of these securities. The decreasing taste of households for municipals may perhaps be attributed to an increasing interest on the part of high-income individuals in growth stocks with low payout, which offer a relatively attractive combination of risk and before-tax return, even though their tax advantage is smaller than that of municipals. Furthermore, in the interests of diversification, these individuals may have been shifting to such other assets as real estate.

Other insurance companies and state and local governments show an increasing interest in corporate bonds. At the same time pension funds and life insurance companies show negative trends in this market, perhaps reflecting the increased attractiveness of corporate stock to both institutions and of mortgages to life insurance companies. In the market for U.S. government securities there is a strong negative time trend in the holdings of pension funds, and there may well have been unfavorable shifts in taste for other investors, as well, though the high correlation between time and the relative supply of governments makes it difficult to isolate these trends through regression analysis. Both types of insurance companies, pension funds, and mutual savings banks showed disproportionately large declines in portfolio weights for this asset.

Corporate Stock. The postwar market for corporate stock has been characterized by relatively modest growth in supply—whether measured in terms of new issues or in terms of overall growth in the earnings accruing to equity. This has been accompanied by a very substantial upward shift in demand, which may be attributed in part to a shift in tastes within investor groups, for reasons previously discussed, and in part to a change in the mix of investor groups making up the aggregate demand for stock, with an increase in the relative importance of such investors as pension funds and mutual funds for which stock investment is particularly attractive. The first of these demand factors is not readily measurable, but we have attempted to approximate it in statistical analysis by some kind of time trend, while the second may be measured by the relative financial wealth of pension funds and mutual funds combined.

The rise in stock prices resulting from this rapid growth in demand (relative to supply) appears to be the dominant force affecting portfolio weights for stock in the period studied. Just as an increase in the relative supply of an asset (with tastes constant) is almost certain to be reflected in a general rise in portfolio weights as the new issues are absorbed, so also a favorable shift in tastes tends to increase portfolio weights, as price is bid up causing the market value of the asset to rise more rapidly than that of assets generally. Portfolio weights will, of course, be most strongly affected by the price rise for those investor groups for which the increase in the asset's relative attractiveness is most pronounced, while other investor groups, if they do not share the favorable shift in tastes, may sell off their holdings as price rises in order to maintain the portfolio weight unchanged (or may even reduce it in response to the decline in yield associated with rising price).

For pension funds and non-life insurance companies, either time or the relative financial wealth of pension and mutual funds (lagged one year to avoid statistical bias) is found to have a positive and highly significant effect on the portfolio weight of stock. When both variables are introduced simultaneously, significance levels are greatly reduced and erratic results obtained. For the non-life insurance companies, the relative wealth variable performs better than the time trend. For life insurance companies, time but not the relative wealth variable is significant, while for mutual funds the relative wealth variable is significantly positive and the time trend negative (especially when combined with the relative wealth variable). As previously indicated, the rise in stock prices has not been associated with an increase in the weight of stock in the portfolios of mutual funds since the very early years of the period studied, which suggests that any favorable shift in tastes has been considerably weaker than for the market generally. For households the relative wealth variable is significantly positive, but the time trend insignificant.

Relative supply, when the quantity of stock is measured in the preferred fashion in terms of command over earnings, is not useful in explaining portfolio weights for stock. When the quantity of stock is measured in terms of market value, the resulting relative supply variable, which must be lagged one year to avoid serious problems of statistical bias, is significant or fairly close to significant for all holders except life insurance companies. The interpretation of this variable is not entirely clear, since it incorporates not only variations in the preferred measure of relative supply but also the increase in the price paid for each dollar of earnings as a result of the demand shifts discussed earlier. In large part, therefore, it serves as a substitute for a time trend or for the relative financial wealth of pension and mutual funds in reflecting the upward shift in demand. It is not useful in combination with the relative financial wealth of pension and mutual funds but performs better than the latter in the case of households.

The shift in demand for stock associated with cyclical variations in monetary stringency is also an important determinant of portfolio weights for stock. The ratio of money supply to GNP (measured as a deviation from its time trend) has significantly positive effects for all holders except life insurance companies (where it is close to significance), but especially for households, which show considerable inertia in their response to short-run price movements. In general, stock prices tended to rise substantially in postwar periods of monetary ease. In part this is the expected result of the increased demand for income-bearing assets generated by a relative over-supply of money. In part monetary ease and rising stock prices may be disparate results of a common cause. To the extent that the topping out of a boom is associated with a decline in stock prices (either because growth expectations, at least for the near term, are adjusted downward or because of the monetary stringency frequently associated with such periods) and to the extent that this decline generates a further cumulative decline, over-shooting a reasonable adjustment to the initial cause, a subsequent recovery of stock prices may be expected. This may coincide with a period of monetary ease engendered by the recession which follows the topping out of the boom.[17]

The variance in the earnings yield on stock over the previous five years might be expected to affect unfavorably investors' tastes for stock through its impact on their perception of the riskiness of stock investment. This variable was found to be significantly negative in regressions explaining the portfolio weights of stock for households, pension funds, and non-life insurance companies, and close to significance for life insurance companies.

The substitution patterns between stock and alternative assets are indicated by the significance of appropriate yield ratios in the portfolio weight regressions either for stock or for the alternative asset. Yield ratios involving a three-year average of the dividend yield plus the percentage capital gain on stock were generally more useful in the stock regressions than those utilizing the earnings yield on stock. However, some bias exists in the first case (tending to increase significance), since any upward movement in current stock prices for whatever reason will tend to increase both portfolio weights and the capital gains portion of the stock yield variable. This bias is somewhat mitigated by the use of an average of the current and two preceding years. (The earnings yield measure used here relates current year earnings to stock price in the last quarter of the previous year and so is not affected by current price.) It is of some interest that in explaining portfolio weights for the alternative assets, ratios involving the earnings yield on stock are somewhat superior.

For households and non-life insurance companies, there is some indication of substitution between stock and both U.S. government and municipal securities, regardless of which stock yield measure is used. However, the measure incorporating capital gains brings better results. For pension and mutual funds there is evidence of significant substitution between stock and both U.S. government and corporate securities when the latter measure of stock yield is used, though for pension funds the yield ratios lose their

---

[17] This pattern is consistent with events observed in 1954, 1958, 1960, and perhaps in 1967.

ROCKHURST COLLEGE LIBRARY

significance when combined with other useful variables. When the earnings yield on stock is used, the only significant substitution found is that between corporate securities and stock for mutual funds. For life insurance companies there is evidence of substitution between stock and mortgages, whichever stock yield measure is used, but in this case the earnings yield performs better.

U.S. Government Securities. The relative supply of governments has a significantly positive effect on portfolio weights for households, both types of insurance companies, commercial and mutual savings banks, and state and local governments (see Appendix Tables 2-18 through 2-25). For pension funds a strong negative time trend dominates all other considerations. The relative financial wealth of commercial banks (or of the three principal holders combined: commercial banks, households, and state and local governments) proves helpful in four cases. The substitution relationships are with time deposits and stock for households; with corporates for pension funds, life insurance companies, and mutual savings banks; and with municipals and stocks for other insurance companies.

Corporate Bonds. The relative supply variable is significant or close to significant for pension funds, both types of insurance companies, and mutual savings banks. Substitution relationships are with stock for mutual funds; with U.S. governments for pension funds, mutual savings banks, and life insurance companies; with municipals for other insurance companies; and with mortgages for mutual savings banks. As previously indicated, time trends are positive in the portfolio weights of corporates for state and local governments and non-life insurance companies and very strongly negative for pension funds and life insurance companies. These time trends are the most significant of the market factors in operation, as indicated by the statistical analysis.

Municipal Bonds. The relative supply of municipals has a significantly positive effect on portfolio weights for households, insurance companies, and state and local governments. A strong positive time trend dominates other considerations for commercial banks, while for state and local governments there is a very strong negative time trend. Negative time trends are also apparent for households and life insurance companies, but the time trend for other insurance companies is positive. Substitution relationships are apparent with stock for households and with all other major asset holdings for non-life insurance companies.

Mortgages. Relative supply is significantly positive for all major holders: life insurance companies, commercial banks, savings and loan associations, and mutual savings banks. The relative financial wealth of major holders is also generally significant and negative, as expected. Substitution relationships are apparent with stock for life insurance companies and with corporates, and perhaps U.S. governments, for mutual savings banks.

Recent Trends

The patterns which characterize the 1950–1967 period as a whole have been somewhat modified in recent years and may be further modified in the future. The exceptionally high percentage growth rates for mutual and pension funds could not continue indefinitely, and they have been substantially moderated. Furthermore, the weight of stock in the portfolios of pension funds cannot continue to rise as rapidly as it has, if only for the mechanical reason that it would soon approach 100 percent. Presumably as earnings yields come to reflect more fully the changing perceptions as to cyclical risk which the postwar record would justify, the favorable time trends in the taste for stock of such investors as pension funds and insurance companies will weaken. These considerations suggest that the growth in the market value of stock may be expected to fall more closely in line with earnings growth and with the growth in other financial assets than was true in the 1950–1967 period.

The decline in the relative importance of U.S. government securities has been substantially moderated since 1958; proceeding at a rate of about 1 percentage point a year up to that time and only half as fast since then. Since 1960, the Federal Reserve banks have absorbed over 40 percent of new issues, with commercial banks showing relatively little interest. The relative importance of both corporate and municipal bonds has been stable since the late 1950s. During the 1960s, commercial banks absorbed almost two-thirds of the new issues of municipal securities, while state and local governments have been the largest buyers of corporate securities, absorbing 40 percent.

The relative supply of mortgages—as well as the closely related asset, time deposits in savings institutions other than commercial banks—has been stable since 1962. The proportion of mortgages held by savings and loan associations has declined slightly since 1964, while the shares held by commercial banks, pension funds, and state and local governments have risen slightly. The imposition in late 1966 of temporary interest rate ceilings on time deposits in institutions other than commercial banks, as well as the reduction in the ceilings for commercial banks, may have helped to stem the outflow of funds from the savings and loan associations and mutual savings banks and hence temporarily helped the mortgage market. However, in the long run the continuation of such ceilings, to the extent that they are effective, might be a factor favorable to household (and overall) demand for both bonds and stocks as well as one unfavorable to the overall demand for mortgages.

Chapter Three

INVESTMENT PERFORMANCE
OF MUTUAL FUNDS

Mutual funds, like other financial institutions, are intermediaries between the ultimate savers of funds and investors in productive goods. Their success in filling the intermediary role can be appraised in either of two ways: The first is to compare the net return the funds provide to those who purchase their shares with that on alternative forms of saving, allowing for differences in risk. The second is to measure the funds' efficacy in helping to channel the money they raise into the most economically desirable investments. The first, or investment performance, approach leads to the traditional measures of mutual fund performance, or overall rates of return (including capital gains as well as dividends), with risk held constant.

The second, or market efficiency, approach examines the relationship between the funds' net purchases of individual portfolio investments and the subsequent earnings on those investments, again as compared with other investment alternatives where risk is held constant. Only one published work applied the "market efficiency" approach to mutual funds. This was the Wharton School *Study of Mutual Funds,* where a few simple tests were carried out to determine the relationship between the funds' net purchases of each of thirty stocks for the period 1953–1958 and subsequent comparative share earnings on those stocks. The results were inconclusive.

Unlike the scarcity of market efficiency analysis of mutual fund invest-

50

ments, there have been many studies of the funds' investment performance. Despite great variation in the sample of funds and periods covered and in the treatment of risk, virtually all the published government and academic studies[1] have indicated that the investment performance of mutual funds in the aggregate is not very different from that of the stock market as a whole, after allowing for the funds' investment outside that market. These studies, however, do not cover the experience of the past few years—when, as many people argue, the advent of the "performance" funds has significantly improved the industry's comparative performance—and for the most part do not handle risk satisfactorily.[2] New results are needed on the investment performance of mutual funds to update earlier performance studies and provide a much more satisfactory treatment of risk.

Before presenting these new results, it should be stressed that such an analysis of investment performance by itself—while of critical interest to investors in mutual funds—may not provide satisfactory evidence of the funds' contribution to market efficiency, of their success in helping to channel funds into the most productive economic investments. A high rate of return on fund shares, even with risk held constant, may reflect a successful anticipation of temporary market fluctuations that have little or no relationship to underlying, intrinsic, or long-run values. If the stock market is a game of musical chairs, the winners need not contribute to economic efficiency. This is especially true if the winners represent a group whose behavior influences that of other investors.

If, however, the stock market itself is efficient, investors who receive above-average risk-adjusted rates of return would be helping to channel funds productively, Thus, if mutual funds have above-average performance, there is some reason to believe that they are contributing to economic efficiency, but the presumption is not strong. A below-average performance would lead to a stronger presumption of misallocated resources, since it seems implausible that fund net purchases of portfolio securities would drive their prices below their long-run values, resulting in temporary market fluctuations adverse to the funds.

Examining the relationship between the funds' net purchases and sales of individual securities and the subsequent performance of these securities over an extended period of time, which we have earlier called the market efficiency approach, provides a better measure of the effect of mutual funds

---

[1] The two basic studies for investment companies in general and for the mutual funds in particular were the original U.S. Securities and Exchange Commission *Report on Investment Trusts and Investment Companies,* Government Printing Office, Washington, D.C., 1940, and the Wharton School of Finance and Commerce, University of Pennsylvania, *Study of Mutual Funds,* Government Printing Office, Washington, D.C., 1962.

[2] The defects in the recent academic treatment of risk in mutual fund portfolios are discussed in Irwin Friend and Marshall Blume, "Measurement of Portfolio Performance under Uncertainty," *American Economic Review,* September, 1970.

on economic efficiency. If the portfolio issues purchased by the funds subsequently have a more favorable ratio of earnings to initial price than other investments, allowing for differences in risk and payout policy, then presumably the funds are helping to channel assets into the most productive economic investments. (The reverse would be true for an unfavorable ratio of subsequent earnings to initial price.) Even here, however, there is no assurance that the clear contribution the funds would be making toward more efficient capital markets is matched by a corresponding flow of economic resources into the more productive types of real investment. Nevertheless, under such circumstances, the funds would be helping the capital market fill its appropriate role in the economy, that of guiding capital into the most profitable real investments.

It should be pointed out that neither the investment performance nor the market efficiency measures are complete indications of the funds' economic performance. While both, and particularly the latter, measure the funds' efficiency in helping to channel resources into real investments with the highest rates of return, they do not reflect all the operating costs expended in attaining this efficiency. Specifically, both are gross of the sales fees initially charged the investor in mutual funds, which typically amount to 9.3 percent of the initial investment (net of sales fees) for noncontractual plans and higher percentages for contractual, or front-end load, plans.[3] The investment performance (but not the market efficiency) measures are net of management expenses, which typically amount to somewhat under 0.6 of 1 percent of assets annually,[4] and commissions on portfolio transactions, which averaged somewhat under 0.5 of 1 percent of assets in the 1960–1968 period and nearly twice as much in recent years.[5]

With these qualifications, we shall analyze, first, the investment performance of mutual funds and, second, the degree to which they help to channel money into the most economically desirable, or most economically efficient, portfolio investments.

Investment Performance for Industry as a Whole

The analysis of mutual fund investment performance covers all funds for which reliable monthly price and dividend data were available throughout any of three periods: January, 1960, through June, 1968; January, 1960,

---

[3] See U.S. Securities and Exchange Commission, *Public Policy Implications of Investment Company Growth,* Government Printing Office, Washington, D.C., 1966, p. 19.

[4] *Ibid.,* p. 98. The advisory fee rate that is included as part of management expenses is on the average somewhat under 0.5 of 1 percent.

[5] The SEC *Statistical Bulletin* shows an average turnover ratio of 0.26 for this period. (It was 0.47 in 1968.) This was multiplied by 2, to allow roughly for both purchases and sales, and by 0.9 of 1 percent to allow roughly for the average commissions paid by mutual funds.

through March, 1964; and April, 1964, through June, 1968.[6] A list of the funds included in this analysis of investment performance is presented in Appendix Table 3-1. The most important omissions from the group of funds covered are the very small funds and those funds formed after April, 1964. Though the funds omitted account for a relatively small proportion of total assets,[7] they may account for a more substantial fraction of the riskier stockholdings.

The overall annual rates of return on investment in these 136 mutual funds averaged .107 for the period January, 1960, through June, 1968, .090 for the period January, 1960, through March, 1964, and .128 for the period April, 1964, through June, 1968. The rates of return are nominal annual rates compounded monthly,[8] reflect all capital gains as well as dividends, are adjusted for all capital changes (stock dividends, splits, etc.), and give each fund an equal weight.[9] These rates for mutual funds might be compared with the corresponding rates of return for all NYSE common stocks, which constitute the major part of the funds' portfolios, or with the average rates of return in a market portfolio invested in NYSE stocks, other stocks, and fixed-interest obligations in the same proportions as the funds.

To obtain the corresponding rate of return for all NYSE stocks, some weighting for each stock must be specified. Two weighting schemes are available for comparative purposes, one involving equal investments in each of the stocks, the other involving proportional investments (the weights are proportional to the value of the stock outstanding). Equal investment in each of the NYSE stocks, that is, unweighted portfolios, would have yielded annual rates of return of .124, .070, and .178 for the January, 1960, through June, 1968, January, 1960, through March, 1964, and April, 1964, through June, 1968, periods, respectively, according to Fisher's combination link relatives.[10] Proportional investment would have yielded annual rates of return of .099, .099, and .098.[11]

[6] All mutual funds listed in the *Wall Street Journal* as of May 31, 1968, were included if the required monthly price and dividend data could be obtained either from the *Journal* or from any of the other financial services.

[7] The funds covered held $43.2 billion in assets on December 31, 1967, accounting for 89 percent of the total assets of mutual funds estimated by the SEC for that date and a significantly higher proportion of the Investment Company Institute total.

[8] The effective annual rates would be somewhat higher than the figures presented.

[9] Giving each fund a weight proportional to its size would raise somewhat the average annual rate of return realized by the funds from 10.7 to 11.0 percent for the period January, 1960, through June, 1968.

[10] These relatives, which were not available at the time of the Wharton School study *(op. cit.)*, are based on data for all NYSE stocks, obtained from the tapes of the Center for Research in Security Prices of the University of Chicago, and were updated for this study. For reasons explained subsequently, they tend to understate the rates of return which would be expected from equal investment in each of the NYSE stocks as compared with the rates of return reported for mutual funds.

[11] The proportionately weighted return was based on the NYSE composite price index adjusted for dividend income. This index is much more comprehensive and more technically satisfactory than the Dow-Jones indexes, which are frequently used for comparative purposes.

Thus, equally weighted or unweighted investment in NYSE stocks would have resulted in a higher rate of return than that achieved by mutual funds in the 1960–1968 period as a whole: a lower rate in the first half of that period, and a much higher rate in the second half. In contrast, proportionately weighted investment in NYSE stocks would have resulted in a lower rate of return in the period as a whole: a higher rate in the first half, and a lower rate in the second half.

A lack of satisfactory data complicates the estimation of the average rates of return which would have been achieved by investing at random the same proportions as the funds in NYSE stocks, other stocks, and fixed-interest obligations. However, the overall market return adjusted for the distribution of the funds' portfolio among these three classes of securities was probably about as high as the rate of return on NYSE stocks alone for the period January, 1960, through June, 1968. As noted earlier, it is estimated that close to 20 percent of the funds' stock portfolio, or 17 percent of their total assets, was invested in non-NYSE stock, mainly American Stock Exchange and over-the-counter stocks. These stocks had a much higher rate of return on the average than NYSE stocks during 1960–1968, especially in the second half of the period. The overall nominal annual rate of price appreciation (compounded monthly) on the National Quotation Bureau index of over-the-counter stocks was 15.5 percent for January, 1960, through June, 1968, compared with 6.7 percent for the NYSE composite price index, while for April, 1964, though June, 1968, the corresponding rates were 25.4 percent for the American Stock Exchange index,[12] 23.2 percent for the NQB index, and 6.5 percent for the NYSE index.

The apparently much higher rate of return on the 17 percent of the funds' assets invested in American and over-the-counter stocks than in NYSE stock might be expected to roughly offset the considerably lower rate of return earned on the 16 percent of the funds' assets invested in net cash and equivalent items, corporate bonds, and preferred stocks. This seems to leave the funds' average rate of return over the 1960–1968 period somewhat higher than that of proportionately weighted investment in the market as a whole, after adjusting for the funds' portfolio composition. However, the margin of error in the available over-the-counter price indices is too large to permit a more precise statement on the relation between the funds' investment return and the corresponding adjusted market return. Moreover, before drawing any definitive conclusions on the comparative investment performance of mutual funds and the market as a whole, it is necessary to consider explicitly not only rates of return but also the associated investment risks.

The overall rates of return on investment in 103 mutual funds classified in three risk groups are presented in Appendix Table 3-2 for the January, 1960, through June, 1968, period. The basic risk measure used—technically

[12] The American Stock Exchange index was not available at the beginning of 1960.

known as a beta coefficient[13]—is a measure of systematic or nondiversifiable risk, i.e., the dispersion in return which cannot be reduced through market diversification. Small beta coefficients correspond to small risks. A beta of around 1 corresponds roughly in risk to a portfolio consisting of all NYSE stocks. Mutual funds typically tend to have beta coefficients somewhat below 1. Another risk measure, the variance in the monthly rates of return, is presented for comparability and will be considered later. The beta coefficient might be considered more applicable for an investor in a mutual fund with other fund or stock investments, while the variance measure is more applicable to an investor in a mutual fund with no other investments in securities.

Appendix Table 3-2 shows that, for the 1960–1968 period covered, the annual rate of return averaged 9.1 percent for the low-risk funds, 10.6 percent for the medium-risk funds, and 13.5 percent for the high-risk funds. The table also gives the corresponding rates of return for 136 random portfolios of roughly equivalent risk. Results are presented separately for random portfolios which reflect an equal investment in each stock and for those in which investment in a stock is roughly proportional to the amount outstanding.[14] The 136 portfolios were selected from a sample of 511 common stocks listed on the New York Stock Exchange throughout the January, 1960, through June, 1968, period.[15]

Initially 200 random portfolios were selected consisting of 100 individual portfolios of twenty-five securities and a like number for portfolios of fifty stocks. A stratified random sampling procedure was used to ensure that we

[13] The beta, or β (for each fund) is defined as the ratio of (1) the convariance between the monthly rates of return for the fund and those for the market as a whole and (2) the variance of the monthly rates of return for the market. The market return refers to Fisher's combination link relatives, updated for this study, and assumes an equal investment in each of the NYSE stocks. While the return on the market portfolio is typically measured, as we do, by some index of common stocks listed on the NYSE, a better measure of market return for purposes of estimating the beta coefficient would be obtained from an index of all wealth whose return is uncertain, but the necessary data for this alternative are not available.

[14] The estimated mean returns for equally weighted random portfolios of NYSE stocks over the 1960–1968 period are higher than those presented earlier for equally weighted investment in all NYSE stocks based on Fisher's combination link relatives. The main reason is that the estimates of period return both for the random portfolios and mutual funds are arithmetic means of the monthly returns, while the Fisher combination link relatives are simple averages of the arithmetic and geometric means of the monthly returns.

[15] A total of 788 common stocks were listed on the NYSE throughout this period, according to the University of Chicago updated tapes from which the data on return for each issue were obtained. The data on amount outstanding for each issue necessary for proportional weighting purposes were available from the Standard and Poor's Compustat tapes for only 511 of these issues. For comparability, the mean returns for both equally weighted and proportionally weighted random portfolios presented in the tables are based on these 511 issues. However, mean returns were also computed for equally weighted random portfolios based on all 788 common stocks listed in the NYSE throughout the period. The mean returns based on the 788 common stocks were quite close to those for the 511 issues for the period as a whole but were somewhat higher in the first half of the period and lower in the second half.

covered the entire spectrum of risk.[16] However, in view of the small number of mutual funds in our sample with beta coefficients below .5 (twelve funds) or above 1.1 (four funds), the results for such funds and random portfolios are not presented.

It appears from these results that random portfolios of New York Stock Exchange stocks with equal investment in each stock performed on the average better over the period than did mutual funds in the same risk class. The differences were fairly substantial for the low- and medium-risk portfolios (3.7 and 2.5 percent respectively per annum) but quite small for high-risk portfolios (0.2 percent per annum).[17]

The differences in rates of return clearly cannot be explained by the trivial differences in beta coefficients of mutual funds and random portfolios in a given risk class, nor by the larger variances in return of the mutual funds, since, everything else equal, larger variances should be associated with higher return. There is no reason to believe that they would be explained by the exclusion of non-NYSE stocks and bonds from the random portfolios as against the inclusion of them in mutual funds: mutual funds are permitted options not open to the random portfolios, American Stock Exchange and over-the-counter stock issues had much higher average rates of return over this period than NYSE issues,[18] and risk is held approximately constant. The relatively better performance of the high-risk than of the lower-risk funds may reflect a greater impact of the former on the prices of the securities in which they are trading (Chapter 5), more extensive investments in ASE and over-the-counter stocks, and perhaps also greater use of letter stock resulting in an element of "instant performance," reflecting the difference between the prices ascribed to and paid for the stock (Chapters 4 and 7).

Another possible reason for the somewhat inferior performance of the mutual funds as compared with equally distributed random stock portfolios

[16] The NYSE securities were ranked in ascending order according to the values of the covariances of the monthly security investment relatives and Fisher's link relatives over the entire sample period. Two portfolios of 25 securities and two of 50 were drawn at random from the first 100 securities. Four more portfolios of the two different sizes were drawn from the securities ranked 9 through 108. This process was repeated again and again, each time increasing the bounds of the stratum by eight securities, until 200 portfolios were obtained.

[17] The differences are lowered by 0.8 percent for the low-risk portfolios and raised by 0.8 percent for the high-risk portfolios, if the random portfolios are selected from the universe of 788 common stocks listed on the NYSE throughout this period. The differences between the mutual funds and these random portfolios taken as a whole are statistically significant as measured by a chi-square test of the differences between the two sets of returns, when the beta coefficients are classified in six intervals with a range of .1 each.

[18] The beta coefficient (covariability with the NYSE price index) was over 1 for the monthly rates of return on the American Stock Exchange index for the April, 1964, through June, 1968, period over which data were available, and below 1 for the National Quotation Bureau index of over-the-counter stocks for both the January, 1960, through March, 1964, and April, 1964, through June, 1968, periods. The variance in the monthly rates of return was higher for the American Stock Exchange and over-the-counter indices than for the NYSE index.

is that the funds' performance is net of management expenses and commissions on portfolio transactions. As indicated above, these might amount to somewhat over 1 percent of assets annually over the 1960–1968 period,[19] which could account for a considerable share of the difference in average performance of the managed and unmanaged portfolios. (Investors in random portfolios would also be paying commissions, but only on the original purchases and reinvested dividends if the portfolios were held throughout the period, and this would typically be less than the initial sales charge by the funds.) However, differences in management expenses and commissions on portfolio transactions cannot explain the apparently superior performance of the high-risk funds relative to the other mutual funds, since the high-risk funds have higher management expenses and higher portfolio turnover and commissions. The effect of management expenses and commissions on performance will be investigated later in this chapter.

The basic reason for the differences in performance between the mutual funds and the random portfolios with equal weight given to each stock held seems to be that the weighting scheme implicit in fund portfolios gives greater weight to the larger issues, which had significantly different rates of return from the smaller issues. Thus, for January, 1960, through June, 1968, the mean rates of return were substantially higher for the equally weighted random portfolios of New York Stock Exchange stocks than for the proportionally weighted random portfolios.[20] If mutual funds do not want to keep much over a hundred stocks in their portfolios, only the small and medium-size funds have the option of investing equal amounts in each of the NYSE stocks without getting involved in potential control of portfolio companies, which may be inconsistent with fund and social policy and could even violate the law. As indicated in Chapter 1, the distribution of fund portfolios among stock issues of different size tends to be intermediate between proportionally and equally distributed investment.

Therefore, mutual fund performance should be compared not only with equally distributed random investments in New York Stock Exchange (or other) stocks but also with proportionally distributed random investments, the weights being proportional to the value of the stock outstanding. The latter type of comparison indicates that the high-risk funds, or more precisely the funds with beta coefficients approximating investment in the NYSE as a whole, clearly outperformed proportionally distributed random

[19] The figure would be considerably higher by the end of the period as a result of the increase in portfolio turnover.

[20] The rather substantial difference between the rates of return on equally distributed and on proportionally distributed random investments in NYSE stocks over the 1960–1968 period raises some questions about the allocational efficiency of the stock market in general. However, it should be noted that a comparison of the equally weighted Fisher index of NYSE stocks with the proportionally weighted Standard and Poor's composite index suggests that the corresponding difference for the 1926–1960 period, while in the same direction, was not nearly as large.

investments in NYSE stock. However, there appears to be less difference in average performance between the low- and medium-risk funds and weighted random investments in NYSE stock. The low-risk funds performed somewhat worse than corresponding random investments and the medium-risk funds somewhat better.

Mutual funds as a whole in 1960–1968 seemed to perform worse than equally distributed random investments in New York Stock Exchange stock but, except for low-risk portfolios, did better than proportionally distributed random investments. Since previous studies had concluded that mutual fund performance was equivalent to that obtained from proportionally distributed random investments in NYSE stock, the new results suggest some improvement in fund performance in recent years. The extent to which this improvement may reflect the impact of the mutual funds on the prices of the securities in which they are trading, corresponding to their increasing importance in the market, will be discussed in Chapter 6.

To determine whether there has been any trend in the relative performance of mutual funds over this period, January, 1960, through June, 1968, was broken down into two equal intervals: January, 1960, through March, 1964, and April, 1964, through June, 1968.[21] Mutual fund representatives have argued that they greatly improved their comparative standing in the second period, which was one of speculative fervor and booming prices of risky issues. The average level of stock prices early in 1969 was midway between the March, 1964, and June, 1968, figures, and at least part of the speculative fervor of the April, 1964, through June, 1968, period had subsided. It is not really possible to tell whether the results for one period or the other are more relevant for the future. The findings for the two subperiods are presented in Appendix Tables 3-3 and 3-4.

Again it appears in both periods that mutual funds as a whole fared somewhat worse than equally distributed random investments in NYSE stocks and somewhat better than proportionally distributed random investments and that the high-risk funds fared better than the low-risk funds in relation to random portfolios of comparable risk.[22] However, in the second period, the high-risk funds performed slightly better than the equally distributed random portfolios, though the difference is not statistically signifi-

[21] The number of mutual funds varies from the overall period to each of the subperiods, reflecting the number of funds for which price and dividend data were available throughout the period or subperiod. The random portfolios for the first subperiod were selected from a sample of 528 common stocks listed on the NYSE throughout January, 1960, through March, 1964, and for the second subperiod from a sample of 706 common stocks listed on the NYSE throughout April, 1964, through June, 1968. The method of selecting the random portfolios was described earlier.

[22] The beta coefficients used for both periods are, of course, different from those for the 1960–1968 period as a whole. The correlation between the betas of the same mutual funds for 1960–1964 and 1964–1968 was .41. For the random portfolios the correlation was .96.

cant, and considerably better than the proportionally distributed random portfolios.

Our analysis of mutual fund performance is based on the measure of risk theoretically most appropriate for investors who take advantage of market opportunities to diversify. However, there is some evidence to suggest that investors in the stock market may be more likely to use the volatility in the rate of return on an investment rather than its covariability with the market to measure its relative risk.[23] We therefore repeated the analysis presented in Appendix Tables 3-2 through 3-4, using the variance in the monthly rates of return of a fund or random portfolio in each of the three periods covered as a measure of its risk over that period. The analysis of random portfolios has been restricted to those with equal weights.

The only noteworthy difference in the results obtained is that there is no longer any indication that, for the 1960–1968 period as a whole, the riskier funds (as measured by variance) fared better in relation to random portfolios than the less risky ones, once variance is held constant (Appendix Tables 3-5 through 3-7). The high-variance funds had a lower rate of return than the equally weighted random portfolios with the same variance over the 1960–1968 period as a whole: a somewhat higher rate of return than the random portfolios in the first half of the period, and a considerably lower return in the second half. Thus, the riskier funds did not perform as well in relation to the random portfolios when variance rather than covariability with the market, or the beta coefficient, is used to measure risk. The main reason for the variation in results obtained from the two different measures of risk (the beta coefficient and variance) is that when the mutual funds and random portfolios are classified by the variance in their return, the random portfolios tend to have higher beta coefficients and the average difference in beta coefficients between the mutual funds and random portfolios is particularly large for the high-variance portfolios.[24]

Investment Performance by Fund Characteristics

It is of interest to determine whether various fund characteristics are associated with investment performance. Prior government and academic

[23] A subsequent analysis of market efficiency in Chapter 4 will relate both market yields and fund net purchases of individual portfolio issues to various measures of risk, as well as to other variables. For a more detailed analysis of the relationship between yields and risk, see Robert S. Parker, "Some Aspects of Long Run Allocational Efficiency: An Empirical Study of the Stock Market," Ph.D. dissertation, University of Pennsylvania, Philadelphia, 1969.

[24] The variation in results obtained from the two different measures of risk is somewhat narrowed when the analysis presented in Appendix Tables 3-5 through 3-7 is confined to those mutual funds and random portfolios where the beta coefficients are relatively constant from the 1960–1964 to the 1964–1968 periods.

studies covering earlier periods of time have generally found no consistent relationship between investment performance and fund size, management expenses, portfolio turnover, and sales charges.[25] The most interesting departures from these general findings are found in two recent academic studies which suggest that performance may be inversely related to management expenses[26] and to portfolio turnover and sales charges.[27]

Appendix Tables 3-8 and 3-9 present the relationships between investment performance and fund size for our sample of mutual funds over the 1960–1968 period as a whole and for the second half of the period.[28] As in earlier studies, there does not seem to be any consistent relation between performance and size once risk is held constant.

Two divergent sets of forces may affect the performance of funds as their size increases: First, the ratio of management and related expenses declines in relation to fund assets, and the absolute amount of resources that can be devoted to investment management increases. Second, some loss in investment flexibility is associated with very large size. The need to purchase portfolio securities in very large blocks may take a substantial amount of time, so that investment opportunities are lost and even in the short run may drive up the price of the securities involved beyond the level at which they were initially attractive. If the portfolio holdings are sufficiently large, the decision to sell may again take substantial time to implement, since the alternative could be a major break in the market for that issue. Moreover, as noted earlier, large funds cannot diversify by investing equal rather than more proportional amounts in all stocks; and the former policy was superior in 1960–1968.

The results, however, do not indicate that these theoretical considerations have had any significant impact on performance of the different size groups covered. It should be pointed out that there is a small upward bias in favor of the larger funds inherent in the classification of funds by their end-of-1967 size (since the better-performing funds move into the larger-asset size groups), but this is not likely to be important enough to affect the results for the 1960–1968 period substantially and should affect the 1964–1968 results only negligibly.

---

[25] For example, see the Wharton School, *op. cit.*, which covers 1953–1958. In the present analysis, the data on fund characteristics with the exception of portfolio turnover were obtained from Arthur Wiesenberger Services. Portfolio turnover was obtained from the SEC Form N1R.

[26] These findings appear in William Sharpe, "Mutual Fund Performance," *Journal of Business,* January, 1966, and C. Hoff Stauffer, Jr., and Robert C. Vogel, *Parameters of Mutual Fund Performance,* Wesleyan University, Middletown, Conn., 1969 (mimeographed). The Sharpe article covers the period 1954–1963; the Stauffer and Vogel paper covers 1955–1964.

[27] Stauffer and Vogel, *ibid.*

[28] Similar tabulations were prepared for the first half of the 1960–1968 period but are not presented to conserve space. The numbers of funds covered in these and other tables relating performance to different fund characteristics will vary somewhat from those covered by Appendix Tables 3-2 through 3-4, reflecting instances where data on fund characteristics were not readily available.

The corresponding relationships between investment performance for 1960–1968 and for 1964–1968 and sales charges as of the end of 1967 are shown in Appendix Tables 3-10 and 3-11. The absence of any clear correlation between these two variables, when risk is held constant, suggests that the size of the sales charges paid by mutual fund investors when they acquire fund shares has little relation to the performance of the fund. Though not shown separately in the tables, it is interesting to note that the rate of return for no-load funds, with risk held constant, was fully as high as for load funds. It might have been expected that higher performance would permit higher sales charges, even though the sales charges largely represent remuneration to the distributors of fund shares rather than to the investment management organization.

If there is a relationship between performance and sales charges, it appears to be negative. The funds with the lowest sales charges (including the no-load funds) seem to perform slightly better than the other funds, but the differences are minor. Moreover, when asset size rather than beta coefficient is held constant, there seems to be even less variation in rates of return of funds with different sales charges. The results seem to be closer to those found in the earlier Wharton School *Study of Mutual Funds* than in some of the more recent analyses.

Appendix Tables 3-12 and 3-13 investigate the relationship between investment performance and the ratio of management expenses to assets, for 1960–1968 and for the second half of the period. Theoretical considerations point to two quite different effects of the management expense ratio on performance. On the one hand, high expense ratios would tend to result in somewhat lower return to investors in fund shares unless the funds with such ratios have superior portfolio management. On the other hand, presumably the higher the management advisory fees, which account on the average for close to 80 percent of all management expenses, the greater the resources which can be devoted to investment research, and the larger the remuneration that can be paid to attract superior management.

While no clear relationship shows up between performance and the management expense ratio, the high-expense funds, to the extent there is such a relationship, seemed to have an edge over other funds.[29] For the second half of the period, April, 1964, through June, 1968, the intermediate-expense group performed better than the other funds. However, the low-expense group performed best in the first half of the period, January, 1960, through March, 1964. As a whole, the results do not support the recent studies which concluded that there was a negative correlation between fund

[29] When asset size rather than beta coefficient is held constant, there is somewhat stronger evidence of a direct relation between mean return and management expense ratio. However, this cannot be taken as evidence of a corresponding relation between investment performance and expense ratios, since higher expense ratios are typically associated with higher beta coefficients for given asset size.

performance and management expense ratios. Rather, they tend to confirm the findings of the earlier Wharton School study, which pointed to the absence of any consistent relation between these two variables.

Appendix Tables 3-14 and 3-15 contain the results of a similar examination of relationships between performance and portfolio turnover. Portfolio turnover might be expected to affect performance in the same fashion as the management expense ratio. Higher turnover results in higher transactions costs, which would tend to lower the return to investors unless management is able to take better advantage of investment opportunities through more active trading. Higher turnover would probably be detrimental to performance, if it is stimulated by the management adviser's desire to generate commission business that can be channeled directly or indirectly to distributors of the fund. If higher turnover is primarily motivated by attempts to take advantage of perceived investment opportunities or if the trading activity itself affects the market in a direction favorable to the fund, turnover may improve performance. Also, fund managers who have been superior performers in a period may feel freer to increase their trading and hence reciprocal brokerage and give-ups to enhance the sale of their shares, so that any positive correlation between performance and turnover might reflect a chain of causation from the former to the latter.

The Wharton School study did not find any significant connection between performance and turnover, which suggests offsetting gains and losses from turnover. The most recent academic study we have seen pointed to a negative correlation between these two variables.[30] Our own results for the period 1960–1968 as a whole provide some evidence of a slight positive relation between performance and turnover, but the results are inconsistent between the two parts of the period. For 1964–1968 there is some evidence of a positive relation, but the reverse seems true of the 1960–1964 period.

The fund's stated investment objective is the last characteristic to be investigated. The investment classifications used are based on those provided by Arthur Wiesenberger Services: growth, growth-income, income-growth, and any combination of income, growth, and stability. There is no separate Wiesenberger classification for performance funds, but presumably these would be included among the growth funds (though a number of growth funds would not generally be considered as performance funds). The relationship between performance and investment objectives is presented in Appendix Tables 3-16 and 3-17.

As might be expected, investment objective is fairly highly correlated with risk class measured by the beta coefficient; the growth funds typically possess a higher degree of risk and the income-growth-stability funds a lower degree of risk than the growth-income or income-growth funds. Again as might be expected, though the riskier investment objectives are as-

[30] Stauffer and Vogel, *op. cit.*

sociated with higher rates of return over the period covered, there is no clear relation between rates of return and investment objective once risk is held constant. Classifying the funds in growth, balanced, and other categories, rather than the investment objective classes, produces similar results.

The findings indicating the absence of any consistent relationships between the characteristics of mutual funds and their investment performance suggest that there may not be any consistent relationship between performance for a given fund in different periods of time. This suggestion seems to be confirmed by the statistically insignificant negative correlations between the mean rates of return of the same funds in the 1960–1964 and the 1964–1968 periods for all funds in a given risk class.[31] This finding does not necessarily mean, however, that there may not be individual funds which have outperformed the market in a larger number of time periods than may be attributed to chance; rather, with the available data and statistical procedures it is not feasible to be certain about the existence of such superior performers.

Ability to Predict General Market

The investment performance of mutual funds over any period is a composite of their ability to predict (or influence) movements in the stock market as a whole and, probably more important in view of the funds' concentration on common stock, of their ability to select underpriced issues (or to affect favorably the relative prices of issues purchased). Their success in portfolio selection, which is closely related to their contribution to market efficiency, will be discussed at some length in Chapter 5. We shall now consider briefly the success of the industry as a whole in forecasting stock market movements as evidenced by the timing of fund flows into and out of the market in relation to the level and movement of stock prices.

For this purpose, we have related the quarterly and monthly net purchases, gross purchases, and gross sales of portfolio stock by all mutual funds to general price movements on the New York Stock Exchange in the same, preceding, and subsequent periods and to the level of NYSE stock prices as a ratio of a longer-term norm.[32] A second set of relationships was also estimated after adjusting the portfolio purchases for the net inflow of money from the sale of fund shares, on the theory that to some extent the funds may have felt it necessary to channel such money into the stock mar-

[31] The coefficients of correlations were — .01 for the 28 funds in the low-risk class ($\beta = .5-.7$), — .05 for the 53 funds in the medium-risk class ($\beta = .7-.9$), and — .19 for the 22 funds in the high-risk class ($\beta = .9-1.1$). The negative correlations may reflect the fact that risk is not completely held constant by the statistical analysis.

[32] The data on fund activity were obtained from statistical releases of the Investment Company Institute. A number of different lag structures were tried.

ket without a prolonged wait. In other words, they may play a less active role in simply channeling new money into the stock market than in shifting their existing resources into or out of common stock. Thus, while the total of net portfolio purchases is the more appropriate variable for measuring the funds' impact on the market, net purchases adjusted for inflow may be more relevant to the funds' ability to predict market movements.

The results in Appendix Table 3-18 do not provide any clear evidence that mutual fund purchases and sales of common stock (with or without the adjustment for net inflow from sale of fund shares) lead monthly or quarterly stock market movements. There is somewhat more evidence that their purchases and sales follow the monthly market movements. Nor is there any indication that fund net purchases are relatively high or low in periods when the level of the market turns out to have been inflated or depressed, when compared with the average level of stock prices over the following year. Fund net purchases exhibit little indication of a quarterly lead or lag relative to stock prices, and only a suggestion of a lag on a monthly basis. Of course, different results might be obtained on a shorter-run basis, but there are no data available for testing this hypothesis. In the Wharton School study covering the period 1953–1958, there was some (but not strong) evidence that monthly net purchases by mutual funds were correlated with general stock price movements in the same month and somewhat stronger evidence of a corresponding correlation between daily net purchases and general price movements.

Some Implications

Our evidence on the investment performance of mutual funds in 1960–1968, analyzed as a whole and by major groups, is mixed. The funds have not generally matched the performance of equally distributed random investments in New York Stock Exchange stock. However, they have fully matched the performance of proportionally distributed random investments in NYSE stock, and high-risk funds—which include the performance funds—have surpassed such random performance, especially in 1964–1968.

Even if the evidence is interpreted as implying that the funds have been no more efficient in their investment policy than the stock market generally, mutual funds may still have served a useful function in our economy. First, they have provided convenient diversification to small investors, who can ill afford large risks, at a cost which was generally not excessive compared to the available alternatives. In the process, they also raised the average return realized by such small investors whose investment alternatives consisted mainly of fixed-interest-bearing obligations.

Second, the very substantial net purchases of portfolio stock by the mutual funds like those by other institutional investors, most notably the pension funds, have probably bolstered stock prices over the post-World War II period and lowered the required rate of return on equity investment. They have funneled money into equities that otherwise would have gone into fixed-interest obligations, and they have been willing to accept a lower premium for uncertainty in view of their ability to diversify. This has served to narrow the differential between the required and realized rates of return on common stock and the much lower rates of return on alternative forms of investment. (The annual rate of return on common stock amounted to close to twice the average corporate bond yield from the latter part of the nineteenth century, which is as far back as the relevant data go, until the past few years.)

To the extent that such institutional developments cut the risk premium reflected in the cost of capital to business, they have stimulated investment demand and economic growth (assuming that realized investment is not completely determined by the supply of saving). The allocation of invest- ment funds among risky and less risky investments may also have been improved, since business probably no longer has had to pay as high a pre- mium for risky investment, typically financed by equity, over less risky investment, financed by a combination of bonds and equity.

There is, however, a very real question whether the decline in the rate of return on common stock implicit in the much higher price-earnings ratios of recent years—a development in which the mutual funds and other institutional investors probably played a significant role—and the rise in bond yields to historic heights may not have completely eliminated (or even reversed) any socially undesirable or excessive risk premium on com- mon stock.[33] Thus, the intensive selling effort of the mutual fund industry may have had a greater payoff for the economy and the individual investor in the past than it will in the future.

Yet, the diversification the funds provide will remain an important ser- vice. The obvious question is whether it can be attained at lower cost. There

---

[33] Under reasonable assumptions, it can be shown that the expected rate of return on stocks as a whole is the sum of the current dividend yield, presently somewhat above 3.5 percent on New York Stock Exchange stocks, and the expected growth rate in per share earnings. The actual growth rate amounted to about 4 percent per annum since the latter part of the nineteenth century—reflecting a 2 percent rate of productivity growth and a 2 percent rate of general price inflation. Thus, if the historical long-run growth rate in per share earnings continues, the ex- pected long-run rate of return for investment in stock at current price levels is somewhat over $7\frac{1}{2}$ percent. This is less than the 9 to 10 percent historical rate of return on stocks, which re- flected not only a higher dividend yield but also an increasing price-earnings ratio resulting from the great disparity between the return on stock and bonds. That disparity has been largely corrected, with the yield on AAA corporate bonds well over 7 percent for long-term outstanding issues. (The yield on new high-grade bonds is even higher but is guaranteed for a much shorter period and is subject to less favorable tax rates.) It is quite possible, of course, that with a higher rate of price inflation in the future than in the past the future growth rate in earnings may ex- ceed 4 percent, or once the current rate of price inflation is substantially reduced, bond yields may decline significantly, but it is difficult to foresee any likely conjuncture of events which will result in a return to the historical disparity between the return on stock and bonds.

is no clear indication that higher sales charges, management fees, or trading expenses are consistently associated with higher or lower performance.

Since there does not seem to be a clear payoff for management and trading expenses, there is much to be said in favor of a new type of mutual fund with minimum management and trading. It would be somewhat akin to the fixed or semifixed trusts of former years, which deliberately duplicated the performance of the New York Stock Exchange stocks as a whole or of some other spectrum of investments. The larger the fund, of course, the smaller are the percentage management expenses, and the easier it is to duplicate the performance of the entire market. Very large funds of this nature, which become sufficiently well known to the investing public, might profitably be sold at commission rates appreciably lower than the sales loads now charged by mutual funds. If the funds are too large, however, they would not be able to take full advantage of the apparent benefits of equally distributed random investments.[34] Brokerage firms would be the obvious sponsors of these funds, and the same firm might offer several funds each in different risk classes.

Funds which duplicate the performance of the market (or of some designated sector) will, of course, not appeal to those investors who would accept the risks of below-average performance for the chance of above-average performance and feel that professional management in existing types of mutual funds will increase the likelihood of their success. Though it is difficult to tell statistically whether a given fund has significantly outperformed the market, investors might reasonably assume that, other things equal, it is preferable to invest their money in those funds that have had fairly consistent above-average performance in the past. Since existing types of mutual funds charge management fees presumably with the expectation of better-than-random performance, it can be argued that these fees should be geared to the difference between the risk-adjusted performance of the fund and the performance of the market. (The calculations would have to cover a sufficiently long period so that, statistically, the probability of being overgenerous in rewarding essentially average or below-average management is rather small.)

Another obvious issue to be raised is the apparent inability of mutual funds, on the average, to clearly outperform the market in spite of their professional investment management. There are several at least partial answers to this question. A sizable fund may have a hundred securities in its portfolio to obtain the very considerable benefits of diversification. Since

[34] It should be noted that the benefits of equally distributed random investments were much smaller in 1926–1960 than they were in the 1960–1968 and especially the 1964–1968 periods. There is reason to believe (e.g., from the higher price-earnings multiples of smaller and riskier issues than of larger and higher-quality issues) that the speculative psychology of the past few years may have relatively overpriced the riskier issues, so that equally distributed investments might not be as attractive in the future as in the past decade.

there will be some differences of opinion as well as investment policy among fund managers, it would not be surprising to find as many as 500 stocks extensively held in the combined portfolios of a hundred or more mutual funds. For obvious reasons the funds will tend to invest principally in the larger stocks among the New York Stock Exchange issues. These 500 issues might be expected largely to duplicate the performance of stock outstanding on the Big Board, since they may account for fully 90 percent of the value of such stock. Moreover, there is a very strong intercorrelation among the annual rates of return for different stocks, with the return on most individual stocks over longer periods tending to concentrate around the average return in the market as a whole. Finally, the inability of the larger funds to invest as much in the smaller and what, at least retrospectively, have turned out to be the more promising investments as they have in others also appears to have harmed their performance results.

While these influences would be expected to greatly mute potential differences between random and professional performance, some residual differences in favor of the mutual funds might still be anticipated. The absence of consistent measurable differences might be explained by the costs of professional management and by the assumption that discrepancies between market price and "intrinsic" value are rapidly dissipated by the action of professional and speculative elements in the market. As a result of such action, the ability of large professional investors like mutual funds to accumulate or dispose of substantial blocks of shares at relatively favorable prices may be extremely limited.

Postscript on 1968–1969 Performance

The performance analysis of the mutual funds previously covered for the period April, 1964, through June, 1968, is extended here to cover July, 1968, through September, 1969, a period of moderate decline in stock prices. For all 143 funds in the sample, the average annual rate of return amounting to —3.8 percent [35] (a loss) was somewhat lower than the —3.3 percent average rate of return (including dividends) on the NYSE composite price index. The funds in the highest-risk (beta) group had the lowest rate of return, while those in the lowest-risk group had the highest rate of return (Appendix Table 3-19). This conforms to expectations in a period of declining stock prices, with the highest-risk group experiencing the largest capital losses. The high-risk funds—the only group for which random investments of the same risk are available—had a lower rate of return (—7.2 percent)

---

[35] Giving each fund a weight proportional to its size would raise the average annual rate of return from —3.8 to —3.3 percent.

than the stocks in the NYSE composite price index, which constitutes a group of proportionally weighted investments of comparable risk.[36]

Again no very strong relationships are found between performance and such fund characteristics as asset size, sales charge, management expense ratio, turnover, and investment objective, once risk is held constant. Though there are no clear differences in investment performance between funds with low and medium expense ratios, those with the highest expense ratios seemed to have the worst performance over this period (Appendix Table 3-20). There is also some evidence of a negative correlation between investment performance and portfolio turnover for low- and medium-risk funds. Other variations in investment performance among funds with different characteristics seemed relatively minor.

[36] The high-risk funds have a mean beta coefficient of close to 1, the same as for the NYSE index.

Chapter Four

MUTUAL FUNDS
AND MARKET EFFICIENCY

A BETTER WAY OF testing the impact of mutual funds on economic efficiency, and especially on long-run market efficiency, compares the cost and subsequent earnings of individual portfolio investments purchased by the funds with the cost and earning of alternative investments. This analysis is carried out for common stocks only, but such investments account for over 80 percent of the total assets of mutual funds.[1] The analysis is performed in two different time periods because of differences in the basic information available. The first period extends from the end of 1953 through 1967. The second period extends from the fourth quarter of 1967 through the second quarter of 1968.

The first period data on annual and quarterly holdings and *net* purchases (in shares) of individual stocks by individual funds were made available to us by Vickers Associates; price, dividends, and earnings data were obtained from the University of Chicago tapes and from the Standard and Poor's annual and quarterly Compustat file.[2] This information covered a high

---

[1] The ratio was 84 percent at the end of 1968 (Investment Company Institute, *Mutual Fund Fact Book*, 1969).

[2] The NYSE price data were obtained from the University of Chicago tapes; other prices, and the accounting data from Compustat. The share volume of net purchases was converted to dollar value by the average price in the period. Where feasible, the data were adjusted for capital changes on the basis of the University of Chicago tapes for New York Stock Exchange stocks and the Standard and Poor's records for other stocks, but a number of non-NYSE stocks had to be omitted for cetain periods where the necessary adjustment data were not available. The Vickers data are reported on a fiscal period (quarter or year) basis.

proportion both in number and value of all New York Stock Exchange stocks, and a very small sample of over-the-counter stocks. The 1954–1967 period begins when mutual funds first became important and ends when a more extensive body of data became available.

For 1967–1968, quarterly data on *gross* share purchases and sales and end-of-quarter holdings of individual New York Stock Exchange and American Stock Exchange stocks by individual funds were provided by the U.S. Securities and Exchange Commission; price and dividends (but not earnings) data were once again provided by Standard and Poor's.[3]

The Vickers data cover the trading activity of a high proportion of all investment companies, while the SEC data are even more inclusive. Both the Vickers and SEC data as well as the other information used were checked for reasonableness.[4] While the SEC data permit types of analysis (separating purchases and sales activity) not possible with the Vickers data, the latter are more useful for analyzing the impact of mutual funds on market efficiency, since they provide information on net purchases for a very much longer period of time.[5]

A simple test of the contribution of mutual funds in directing capital into investment areas which ultimately prove the most profitable involves comparing the average ratios of subsequent earnings to initial prices for stock issues held or purchased on balance by all mutual funds with the corresponding ratios for the stock market as a whole. However, this test is too simple, since a high proportion of NYSE stock is held by at least one fund, and it is highly desirable to properly weight stocks held or purchased by mutual funds by their relative importance in fund portfolios or activity. Moreover, if the ratio of terminal earnings to initial prices is to be a satisfactory measure of the economic desirability of investment in a specific stock, dividend payout and risk must be held constant. The statistical analysis used attempts to weight fund activity appropriately and to hold both payout and measures of risk constant (at least in a linear fashion). It compares net dollar purchases (gross purchases less sales) rather than dollar holdings to the ratios of the subsequent earnings to initial price. This comparison makes it easier to determine the timing of any changes in the funds'

---

[3] The quarterly data on gross purchases and sales were first collected by the Securities and Exchange Commission in the fourth quarter of 1967. These data, which are reported on a calendar quarter basis, have also been adjusted for capital changes where necessary and feasible.

[4] We eliminated data where computer checks of reasonableness suggested a likelihood of error.

[5] It should be pointed out, however, that a substantial volume of reported fund activity was eliminated from the Vickers data because of questions about the accuracy or consistency of the data or because of inability to obtain needed price information. In addition, only funds reporting in the fourth quarter of the year were included in the annual analysis of these data, and only funds that reported for all quarters during which Vickers carried their transactions were included in the quarterly analysis. As a result the Vickers data on net fund transactions in portfolio stock which were used in our analysis accounted for only about three-eighths of total fund activity, but a higher proportion of activity in NYSE stocks. As of December 31, 1967, the market value of fund common stock holdings covered by our analysis amounted to over $15.1 billion.

investment efficiency. The Vickers data have been used primarily for reasons already indicated.

Long-run Efficiency

Appendix Table 4-1 presents the results of this analysis annually for the years 1954, 1957–1959, and 1964–1967, for New York Stock Exchange stocks only. Quarterly results which were carried out for the periods 1958–1959 and 1964–1968 for NYSE stocks are not presented for reasons of space. In almost all respects, this quarterly analysis would lead to the same conclusions as the annual. For the annual data, the prices paid by mutual funds for their net purchases of each issue were estimated as an average of twelve month-end prices of that issue, while for the quarterly data end-of-fiscal-quarter prices were used.

The aggregate fund net purchases of each stock in a period were expressed as a linear function of the stock's risk, dividend payout ratio, and the ratio of subsequent adjusted earnings to the market price of the stock at the beginning of the period. For constant risk and dividend payout, a significant positive association between net purchases of a stock and its ratio of subsequent earnings to initial price would indicate a contribution by the funds to market efficiency, while a significant negative association would indicate the reverse. If the funds do make a positive contribution to market efficiency, net purchases might be expected to be more highly correlated with the ratio of near-term future earnings to initial price than with the ratio of subsequent earnings to initial price, but both correlations should be positive. The correlations might be expected to decline for two reasons: First, it is easier to predict what will happen in the next quarter or year than what might happen ten years from now. Second, as more capital flows into undervalued companies and industries through the stimulus of their rising-earnings ratios, the relative level of earnings of these companies should be reduced in the absence of monopolistic power.

Mathematically, the basic relationship may be shown in the form

$$\frac{NP_i}{H} = a + bR_i + C\,\frac{D_i}{E_i} + d\,\frac{E_{ni}/P_{0i}}{E_{nm}/P_{0m}}$$

where NP_i represents the dollar value of net purchases of the ith stock (any given stock) in the indicated quarter or year by all mutual funds reporting in any month of that quarter or year; H is the dollar value of initial holdings of all stock by funds reporting in that month;[6] R_i is a specific measure

---

[6] The reason for deflating NP_i by H rather than by variables such as O_i, the value of all outstanding shares of the ith stock, is that since the Vickers data are compiled each month for mutual funds with fiscal periods ending in that month, it was desirable to devise a method for appropriately combing or weighting the data reported by the sample funds in different months

of risk, i.e., variance of monthly rate of return, and covariance of rate of return with market;[7] D_i/E_i is the average dividend payout ratio of the stock over a four-year period; E_{ni} and P_{0i} are the terminal earnings and beginning-of-period market price of the stock,[8] and the E_{nm}/P_{0m} ratio used for the market as a whole is the mean of the ratios for the individual stock issues reported on Compustat.

Mutual funds as a whole, according to our results, are neither especially good nor especially bad at directing capital into profitable areas of investment. They seem as likely to invest in a NYSE stock that is overvalued in relation to its subsequent earnings as in one which is undervalued. Actually, there seems to be more evidence of funds purchasing NYSE stock that in the subsequent three to eleven years turned out to be overvalued than of funds purchasing NYSE stock that turned out to be undervalued, but these results, generally, are not statistically significant. The funds tended in 1966 to purchase NYSE stock that showed relatively favorable earnings in the same and following years but tended to do the reverse in 1964. These results are insensitive to the particular way risk is measured.[9]

It was infeasible to repeat this analysis of market efficiency for fund investments in non-NYSE stocks. While the Vickers data did cover American Stock Exchange issues, long-term continuous series of prices and capital adjustment factors were not readily available for a substantial fraction of these issues. However, a much more limited analysis of ASE stock will be reported subsequently on the basis of data provided by the SEC. We have not been able to carry out any separate analysis of market efficiency of fund in-

---

in order to arrive at quarterly (or annual) totals which were reasonably comparable from one period to the next. This procedure, it should be noted, introduces no appreciable timing errors into the estimated statistical relationships, since the initial and terminal periods used in computing E_n and P_0 are adjusted to the reporting period of the fund.

[7] The variance and covariance measures were computed only if there were at least sixty months of data for the NYSE stocks. These measures (and also the average dividend payout ratios) were computed with data from December, 1953, through March, 1961, for the analysis prior to 1964, and with data from April, 1961, through June, 1968, for the analysis after 1964. Other measures of risk and related variables used included one-half the interquartile range and skewness. The objective variance and covariance measures explain a sizable proportion of the variation in quality ratings, a subjective measure of risk. Moreover, on the basis of their relationship with return, variance and covariance seem to be somewhat better proxies for investors' risk assessments than the rating variable (Robert S. Parker, "Some Aspects of Long Run Allocational Efficiency: An Empirical Study of the Stock Market," Ph.D. dissertation, University of Pennsylvania, Philadelphia, 1969). The Parker study also finds little evidence of any nonlinear relation between risk and return.

[8] Different relationships of the same form have been estimated where feasible for $n = 0$, 1, 3, 5, 8, and 11 years after period of net purchase. E_0 represents the first annual earnings report after the P_0 date, E_1 the earnings report for the next year, etc.

[9] The effect of these risk measures is generally quite small and not infrequently has a sign contrary to what would be expected. The measure of skewness is not usually regarded as a risk measure but is another characteristic of the distribution of returns of interest to investors, who presumably prefer positive skewness.

vestments in over-the-counter stock or in letter stock. Over-the-counter issues account for somewhat over 10 percent of the value of all stock held by mutual funds,[10] while letter stock is much smaller though of substantial interest in its own right.[11] NYSE stocks, to which our long-term efficiency analysis is confined, consistently accounted for the preponderance of total assets of the mutual fund industry and even more so of their common stock holdings.

The fact that mutual funds do not appear to show any superior ability to select those stocks with the best long-run earnings potential tends to confirm our tentative conclusion on market efficiency drawn from the analysis of fund investment performance. However, this new finding suggests that it is the impact of their trading activities on the market or their perception of short-run trends in individual securities rather than their foresight in finding fundamentally undervalued issues which may have accounted for the funds' above-average performance in recent years relative to proportionally weighted random portfolios of NYSE stocks. It might also indicate that while the funds are not able to select stocks with favorable earnings trends, they may have some ability to select stocks whose price-earnings ratios will tend to increase in the long run in relation to the market as the market changes its evaluation of their risk.

A quarterly analysis to test this hypothesis was carried out for the periods 1958–1959 and 1964–1968 and stocks covered above. One test consisted of relating aggregate fund net purchases of each stock in a period (divided by fund holdings) not to the ratio of subsequent earnings to beginning-of-period market price of the stock as in the preceding analysis but to the ratio of end-of-period market price to end-of-period earnings (divided by the corresponding ratio for all stocks), again holding the beta coefficient and dividend payout constant. Another test also held constant the ratio of beginning-of-period market price to beginning-of-period earnings (again divided by the corresponding ratio for all stocks).

The results indicated that funds tended to select those stocks which had rising price-earnings ratios relative to the market over the subsequent one to eight years somewhat more often than stocks with declining price-earnings ratios, but the differences were not marked, consistent, or generally

---

[10] This is a rough estimate. The figure as of September, 1958, was 10.6 percent (Wharton School of Finance and Commerce, University of Pennsylvania, *Study of Mutual Funds,* Government Printing Office, Washington, D.C., 1962, p. 185). The estimated ratio of mutual fund holdings of NYSE stock (including preferred) to the market value of their net assets changed very little—71 to 70 percent—from the end of 1958 to the end of 1968 (Investment Company Institute, *op. cit.*). The fund ratio of all common stock holdings to net assets was also relatively unchanged, rising from 83 to 84 percent over this period (*ibid.*).

[11] The SEC has released an estimate of letter stock held by mutual funds as of the end of 1968 (Investment Company Act Release No. 5847, Oct 21, 1969), but the estimate seems to be too high and is being reexamined by the Commission.

statistically significant.[12] The analysis in Chapter 5 will provide some additional insights into the funds' impact on the market as distinguished from their predictive ability.

Short-run Timing

Though the funds display no superior ability to select stocks with the best long-run earnings potential, they may be able to predict or influence short-run movements in the price behavior of individual issues relative to the general market. We ran tests of this relationship that parallel some of the earlier tests of the funds' ability to predict general market movements. Obviously, in the short run, the overall rate of return on a stock is dominated by its price experience. Therefore, the new results can be regarded as tests of the short-run market efficiency of the funds' stock trading, with qualification that the results do not distinguish situations in which the funds displayed superior insight from those in which their activities affected the market.

The same quarterly Vickers data for New York Stock Exchange stocks were used as in the analysis of long-run efficiency. The price changes over a quarter in individual stocks (relative to the market) were expressed as a function of aggregate fund net purchases (relative to aggregate fund holdings) of that stock in the same and in the two preceding quarters, of the stock's risk, and of its price changes (relative to the market) in the period preceding that covered by the purchase data. The use of preceding-period values of price changes is an attempt to hold constant other influences not explicitly allowed for.

The pooled results for all quarters in the 1958–1959, 1964–1965, and 1966–1967, periods covered are presented in Appendix Table 4-2. They indicate some tendency for mutual fund net purchases of a NYSE stock in a quarter to be associated with a rise in the stock's price relative to the market, especially in the 1958–1959 and 1966–1967 periods, but it is not clear whether this tendency is statistically significant.[13] The evidence on the relationship between fund net purchases of a NYSE stock and its price behavior in the following quarter is more mixed: a moderate positive correlation in 1966–1967, and weaker negative correlations in 1958–1959 and 1964–1965.[14] Thus,

---

[12] For example, using the traditional .05 test of significance, which tends to overstate the reliability of results, the funds' purchases were useful in only two out of eight quarters for anticipating changes in price-earnings ratios over an eight-year period, in no quarter out of the eight covered for anticipating changes over a five-year period, and in no quarter out of thirteen for anticipating changes over a three-year period.

[13] Since the distribution of stock price relatives — and probably also of the ratio of relatives — is not normal, it is necessary to use somewhat more stringent standards of significance than those customarily applied.

[14] The generally positive correlation between relative price performance and risk (as measured by the beta coefficient) reflects the fact that the quarters covered are typically periods of rising stock prices.

any ability of the funds to predict short-term relative price movements of individual stock issues is confined mainly to the same quarter. Even in the same quarter, however, it cannot be ascertained from these results whether funds purchased stock before or after the favorable price movement.

Recent Short-run Results

The SEC data available from the fourth quarter of 1967 through the second quarter of 1968 make it possible to examine the funds' and other management investment companies'[15] purchases of individual portfolio issues separately from their sales and to analyze issues listed on the American Stock Exchange as well as those listed on the New York Stock Exchange. Unfortunately, the information does not permit the types of long-run analysis carried out with the Vickers data. Due to the brief time span covered by the SEC data, we confined our analysis to the relationship between the short-run price behavior of issues purchased and sold by the investment companies and that of the general market. The price changes over a quarter in individual stocks relative to the market were expressed as a function of the aggregate fund gross purchases and gross sales of that stock relative to the amount of the stock outstanding.[16] In some cases, the preceding quarter's ratios of purchases and sales to outstanding stock were added as additional explanatory variables, and in others the ratio of fund holdings to outstanding stock was also added. Separate relationships were computed for NYSE and for American Stock Exchange stock as well as for the two combined.

The most important results of this analysis are presented in Appendix Table 4-3. The higher investment company purchases of a stock issue during a quarter, the better was the price performance of the issue from the beginning to the end of that quarter. The reverse is true of investment company sales; i.e., the higher the sales of an issue, the poorer its price performance. While both results are probably statistically significant[17] and the same results are obtained in each of the periods covered, investment company purchases and sales do not explain a high proportion of the variation in the price performance of different issues. However, their transactions appear to cause, or to anticipate correctly, or to be motivated by, some of the short-run relative price fluctuations in individual issues. Investment company purchases and sales of the preceding quarter are much less closely related

[15] While all management investment companies, closed-end as well as open-end, are included in the SEC data, the great bulk of the activity covered by these companies is accounted for by mutual funds.

[16] It was necessary to eliminate a small number of issues because of difficulties with the capital adjustment corrections. Several different forms of the gross purchases and gross sales variables were tested, including deflation by volume of trading, but deflation by the amount of stock outstanding seemed most reasonable and gave the best statistical results.

[17] For reasons explained earlier, it is necessary to use somewhat more stringent standards of significance than those customarily applied.

to the price performance of an issue in a given quarter, and the negative correlations between the measures of price performance and both previous quarter purchases and sales are probably insignificant.[18] These findings generally were somewhat stronger for NYSE than for American Stock Exchange issues. Investment company holdings of a stock do not seem consistently to affect the issue's price performance over a quarter.

Further insights can be gained into the nature of this relationship between investment company purchases and sales of individual issues and the short-run price behavior of that issue by relating the purchases (or sales) in one quarter to the purchases and sales in the preceding quarter, to the relative price performance of the issue in each of the same and preceding quarters, and to the investment company holdings of that issue.[19]

The investment companies tended to purchase the issues which they had purchased in the preceding quarter and those which performed well in the preceding or in the same quarter (Appendix Table 4-4). The companies tended to sell those issues which they had sold or (to a lesser extent) purchased in the preceding quarter, those in which they had sizable holdings, and those which performed badly in the same quarter. There is some evidence that the investment companies followed market trends in their portfolio purchases during this period, though much less so in their sales.[20] However, it is not possible to say from these data whether the companies caused or anticipated the positive relation between their net purchases and price movements during the same quarter.

Since the mutual funds did not show any superior ability in selecting those stocks with the best long-run earnings potential, it could be argued that the positive relation between their net purchases and price movements during the same period may reflect the effect of their trading activities rather than their predictive ability. Nevertheless, such evidence is at best only suggestive. Other tests of the extent to which the funds anticipate or cause stock market movements are carried out in Chapter 5 in an analysis of the impact of mutual funds on fluctuations in the stock market.

An additional result of this analysis is that mutual funds do not have a monolithic investment policy. Often, within a quarter, one group of funds

[18] A negative correlation between price performance in one quarter and purchases in the preceding quarter makes little sense unless destabilizing purchases are followed by a movement toward market equilibrium.

[19] In the statistical relationships estimated, end-of-quarter holdings were used for computational reasons instead of the more appropriate beginning-of-period holdings. While this procedure poses no problem in Appendix Table 4-4, it does somewhat bias those relationships in Appendix Table 4-5 which include holdings as an explanatory variable, though the effects are not believed to be large.

[20] If investment company purchases and sales of an issue are deflated by the total volume of trading (V_i) in that issue rather than by the total amount of outstanding shares (O_i), the companies appeared to follow market trends more in their sales than in their purchases. However, the correlations are consistently higher when O_i is used instead of V_i.

will buy issues that another group is selling (and at times individual funds will buy and sell the same issue).[21] Funds also frequently buy or sell the same issues in successive quarters.[22] Further investigation is needed on the relationship between patterns of purchases and sales of individual issues by different groups of funds. Perhaps the most interesting question here is the extent to which certain groups of funds are the leaders and others followers in setting investment fashions.

Concordance of Portfolio Activity among Management Investment Companies

The stock market (especially in ebullient periods) has always provided evidence of follow-the-leader behavior. The attention paid in recent years to the performance of funds having high rates of return or high growth rates suggests that these funds may have significantly influenced the behavior of other funds, and presumably other investors as well. The quarterly net purchases of individual securities by individual funds are generally made public within several weeks after the end of the quarter in the funds' reports to their stockholders. Sizable purchases are frequently known to other funds and professional investors shortly after they occur. Indeed, once an acquisition or liquidation program has been completed by a fund, it has no incentive to conceal its action and, under certain circumstances, may gain from the immediate disclosure.

To test whether mutual funds or other management investment companies have shown any evidence of such follow-the-leader behavior we analyzed the relationship between the investment behavior of the relatively successful management investment companies in the first quarter of 1968 and that of all other investment companies in the following quarter, based on the SEC quarterly data on each company's purchases and sales of portfolio stock referred to earlier. For the first set of relationships, the gross volume of purchases of a given stock in the second quarter of 1968 by the "followers" was expressed as a function of the "leaders'" gross purchases in the first quarter and the followers' gross purchases in that quarter. All variables were expressed as a ratio to the number of outstanding shares of that stock. (The purpose of the last term in the equation, the lagged gross purchases by the followers, is to hold as constant as possible the basic short-run investment policy of these companies.) Similar relationships were estimated by adding such variables as lagged sales of both the leaders and the fol-

---

[21] The simple pooled correlation between the P_i/O_i and S_i/O_i quarterly ratios was .34 for the fourth quarter of 1967 and first quarter of 1968.

[22] The simple correlation between the successive P_i/O_i ratios for the fourth quarter of 1967 and the first quarter of 1968 was .48 and between the successive S_i/O_i ratios .46.

lowers. Identical types of relationships were estimated to explain the sales of followers.[23]

In those relationships explaining purchases by the followers, a significantly positive coefficient of the variable representing lagged purchases by the leaders would suggest a follow-the-leader behavior, but this would not be conclusive. Such a result might simply reflect similar behavior in both leaders and followers and serial correlation between the behavior of each group of funds in successive quarters; or it might reflect the deflation of both dependent and independent variables by the same variable, i.e., the number of outstanding shares. Therefore, a second set of relationships was estimated to test further the presence of follow-the-leader behavior. The gross volume of purchases of a given stock in the second quarter of 1968 by the leaders was now expressed as a function of its gross purchases by leaders and followers in the preceding quarter. All variables were again expressed as a ratio to the outstanding shares. The conclusion we might draw from a significantly positive coefficient of lagged purchases by the leaders in the first set would be strengthened considerably by an insignificant coefficient of lagged purchases by the followers in the second. Such results would indicate that the followers' purchases of a stock truly lag behind the leaders' purchases, and that this is not just a statistical quirk.

Two criteria were used to distinguish the likely leaders among the management investment companies: their rate of return of growth over some preceding period and their size. It was statistically most convenient to use the investment company's rate of growth in the first quarter of 1968, though rate of return might be preferable to rate of growth, and return or growth over a longer span of time might be preferable to growth over a quarter. Six classifications of leaders were tested: the twenty-five investment companies with the highest growth rates in the first quarter of 1968 and with a market value of common stock over $15 million, over $50 million, and over $100 million at the end of that quarter, and the ten top companies within those twenty-five. All other funds reporting to the SEC were classified as potential followers. Qualitatively, the results obtained from the different classifications are similar, but the best results were derived by classifying as leaders either the twenty-five companies with the highest growth rates of those with a common stock portfolio worth over $15 million or the ten companies with the highest growth rates of those with a common stock portfolio worth over $50 million.

---

[23] An attempt was also made to analyze the parallelism of action among all investment funds, the leaders and the followers in their portfolio decisions. The procedure used was to rank, for each fund, the quarterly net purchases divided by the outstanding shares for each stock on the New York Stock Exchange and American Stock Exchange. Since there were many issues which a fund neither purchased nor sold, there were numerous ties in the ranks, making such measures as Kendall's G concordance coefficient inappropriate for measuring parallelism of action. These results are therefore not presented in the text.

The results in Appendix Table 4-5, as well as other results not presented, suggest that there is a statistically significant amount of market leadership in stocks purchased by mutual funds. In spite of our primitive definition of market leadership and the need to impose a rather unrealistic fixed one-quarter lag, there is evidence that a number of investment company managers do, at least to some extent, follow their more successful colleagues' investment behavior.[24] There is no reason to believe that such behavior by investment companies that were not in the top-growth group paid off in better-than-random performance, in view of the industry's investment performance discussed earlier. The extent to which the top-growth companies influence the stock purchases by other companies is relatively modest, but this may be a deficiency of the data available to us.

One interesting sidelight on the different trading patterns of the top-growth and other funds is indicated by the high correlation between the sales of the second quarter of 1968 and the purchases of the first quarter for the top-growth group and the much more moderate correlation for other funds.[25] This reflects the fact that the top-growth funds had high portfolio turnover.

[24] These results may also reflect some tendency by investment companies as a whole to purchase stocks which had already risen in price.

[25] The coefficient of determination adjusted for degrees of freedom ($\bar{R}^2$) was .84 for the former group and .20 for the latter.

Chapter Five

IMPACT OF MUTUAL FUNDS ON MARKET MOVEMENTS

THE ANALYSIS IN Chapters 3 and 4 examined some aspects of the relationship between movements in the market and the purchases and sales of securities by mutual funds. There was no significant evidence that mutual funds have the ability to predict or to influence quarterly or monthly movements in the stock market as a whole, as measured by the timing of their flows into and out of the market in relation to the changes in the level of market indices. However, when quarterly portfolio transactions and price movements in individual stocks were examined, the results suggested that the funds either correctly anticipated or possibly affected subsequent trends in the issues they purchased. The analysis of the overall investment performance of mutual funds using proportional weights indicates that these funds had some ability to predict or influence market movements—presumably in individual issues—during the 1964–1968 period, though not for the other periods covered. There was some evidence in the 1964–1968 period that the funds with higher relative trading activity (as measured by the turnover ratio) tended to perform better than other funds, though the margin of difference was small.

While this evidence is hardly impressive, it does provide some indication that mutual funds may in their trading of individual issues either anticipate or cause subsequent abnormally large price movements. The first analysis of the chapter measures the comparative success of stocks funds purchased and sold. It provides a somewhat more satisfactory test of the wisdom of the funds' trading activity. This test does not permit any inferences to be drawn on the predictive ability versus the market impact of the funds except in the unlikely contingency that stocks purchased by the funds in a given period on average subsequently performed worse than stocks sold by the funds in that same period. The second test of the chapter measures the funds' success in timing their purchases and sales of individual securities. This analysis does distinguish, under some conditions, the predictive ability of the funds from their market impact upon the prices of individual issues.

Subsequent Performance of Stocks Purchased and Sold

A sensitive test of the success of the funds' trading activity, at least before transaction costs, is the comparison of the average rates of return subsequently achieved by stocks in different risk classes purchased by the funds with the average rates of return subsequently achieved by the stocks in corresponding risk classes sold by the funds. Although this comparison does provide a satisfactory basis for determining whether, when funds turn over their portfolios, the stocks they buy do better than the stocks they sell, it will not, under most conditions, distinguish between the predictive ability of the funds and the impact effects of their trading.

The analysis of the relationship between the overall investment performance of mutual funds and the turnover rates of their portfolios in Chapter 3 suggests as one possibility that in the 1964–1968 period their trading activity tended to be successful even after commission expenses and that in the earlier periods their trading activity, if successful at all, was not on average sufficiently successful to cover the transaction costs. However, the results in Chapter 3 are consistent with two other equally tenable hypotheses: First, superior or inferior investment performance in any period may reflect the classes of securities held by funds (e.g., glamour stocks, letter stock) rather than the results of their trading activity; in fact trading activity itself may be a good surrogate for the classes of securities held. Second, it is possible that funds with a superior record of performance might feel freer to increase their trading activity and hence brokerage fees and the corresponding give-ups to enhance the sale of their shares or, if the external adviser is connected with a brokerage firm, his income.

The data used to test the comparative record of stocks purchased and sold are the quarterly Vickers data for the New York Stock Exchange stocks, covering the periods 1958–1959, 1964–1965, and 1966–1967. These data were described extensively in Chapter 4.

The subsequent performance of the individual securities purchased and sold by mutual funds, for these three periods for four different risk, or beta, classes, are analyzed in Appendix Table 5-1. The performance itself is measured by the ratio of the rate of return (including the reinvestment of dividends) subsequently realized by the security to the rate of return subsequently realized by a typical security of the same risk. The return on a typical security of a given risk was measured as the unweighted average of the returns of all securities that had roughly the same risk characteristics as measured by the beta coefficient.[1] An unweighted average, as pointed out in Chapter 3, may be substantially different from a value-weighted average.[2] These ratios, which therefore should be interpreted as rough and not exact measures of performance, were expressed as rates of returns by subtracting 1. In the future they will be called abnormal rates of return—abnormal in that they abstract from the return that would typically be realized by a security of the same risk picked at random. A positive percentage would indicate superior performance; a negative percentage inferior performance; and a zero percentage neither superior nor inferior performance.

These abnormal rates of return were calculated for each security covered in the Vickers data which was purchased or sold by a mutual fund during the three periods mentioned above. In the case of a purchase, any security held less than three months was ignored. These rates were derived for the three-, six-, twelve-, eighteen-, and twenty-four-month periods following the quarter in which the security was purchased or sold. The use of the return in the interval following the reported quarter in which the transaction took place will produce a slight understatement of the success of mutual

[1] The construction of indices of returns for each class proceeded as follows: For, say, February, 1958, the beta for each stock on the New York Stock Exchange was estimated using the sixty previous months of data including that for February, 1958, by regressing these monthly returns on the corresponding values of the Fisher combination investment performance index. The securities were then classified in four risk classes, whose beta values were respectively .4 to .8, .8 to 1.2, 1.2 to 1.6, and 1.6 to 2.0.

For the lowest beta class, .4 to .8, the percentage increase in the value, including the reinvestment of dividends, of each security was calculated from the end of February, 1958, through the end of May, 1958—a three-month period. Percentage increases in values were also calculated for six-, twelve-, eighteen-, and twenty-four-month periods from the end of February, 1958. These percentage increases were then averaged, giving equal weight to each security to determine indices of return. Similar indices were also constructed for the returns during the fourth through the sixth month, seventh through the twelfth, thirteenth through the eighteenth, and nineteenth through the twenty-fourth. The above process was repeated for each risk class and for each month for which the Vickers data contained quarterly net purchases.

[2] Chapter 3 examined in detail the problems of using an equally weighted rather than a value-weighted index as a criterion of comparison. During the 1960–1964 period, the return given by an equally weighted index was 2.9 percent less than the return given by the value-weighted index, and during the 1964–1968 period, the return given by equally weighted index was 8.0 percent greater than the return given by value-weighted index. The measures of performance described in the text will therefore tend to be biased upward in the earlier period and downward in the later period if the value-weighted index is preferred.

funds' trading activity if this activity is successful. The reason for this is that the measure of return does not begin immediately after the transaction and may not begin to record the performance of the security until up to three months after the purchase or sale. For a purchase, this would tend to understate the realized return and the reverse for a sale, if the trades were justified.

These abnormal returns were then averaged for each risk class and each period to yield the figures contained in Appendix Table 5-1. For ease of interpretation, these averages are expressed as "annualized rates of return." This means that the rates are comparable regardless of the number of months over which the performance was measured. An abnormal return of 6 percent, for instance, in the three months subsequent to the purchase indicates that the security had an abnormal increase in value of somewhat less than 1.5 percent during this three-month period. The averages themselves are weighted by the absolute dollar value of the net quarterly purchases or sales rather than by an equal weight for each purchase or sale. The number of different quarterly purchases and sales covered in these different averages, as opposed to the dollar value of the purchases and sales, is also given in this table.

In the 1958–1959 period, the subsequent performance of the purchases is roughly the same as the subsequent performance of the sales as measured by the abnormal rates of return. For the three months subsequent to the transaction, the sales outperform the purchases two times out of four. If there is any tendency for the trading activity of mutual funds (as measured by the abnormal rates of return in these three months) to be successful at least before transaction costs, the success would be confined to the highest two risk classes of securities. By the end of the twenty-four-month period following the quarter in which the transaction took place, there is no evidence that the securities purchased outperformed the securities sold.[3] Mutual funds, however, may have realized abnormal returns on some of their purchases if they did not hold the securities for the full two-year period, particularly the higher-risk securities.

In the 1964–1965 period, success in their trading activity seems to be confined to transactions in the two highest risk classes, as measured by the performance in the three months following the purchase or sale. The magnitude of their success in the highest-risk stocks is particularly pronounced: an abnormal return of 36.5 percent for the purchases and -2.6 percent for

---

[3] As discussed earlier, there is possibly some bias in these abnormal rates of return, so that a value slightly less or greater than zero may not indicate significantly better or worse performance. Since there is no reason to believe that this bias, if present, would affect the abnormal rates of return for the securities purchased differentially from those for the securities sold, the comparison of the success of sales versus purchases can be done without fear of any statistical biases.

the sales. This means that during the three months after the quarter of the transaction, the securities purchased increased somewhat less than 9 percent in value and the securities sold decreased somewhat less than 0.7 percent. Insofar as the funds sold their holdings of these high-risk securities in less than twelve months, the magnitudes of the abnormal returns indicate that the profit from such trading activity would more than cover the commission cost. Therefore their trading activity would be deemed successful from the point of view of the investor. The funds' trading activities in the two lowest-risk classes do not appear to have produced any abnormal returns (as measured by any period up to twenty-four months after the transactions). There is no evidence that the stocks purchased performed any better than the stocks sold by the end of the twenty-four months. In fact, for the high-risk class of securities, there is some evidence that the stocks purchased performed substantially worse than the stocks sold.

In the 1966–1967 period, the abnormal rates of return for the purchases for the three months following the transaction exceeded the corresponding returns for the sales for all risk classes. The differences between the abnormal returns on the purchases and sales for the two highest-risk classes is pronounced. For the twelve-month period following the transactions, which is the longest interval analyzed because of the availability of data, the securities purchased exhibited better performance than those sold for all but the lowest-risk class, with the magnitude of the differences in performance increasing with the risk of the securities bought or sold.

In summary, the performance of the securities purchased was not substantially different from that of the securities sold by the end of two years after the transaction in the 1958–1959 and 1964–1965 periods, although in the latter period and to some extent the former period the high-risk stocks purchased by mutual funds performed better than the stocks sold in the three months after the transaction. This tendency for short-run success of purchases relative to sales in the higher-risk securities is even more pronounced during the 1966–1967 period with this success extending to moderately risky securities. These results are consistent with the finding of a positive relationship between turnover and performance of mutual funds in the 1964–1968 period, since the funds with the highest turnover tend to hold the high-risk securities.

It is not surprising that mutual funds appear to demonstrate some success in picking those high-risk stocks which will rise and those which will fall in the short run in relation to a typical stock of the same general characteristics. These stocks typically represent the smaller, less seasoned companies, whose securities probably are not as well priced as the larger, more seasoned companies. The predictive hypothesis would argue that funds perceive which securities are under- or overvalued and by their transactions help to drive the prices of these high-risk stocks back to equilibrium. The trouble with this explanation is that it does not explain why no tendency was observed for the securities purchased to outperform the securities sold in the 1958–1959 or 1964–1965 periods, for the twenty-four-month period following the transactions. The superior performance of the higher-risk stock for the twelve-month interval following the transaction in the 1966–1967 period suggests that if these performance figures could be extended to twenty-four months, the securities purchased might very well outperform the securities sold. Thus, the funds in this last period may have demonstrated more predictive ability than they did in the earlier periods. Yet, in view of the increased differences between the short-run performance of the purchases and sales in the recent years and the increase in institutional trading in these same years, the data are also consistent with the market impact hypothesis: it is impossible to distinguish between the two hypotheses using these data.

The Success of Timing

The previous analysis ignored the problem of the timing of portfolio purchases and sales in judging the success of the trading activity of mutual funds. Thus, it could not tell whether mutual funds realized capital gains in those securities that had abnormally high returns. To analyze this aspect of mutual fund trading activities, the abnormal rates of return for the securities purchased in Appendix Table 5-1 were broken down according to the length of time a security was held in a fund's portfolio.

Appendix Tables 5-2 and 5-3 present this breakdown for securities which were held from four to six months and those held more than six months. A purchase was classified in the holding category of four to six months if it was followed by a sale of any size of the same security by the same fund in the four to six months following the purchase. If there was a sale in less than four months, the purchase was ignored, because the data did not permit a fine enough resolution of the timing to allow a meaningful analysis. Otherwise, the purchase was classified in the holding period of seven or more months. The averages are weighted by the dollar value of the purchases and expressed as "annualized rates of return," as they were in Appendix Table 5-1.

This scheme for classifying a purchase in one of these two categories and for weighting the average by the value of the purchase is not as clear-cut as it might seem at first glance. For a security in which a mutual fund established its complete position in one quarter and eliminated its complete position during the four- to six-month period following the purchase, this classification gives theoretically correct results. If, however, the taking of a position or the reduction of this position took more than one quarter, the classifications and the weightings are not precisely correct. For instance, if 50 percent of a position were taken in one quarter and 50 percent in the next and if then in four to six months the position were eliminated, half of the position would be classified in the four- to six-month holding period and half in the over-six-months holding period. From the viewpoint of the mutual fund manager, it is not clear whether these purchases should be split this way: the decision to take this position may have been long-term, but the sequence of the execution of the purchase orders resulted in the classification of part of the decision as short-term. Yet, from the viewpoint of the market as a whole, this classification and weighting scheme is reasonable, because the market observes the transactions and not the decision to make the transactions.

The results for the 1958–1959 and the 1964–1965 periods are similar, so they will be treated together. Any substantive differences will be noted. The numbers of quarterly purchases analyzed in each entry of Appendix Tables 5-2 and 5-3 are given in Appendix Table 5-4. The few purchases analyzed in the abnormal returns for securities held four to six months for all risk intervals in the 1958–1959 period and for the highest-risk interval in the 1966–1967 period may produce large sampling errors, and any conclusion based upon these particular performance figures would be suspect. The remaining abnormal returns in Appendix Tables 5-3 and 5-4 are all based on sample sizes ranging from a low of 109 to a high of 1,797 and thus can be taken with some confidence.

In the 1958–1959 and the 1964–1965 periods, there are no discernible differences between the returns subsequently realized in the twenty-four-month period following the purchase on securities held only four to six months and on those held more than six months. The sole surprising figure is the 23.3 percent annualized abnormal return for the 1964–1965 period for stocks with betas between 1.6 and 2.0 and held only four to six months. Since, for all funds, these highest-risk securities represent a small proportion of their total assets, the timing of the purchases and sales of the high-risk stocks would have little impact upon aggregate performance, although it may have important effects on individual funds.

A more careful examination of Appendix Table 5-3 discloses that all the abnormal returns measured for the twenty-four-month period after the quarter of the purchase for the 1958–1959 period are negative, that four out of eight for the 1964–1965 period are negative, and that all for the twelve-month period after the purchase for the 1966–1967 period are negative. These findings are consistent with those in the previous section.

The same results are evident in Appendix Table 5-3, which gives a better view of the periods in which the returns were negative. During the twelve-month period following the purchase, the returns are predominantly positive for the 1958–1959 and 1964–1965 periods and then for the next twelve months predominantly negative. For the 1966–1967 period, the abnormal returns are half positive and half negative in the one- to three- and the four-to six-month intervals following the purchase and are all negative during the seven- to twelve-month period. This means that the prices of stocks purchased by mutual funds tend to rise in relation to the market after the purchase and then fall in relation to the market. This pattern of increase and subsequent decrease takes place more rapidly in the 1966–1967 period than in the earlier periods.

These results are consistent with the hypothesis that there is some positive dependence in the changes in security prices, so that stocks tend to move gradually out of equilibrium and then back into equilibrium. This evidence cannot be used definitively to decide whether funds predict prices or affect them, although the market impact hypothesis seems more plausible than the predictive hypothesis. Since the securities they purchased tended to show abnormally high and then abnormally low returns, the large sums available to them would tend to make one believe that their purchases might have even increased the magnitude of this disequilibrium. In any case, one must conclude that their trading activity did not help to stabilize the market.

The pattern of the three-month returns for the high-risk stocks (measured by betas between 1.6 and 2.0) for the 1964–1965 period is strikingly different from those associated with the lower beta stocks in this period.[4] For stocks held four to six months, the three-month annualized return for 1964–1965 is 52.8 percent, whereas the same return for stocks held more than six months is 28.0 percent. Thus, the trading activity of mutual funds in these high-risk stocks must be deemed extremely successful. Whether this success results from their predictive ability or from their market impact must be assessed to determine whether mutual funds help to stabilize or destabilize the market and thus the economy.

An explanation, and it will turn out that this is the most likely one, is that mutual funds in their trading activity do have an effect upon market prices of the high-risk stocks which would tend to include the smaller, less seasoned companies. If mutual funds did have such an effect, one would expect that as they purchased a security, the price would be driven up, and as they sold the same security, the price would be driven down, resulting in an abnormally high return and then an abnormally low return. The high-risk securities held four to six months behaved this way, as indicated. The abnormal return was 52.8 percent for the three months after the quarter of the transaction and -22.0 percent for the quarter in which they were sold.

After the mutual funds complete their selling activity, the stock should recover from its oversold position, although it may not return to its same level as before the trading activity took place, due to possible fundamental changes in the company either predicted or caused by their trading. These

---

[4] The stocks held four to six months with betas between 1.6 and 2.0 for the 1958–1959 and 1966–1967 periods will not be analyzed because of the small sample. Even for the 1964–1965 period, the sample size is not impressive, but it is probably large enough to yield reliable results.

recoveries did occur. In the seven- to twelve-month interval following the quarter of the initial purchase of the security, the securities held four to six months recovered 38.4 percent. These recoveries resulted in a cumulative abnormal return of 25.8 percent from the quarter of purchase.

The abnormal returns for the high-risk stocks held seven or more months are also consistent with the hypothesis of market impact. During the six months following the quarter in which the purchase occurred, mutual funds would either be holding this stock or increasing their holdings, thereby driving up the prices. After the sixth month, the mutual funds could be reducing their holdings, doing nothing, or increasing their holdings, so that the market impact hypothesis would imply nothing about the direction of the future price changes. The empirical results in Appendix Tables 5-2 and 5-3 are consistent with this description. For the first two quarters following the transaction, the returns are abnormally high; thereafter, they tend to fluctuate about zero.

The hypothesis that mutual funds tend to have a substantial impact upon the prices of high-risk securities, which would include the smaller, less seasoned companies, provides a very good description of the data. There are of course numerous other hypotheses which might possibly be consistent with the data.

The most obvious alternative hypothesis is that mutual funds have some ability to predict future price movements and therefore help to stabilize the market by making the adjustment take place sooner. This hypothesis, although it can explain some of the observed data, cannot explain all the data as adequately as the impact hypothesis.

For the stocks held four to six months, the predictive hypothesis would proceed in this way: Mutual funds would perceive that certain securities were undervalued and would purchase them. This trading activity would of itself tend to drive up the price and would secondarily, but possibly more importantly, draw attention to the undervalued situation. The stock price would then adjust upward to its new equilibrium, causing an abnormally high return. When the adjustment had taken place, the mutual fund would withdraw its money, taking a large profit, and would have performed a useful social service. So far, the data are consistent.

After the sale, a naïve version of the predictive hypothesis is that the security would be at its new equilibrium and in the future the security would exhibit neither consistently abnormal high nor low returns. The data, of course, are inconsistent with this prediction, because there are large negative returns on average in the quarter of sale. Yet, a more sophisticated version of the predictive hypothesis could explain these negative returns in conjunction with the method by which Appendix Tables 5-2 and 5-3 were constructed.

The reasoning would go as follows: There are two classes of highly risky stocks. First, there are those securities whose earnings fluctuate widely, possibly due to changes in GNP or defense expenditures, but which can be accurately predicted in relation to these factors. Since future earnings behave in predictable ways, the nature of the risk attached to these securities would be known with reasonable certainty and the chance of a failure would be remote; thus these securities might be held for the long term. Second, there are those securities whose future earnings are very uncertain due, possibly, to new technology or products. Some of these securities will succeed, and others will fail. An efficient capital market will channel funds to these companies, fully realizing that some companies will fail and others will succeed handsomely. The securities of such new technological companies will have spectacular returns in the short run, and as information about the success of the companies becomes available, the securities will adjust upward or downward. The proponents of the predictive hypothesis might argue that mutual funds invest in these latter types of securities and due to their superior skill unload in a very short period of time those companies which are subsequently doomed to failure. Moreover, the method of constructing Appendix Tables 5-2 and 5-3 leads to the classification of the failed firms in the four- to six-month holding periods and the successful firms in the longer holding periods.

Although one could, using the predictive hypothesis, justify the negative abnormal returns in the quarter in which the funds sold, one would be hard pressed to explain the observed recovery in the following quarters (the seven- to twelve-month interval following the purchase). Careful consideration discloses no reasonable explanation under the predictive hypothesis. Thus, the data for the high-risk stock for 1964–1965 lend some support to the market impact hypothesis over the predictive hypothesis.

The evidence in this chapter indicated that in the more recent years the high-risk stocks purchased by mutual funds tended in the short run to outperform the stocks of the same risk sold by mutual funds. This tendency was more pronounced and covered a larger spectrum of risky stocks in the 1966–1967 period than in the 1964–1965 period. There was some evidence that this tendency was also present in the 1958–1959 period, although the magnitude of the difference was inconsequential. These tendencies are compatible with either the hypothesis that mutual funds can predict future price changes or that the trading activity itself of the funds affects prices. An analysis of the performance of high-risk securities by the length of time held in the 1964–1965 period gave some weak support to the market impact hypothesis over the predictive hypothesis. If, as this evidence suggests, mutual funds' trading activity does have some impact upon the prices of the higher-risk stocks (which are typically the smaller, less seasoned companies), there is some presumption that mutual funds' trading activity on the American Stock Exchange and the over-the-counter market would have considerably more impact. These stocks are usually smaller and less seasoned than those on the New York Stock Exchange.

For the two years following a transaction, there is no evidence that the funds' purchases outperformed the sales in the 1958–1959 period and the 1964–1965 period. In view of this finding, the trading activity of the funds had virtually no impact upon prices in the medium term, and any short-run abnormal profits made by the funds therefore result from their anticipating or causing transient changes in prices of individual securities. Although the data were available only for one year, there was some suggestion that the securities purchased might have outperformed the securities sold in the two years after the transactions in the 1966–1967 period, so that in this period funds might have anticipated or caused longer-term price movements than in earlier periods.

Chapter Six

IMPACT OF INSTITUTIONAL INVESTORS ON MARKET EFFICIENCY

DID THE INCREASED stockholdings and trading by mutual funds contribute to or subtract from stock market efficiency? The analysis in the preceding chapters did not indicate that on balance either effort was significant. That analysis was primarily directed to the funds' contribution to intermediate and longer-term market efficiency in NYSE stocks, because only limited information was available on trading in other stocks or on trading in NYSE stocks within three-month intervals and no data were available on individual transactions or on trading for periods shorter than a month. The evidence was stronger on the funds' contribution to long-run market efficiency than on intermediate-run efficiency, since the rate of return on a stock over several years (including price appreciation) is much less likely to be affected by the funds trading in that stock than quarterly or monthly rates of return. Thus, it is easier to isolate the funds' ability to select stocks with the best earnings potential from long-run than shorter-term data.

Unfortunately, we do not have data permitting a comparable evaluation of the contribution of pension funds or other institutional investors to market efficiency along the lines carried out for mutual funds. However, we can use the University of Chicago and Standard and Poor's data for New York Stock Exchange stocks described in Chapter 4, covering the periods 1958–1959, 1964–1965, and 1966–1967, to obtain some insights into the impact of all institutional investors on trends in intermediate and longer-run market efficiency. Since we do not have trading data for institutional investors other than mutual funds, the only course open to us is to determine whether there have been any significant changes in market efficiency over the period covered—a period when institutional investors were becoming increasingly important. Obviously, many factors apart from institutional trading affect market efficiency so that any changes in efficiency observed over these years do not necessarily reflect institutional activities. On the other hand, it is difficult to conceive of any development that had a larger impact on the stock market in recent years. If institutional net purchases and trading do have any marked effect on market efficiency, it might be expected that this should show up over a period in which institutional stock ownership and trading increased so greatly.

The ability of the stock market to maintain equivalent rates of return on comparable investments was used to measure market efficiency over the periods covered. To the extent that the market has this ability, it would help to ensure that funds are channeled from savers to those users who will apply them most profitably, in view of the close relationship between rates of return and costs of financing. Comparable investment opportunities would find access to new funds at comparable costs. The most profitable investments for given risk would be able to bid funds away from investments offering lower rates of return. The efficiency of this process can be assessed retrospectively by the extent to which there are variations in return among different stocks and by the extent to which these variations can be explained by differentials in risk. There are, of course, other tests of overall market efficiency, including tests of short-term price continuity and rapidity of response to changes in underlying economic conditions. However, the test used in this chapter seems to us to be the most relevant to the basic concept of efficiency in the allocation of economic resources. Furthermore, it has the very practical advantage that the necessary data were readily available to us as a by-product of the analysis in Chapter 4.

The test of market efficiency in this chapter relates, for each quarter covered, the adjusted ratio of subsequent earnings to beginning-of-period price of each of the NYSE stocks covered to measures of the stock's risk and average dividend payout, and it uses measures of goodness of fit of this relationship as an indication of market efficiency. The adjusted ratio of subsequent earnings to beginning-of-period price of the stock is the ratio of end-of-period earnings to beginning-of-period price divided by the corresponding ratio for the market as a whole. The risk measures are the beta coefficient (β), indicating the covariation of the monthly rate of return with the market, and the variance of the monthly rate of return (σ^2). (See Chapter 4 for details of measurement of adjusted earnings-price ratios, average dividend payout, and risk measures, as well as the stocks covered.)

The measures of goodness of fit are the adjusted coefficient of determination (the square of the correlation coefficient adjusted for degrees of free-dom $\bar{R}^2$) and the standard error of estimate of the relationship. To the extent that the variables explaining the adjusted terminal earnings–initial price ratios account for a high proportion of the variation in these ratios (i.e., the correlation is high), the coefficient of determination (or the cor-relation coefficient) might be considered the more appropriate measure of market efficiency. However, if the correlation is low (i.e., the model used is not very helpful in explaining variations in earnings-price ratios), the standard error of estimate is the preferable measure of market efficiency. Under such circumstances it should be quite close to the dispersion of the original values of the ratios of the end-of-period earnings to beginning-of-period price. The correlation would not generally be expected to be very high, since no provision could be made for one of the most important sets of variables affecting the earnings-price ratios, anticipated and unanticipated growth rates in earnings. An increase over time in the correlation coef-ficient or a decrease in the standard error, or both, would point to an im-provement in market efficiency.

Summary results of these statistical tests are presented in Appendix Tables 6-1 and 6-2. For each quarter in the period covered, a number of statistical relationships are computed expressing, as a function of dividend payout and risk, the adjusted ratios to initial price (P_0) of the first annual earnings after the price date (E_0), and for some of the earlier quarters the adjusted ratios to initial price of subsequent annual earnings up to eight years later (E_8). The correlation indicated by these relationships is as a whole extremely low, so that the standard error of estimate is likely to be a superior relative measure of market efficiency for different periods.

For the period from the first quarter of 1958 through the first quarter of 1960, the standard error of estimate shows no trend in the adjusted E_8/P_0 ratios, and the correlation for the regression explaining this ratio actually declines. The standard errors and correlation coefficients of the adjusted E_5 /P_0 and E_3/P_0 ratios again show no consistent trends, while the standard errors of the adjusted E_1/P_0 and E_0/P_0 relationships evidence some ten-dency to increase with no corresponding changes in the correlations.

As a result, there is no indication of a significant change in market effi-ciency over the 1958–1960 period covered, though there is more suggestion of a decline than of a rise in efficiency. On the other hand, the analysis of the E_3/P_0, E_1/P_0, and E_0/P_0 ratios points to some, though probably statisti-cally insignificant, improvement in market efficiency for the 1958–1960 pe-riod to the mid-1960s and some, again probably insignificant, decline in ef-ficiency from the mid-1960s to the first quarter of 1968, the last period covered. The analysis of the E_1/P_0 and E_0/P_0 ratios which cover the largest span of years does not indicate any change in market efficiency from the 1958–1960 to the 1967–1968 quarters covered.

Thus, there does not appear to be any noteworthy trend in market efficiency from the 1958–1960 to 1967–1968 periods in spite of the greatly increased stock activity by institutional investors over these years. This result parallels and is supported by the more firmly based finding that mutual funds showed neither superior nor inferior ability to direct capital into those areas of economic investment which subsequently turned out to be the most profitable.

Chapter Seven

SOME POLICY ISSUES

THE MAIN POLICY issues arise out of the rapid and continuing growth of institutional equity investment: First, are there undesirable effects associated with that rate of growth, and, if so, should it be controlled? Second, are there characteristics of institutional equity investment, especially in the areas of portfolio company policies and trading practices, which should be altered? Third, are new measures required to protect the stockholders or beneficiaries of the institutional investors themselves from possible conflicts of interest with management groups? All these issues apply to every type of institutional investor, though the third appears to be especially applicable to mutual funds and much less so to pension funds, the other major group of institutional equity investors.

Restrictions on Growth of Institutional Equity Investment

Some students of finance have suggested that the rapid growth of institutional equity investment (with institutional net purchases of stock far exceeding the net stock issues by other corporations) will, in the absence of a substantial rise in new stock flotations, lead to dangerously high stock prices and may require the imposition of curbs on such investment.[1] Our analysis does not lend much support to this concern, though there is reason to believe that the pension funds and mutual funds have contributed to the postwar rise in stock prices. So far, it appears that the growth in institutional investment has helped to eliminate the former substantial disparities between the returns on equities and those on other investments rather than to inflate stock prices in relation to prospective returns. There is no reason to expect that in the future, even if the rate of new stock flotations remains low, institutional investors as a whole would be any more irrational than other investors in bidding up the prices of stock beyond their intrinsic values. It could be argued that mutual funds might pose an exception to this general rule since, even if stock prices were bid up excessively, the uncertain returns associated with stocks may provide a more effective basis for promoting sales of fund shares than the relatively certain returns on other portfolio investments. However, any such danger should be greatly moderated by some of the steps recommended subsequently to reduce conflicts of interest between fund management and shareholders with respect to the sale of fund shares.

A growing rate of institutional equity investment might, of course, be detrimental to the economy, not only due to the dangers of an unduly high level of stock prices, but also if—because of faddism, excessive speculativeness, or other reasons—the structure of stock prices were distorted in such a way as to diminish market efficiency and the stability of stock prices were adversely affected. Again, however, the evidence presented in this study suggests that mutual funds, at least, were about as efficient in their equity investments as the market as a whole and did not substantially affect market stability. While comparable information is not available for other institutional groups, there is no reason to believe that they are more likely to engage in faddism or speculative activity than the mutual funds. Moreover, the stock market as a whole apparently showed little change in efficiency over the postwar period during which institutional investors were rapidly growing in relative importance.

Restrictions on Portfolio Company Policies and Trading Practices

The concentration of power over portfolio companies (corporations whose shares are owned by the institution) implicit in the growth of a number of giant organizations oriented toward equity investment has been a basis for

---

[1] For example, see Raymond W. Goldsmith, *Financial Institutions,* Random House, Inc., New York, 1968, pp. 196–197. Dr Goldsmith suggests that it may become necessary to set upper limits on the share of funds that at least some groups of institutional investors may invest in common stock.

concern totally apart from the other economic implications of the growth in institutional equity investment. Excessive concentration of power not only may have adverse economic consequences but is frequently regarded as detrimental to the maintenance of a democratic society. However, it is known that mutual funds have not been especially active stockholders and have usually indicated their reaction to portfolio company management by purchasing or selling the company's shares rather than by attempting to influence its policy. (They are presumably somewhat more active than the smaller individual stockholder and considerably less active than the very large individual stockholder.) We suspect that the same situation generally characterizes other institutional investors as well. There is, however, always the danger that as institutional investors own more and more of the available stock and it becomes more difficult to dispose of the larger and larger blocks of stock involved, they may take a more dominant role in the affairs of portfolio companies.

We do not feel that this danger is sufficiently great to warrant restrictions on the size of institutional investors at this time, though perhaps restrictions on the amount of investment in stock of individual portfolio companies by institutions other than mutual funds may be in order. There does not appear to be much evidence that mutual funds so far have had an undue or detrimental influence on portfolio company affairs. These funds—partly for liquidity considerations—are already restricted in 75 percent of their investments to holdings not exceeding 5 percent of their assets or 10 percent of the voting stock of the portfolio company. Moreover, if a mutual fund (or other diversified management investment company) owns more than 5 percent of the stock of a portfolio company, most transactions between the fund and the company require prior SEC approval. Comparable types of restrictions might be enacted for other institutional investors, but, in the absence of data on the investment policy of such investors, especially the pension funds, we have little basis for assessing the need for, or effect of, such a legislative change. Moreover, there are generally not the same liquidity grounds to justify such restrictions. What does seem to be urgently required is the periodic collection of portfolio and other data from pension funds and other important groups of equity-oriented institutional investors which do not now submit such information.

If institutional equity investors continue to increase in relative importance and also participate more actively in the affairs of portfolio companies, it may become desirable to enact further restrictions on the role they play in these companies. Even under such circumstances, however, it is not clear that there would be adequate reason to limit the size of the institutional investors. Mutual funds (and other institutional investors for which data are available) exhibit significant economies of scale in their operating cost; large funds seem to have fully as good investment performance as the smaller ones. The reduced operating costs of the larger organizations may be offset, to some extent, by increased investment inflexibility. Perhaps the best approach to avoiding the dangers of monopolistic control of portfolio companies by large institutional investors would be to strengthen, when necessary, the current limitations on the percentage of voting stock of individual portfolio companies that may be held by a single mutual fund complex and to extend such restrictions to other institutional investors.[2]

An alternative mechanism would limit institutional holdings of equity issues in portfolio companies to nonvoting stock (i.e., to stock which is nonvoting while held by institutional investors). The latter approach has the advantage of avoiding arbitrary percentage restrictions on stockholdings but has four shortcomings: First, if the institutional investors were truly divested of power by the use of nonvoting stock, it would be easier than ever for other stockholders (not necessarily aligned with management) to gain control, with a relatively small investment, of portfolio companies largely owned by institutional investors, and proxy fights would probably be greatly encouraged. Second, it is doubtful that institutional investors with very large blocks of stock would be divested of power simply because their stock was nonvoting, since a threat to liquidate such holdings would be quite potent. Third, for mutual funds and perhaps certain other institutional investors, there is the need to ensure portfolio liquidity. Fourth, institutional investors may well be more informed stockholders than most of those permitted to vote.

Institutional ownership of large blocks of stock in portfolio companies also raises a number of questions about the need for protecting other stockholders from the consequences of institutional activities. Institutions, because of their resources, may have better and faster access to information about the company's affairs. This could work to the disadvantage of most of the other stockholders, who are typically much smaller in size. There have been enough news stories to indicate that, in spite of the safeguards under present securities regulation, institutions as well as other large investors have a significant advantage over the smaller investors in the dissemination of corporate information.[3] It seems reasonably clear that securities regulation should attempt to ensure that no stockholder, no matter how large, be given access to important information which is not made available to any other stockholder, no matter how small.

Only one real issue seems to be in question here. Should management make available to any stockholder who seeks it significant information that

[2] It might be noted that there is no evidence that the existing restrictions of this type, which tended to widen the coverage of stocks in fund portfolios, impaired the investment performance of mutual funds (see Chap. 3).

[3] That they may also have a comparative disadvantage by readier access to corporate misinformation is suggested by institutional losses in Parvin/Dohrmann stock (*Fortune,* December, 1969, pp. 163–168).

would not be available to other stockholders simply because they do not request it? Despite the costs involved in interfering with the free flow of information of this type, simple equity among stockholders seems to require that to the extent possible no important information be given to one group of stockholders which is not given to all stockholders at the same time (or where it is given, e.g., to stockholders who are also insiders, that restrictions be placed on their ability to profit by it). Obviously, one way to minimize the costs of this policy to market efficiency would be to ensure that all important information be disseminated to stockholders as soon as feasible.

As a practical matter, dissemination of information to stockholders in a large publicly owned corporation is tantamount to disclosure to the general public. A problem arises, and exceptions to the general rule of immediate disclosure might be warranted in certain cases, when management desires to withhold information for a limited period for the company's welfare (as distinct from the welfare of a particular group of stockholders). However, since equity as well as the philosophy of securities regulation requires the fair treatment of potential as well as actual stockholders, there may be a conflict between the responsibility of management to potential stockholders (to provide relevant disclosure of material facts) and their responsibility to actual stockholders (to maximize their risk-adjusted returns). Presumably, the legal basis for resolving this conflict should take into account the prospective damage and benefits to the two groups. The optimal resolution of the conflict depends largely on the relative responsibility management is considered to have toward actual and potential stockholders.

One tenable resolution—which rests on the premise that the basic responsibility of management is to maximize risk-adjusted return (or market value) for the company as a whole—would permit the temporary withholding of material information, so long as there were a legitimate reason for doing so from the viewpoint of the company's welfare[4] and no group were permitted to profit from advance knowledge. This apparently is close to the present law. The rationale for this position, from the viewpoint of the potential stockholders who might be adversely affected, would be that temporary withholding of information for the company's welfare may be regarded as an ordinary market risk (which enters into the pricing of stock) and management cannot be expected to protect potential stockholders from such risks at the expense of actual stockholders. One attractive way to cut down on the prospective damage to potential stockholders is to institute a stricter construction of the legitimacy of business reasons for withholding material information and of the justified withholding period.

A second, quite different, but still theoretically tenable resolution of this

[4] This would presumably occur mainly when a significant change in the company's position becomes likely but is not certain and the immediate disclosure of that prospect would affect the probability of its occurrence or of some related event affecting the company's welfare.

conflict of interest between potential and actual stockholders would be for management again to conduct its affairs so as to maximize risk-adjusted return for the company as a whole, which as before might require the withholding of material information, but then to compensate any purchasers (or sellers) of stock who have suffered substantial losses as a result of this action. However, this second position would be extremely difficult to implement in practice, and has the further limitation that it might inhibit management in maximizing risk-adjusted return with a resulting social cost to the economy.

Institutional ownership of large blocks of stock in portfolio companies is sometimes considered to be detrimental in still another way to the interests of other stockholders and potential investors in the portfolio companies. In view of the size of their stockholdings in individual companies, institutions have been largely responsible for the rapid growth in block transactions. The sale or purchase of large blocks of stock may cause major discontinuities in the market, with such sales, at times, sharply reducing prices for other stockholders (to the advantage of potential investors) and purchases sharply increasing prices for other potential investors (to the advantage of stockholders). However, so long as institutional investors make as informed decisions in their sales or purchases as other investors (and do not have greater access to inside information),[5] there is little reason to consider the prices at which they consummate their transactions to be less fair or less desirable than those achieved through a larger number of transactions, assuming that institutions attempt to use the best market outlets. Thus, it is important to observe that the previously discussed evidence on the market efficiency of mutual funds and on the postwar trend in the efficiency of the stock market as a whole does not point to significant costs of the trend toward block trading.

The continued rise in the relative importance of block transactions might be undesirable in one repect: the transactions cost for a given volume of stock trading may be increased somewhat (though this is not certain), and the transaction-to-transaction price continuity of the auction markets would probably be somewhat impaired. The short-term trading data for assessing the extent to which such developments have occurred are not available. Since intermediate and longer-term market efficiency have not been impaired, there is little reason to believe that significant economic costs have been associated with block trading. However, it is possible that a detailed examination of block trades would indicate the possibility of effecting improvements to the short-run behavior of the stock market through restrictions on the disposition of large purchase and sale orders.

[5] Inside information here should be construed to include restricted market information about the company's stock as well as restricted information about the company's affairs.

Restrictions on Conflicts of Interest

While conflicts of interest between stockholders and management groups characterize every major type of institutional equity investor, and indeed virtually all corporate enterprise, they are especially troublesome for mutual funds for reasons developed in Chapter 1, including the customary control of fund management by external investment advisers. For pension funds, the other major group of equity-oriented institutions, the corporate sponsor of the fund is quite independent of the external investment adviser (typically a commercial bank), and the corporate management and the fund's beneficiaries have similar interests in maximizing fund return and minimizing costs of operation. Moreover, the beneficiaries' interests are further protected by their unions.

The conflicts of interests in insurance stock companies are probably not very different from those of most other corporations of comparable size. The conflict problems for mutual insurance organizations are presumably similar in general nature though not in specific form to those of internally managed mutual funds, with the problems likely to be more serious in certain state jurisdictions than in others.[6] Bank trust funds, which are frequently classified as institutional investors, have some of the same potential conflicts of interest as externally managed mutual funds, but the necessary data for assessing the extent and consequences of these situations are not available.

For mutual funds, the interests of the external adviser in maximizing the fund's size and the management fee may be quite different from those of the fund shareholders. Historically, as documented in Chapter 1, this has been evidenced most strongly in the areas of management fees, the disposition of commission income associated with portfolio turnover, and sales charges. In recent years, the rapid growth of fund holdings of letter stock (Chapter 4) has also provided a significant potential for conflict, since they can be used as a device for stimulating sales of fund shares through "instant performance" reflecting the difference between the prices ascribed to and the prices paid for the stock. Overvaluation of letter stock would further serve to raise management compensation unduly.

In October, 1969, the SEC—apparently mainly on liquidity grounds—took some initial steps toward limiting investment in letter stock to 10 percent of a fund's assets. The SEC pointed out the fiduciary responsibility of the directors in ascribing a fair value to such stock, required that data used for valuation of the stock be retained for inspection, and noted that there

---

[6] The conflict problems in the administration of investment funds and perhaps other activities of nonprofit institutions may also have some similarity to those of other mutual internally managed organizations.

should be public disclosure in the prospectus of "all matters" relating to this valuation, including the original price. Obviously, letter stock, if properly used, may be advantageous to the fund shareholders, since the stock is obtained at a discount from the estimated market value, but the dangers seem sufficiently great both on liquidity and conflict grounds to warrant the general form of the restrictions proposed by the SEC. The full disclosure and fiduciary responsibility requirements are the *sine qua non* of responsible regulation in this as well as other areas and are necessary to minimize liquidity and conflict problems. However, the precise percentage limitation of assets is arbitrary and must be justified more by liquidity than by conflict of interest considerations. An approach which might well be used to supplement the recent SEC action is to require that the estimated discount from market value normally be amortized over some suitable period of time. This would substantially modify the appearance of instant performance, which ordinarily could not be realized in the marketplace. The amortization policy would not be followed where there is strong reason to believe that it would not lead to a fair value of the underlying stock.[7]

In the other and more basic conflict-of-interest areas affecting mutual funds, the SEC and the Congress have watered down the original SEC proposals as a result of industry opposition. The most recent proposals at the time of this writing are embodied in S. 2224 passed by the Senate and now before a House Commerce subcommittee. As noted in Chapter 1, the original SEC proposal to ensure more equitable management fees required that all compensation received by any person affiliated with a mutual fund or other registered investment company be reasonable as measured by stipulated standards. It has since been modified to affirm the fiduciary responsibility of investment advisers, but also to direct the courts that, in any legal adjudication of management fees, appropriate weight be given to the directors' approval and shareholders' ratification of such fees.[8] (Apparently, there is an element of ambiguity about the implications of this modification, and some industry representatives have argued that it is no less objectionable to them than the original recommendation on management fees, while some lawyers who have been active on behalf of minority shareholders have

---

[7] The SEC has taken a position in opposition to the principle of automatic amortization of the estimated discount (Investment Company Act of 1940 Release No. 5847, Oct. 21, 1969) largely on the grounds that this would be inconsistent with the requirements of the Investment Company Act that each security for which a market quotation is not readily available "be valued at fair value as determined in good faith by the board of directors." However, it is desirable to set some general guidelines for valuation in view of the intrinsic difficulties of valuing securities which have no exact market counterpart. The SEC seems to display undue confidence in the directors' ability to value such stock and undue skepticism about the usefulness of the available objective market evidence.

[8] See the statement by SEC Chairman Hamer H. Budge before the Subcommittee on Commerce and Finance of the Committee on Interstate and Foreign Commerce, U.S. House of Representatives, Dec. 11, 1969.

maintained that it is little if any improvement over the present state of affairs.)

The proposal that sales charges of mutual funds be limited to 5 percent of their net asset value was modified to give the National Association of Securities Dealers (NASD) power to fix reasonable sales charges, subject to general SEC review. The prohibition of front-end load plans was replaced by a rule allowing two alternative means for selling such plans. The first alternative provided for a refund on early redemptions, so that if an investor redeemed his underlying shares during the first three years of his contract, he would be entitled to receive, in addition to his net asset value, a refund of any sales charges in excess of 15 percent of his total payments under the plan. The second alternative for selling such plans that could be elected by the plan sponsors would stretch out the period for collection of sales charges, so that the load could not exceed 20 percent of any payment or average more than 16 percent annually over the first four years.

The current (early 1970) SEC proposal for regulating management fees by formalizing the fiduciary responsibility of investment advisers may require clarification, but some form of this proposal seems to be the minimal legislative change required to protect fund shareholders against inequitable management fees.[9] This proposal can be justified both on equity and economic grounds, though the SEC seems to have been primarily motivated by equity considerations. The Commission's stated purpose is to ensure that "those who derive benefits from their fiduciary relationships with investment companies can charge them no more for their services than if they were dealing with them on an arm's-length basis."[10] There is overwhelming evidence cited in Chapter 1 that most investment companies do charge their stockholders more management compensation than would be associated with arm's-length bargaining. Neither the extent or cost of services nor the quality of investment performance can explain the differences in management expenses between the typical externally managed mutual funds and either nonfund clients of the same external advisers or mutual funds without external advisers.

Contrary to the industry's position, the large number of mutual funds, including many of substantial size, do not ensure competition in management fees or in other practices. It is the behavior of prices and costs that

[9] The position on the SEC proposals taken here is similar to that expressed by one of the authors in *Mutual Fund Legislation of 1967: Hearings on S. 1659 before the Committee on Banking and Currency, United States Senate, 90th Congress,* August, 1967, part 2. It is interesting to note that the recommendations made in the recently published *Report of the Canadian Committee on Mutual Funds and Investment Contracts,* Queen's Printer for Canada, 1969, are generally consistent with this position, especially with respect to sales charges but substantially also with respect to management fees and front-end loads.

[10] U.S. Securities and Exchange Commission, *Public Policy Implications of Investment Company Growth,* Government Printing Office, Washington, D.C., 1966, p. 13.

measures the effectiveness of competition, not the number or size of companies. There is, essentially, only one sponsoring organization determining fees and selling the shares of a specific mutual fund. Therefore, if contrary to the facts developed in Chapter 3 the potential investors are led to believe that higher fees indicate a superior product, competition is ineffective and does not take the place of arm's-length bargaining.

The elimination of the original SEC proposal to limit sales charges on mutual fund shares to 5 percent of their net asset value is probably a move in the right direction. Government price fixing is not desirable except in special circumstances (e.g., in industries or activities where competition is not feasible or during periods of severe economic disruption), since it ordinarily leads to inefficiency in the allocation of economic resources and frequently to inequities as well. On the other hand, giving the NASD limited powers over the size of sales charges is not likely to be a very effective means of ensuring meaningful competition in the mutual fund industry. The grant of these powers to the Investment Company Institute, recently proposed by the industry, is similarly open to serious question.

Competition in this industry has not served its traditional function of reducing price to the purchaser. As noted in Chapter 1, there was an appreciable rise in the average percentage sales charge from 1950 to 1966. There may also have been a rise in the average "reciprocity ratio," which is another form of dealer compensation.[11] There did not appear over this period to be any correlation between performance and sales charges, which may be considered the price of fund services to the purchasers. (Management and commission expenses are already reflected in investment performance.) The weakness of the ordinary competitive forces in the industry is further highlighted by the availability of similar investment media (such as the no-load funds) of comparable portfolio performance and diversification which, however, in spite of their much lower price, made no substantial inroads on the sales of the more expensive funds.

More effective price competition might be achieved by either removing the retail price maintenance provisions of Section 22(d) of the Investment Company Act or providing potential investors with more complete disclosure. The SEC gave a number of reasons for originally recommending a maximum sales load in preference to amendment of 22(d), but apparently the most cogent argument in the Commission's view related to the "unsettling and unforeseeable effects which abolition of retail price maintenance might have on the broker-dealer community." One can argue, however, that freeing competitive forces via 22(d), permitting retail dealers to attract investors by offering lower prices, would be preferable to government or in-

---

[11] In addition to the typical 8.5 percent sales charge of which the dealer might receive 6.5 percent, the dealer might be paid as much as an additional 5 percent in the form of reciprocal brokerage.

dustry price fixing. The expected result of such competition would be a much higher proportion of fund business flowing to the more efficient and lower-cost members of the financial community.[12]

If potential investors were provided with "full disclosure," they would be aware of the performance and costs of the fund offered to them compared with the broad alternatives, including other load funds, no-load funds, and closed-end investment companies (the latter frequently selling at a discount). This is another approach to more effective price competition in the setting of sales charges, one not considered by the SEC in its 1966 report on investment companies. This is, at least in theory, more attractive than a maximum sales load and may be less unsettling than a revised 22(d). To implement this approach the SEC might prescribe a way of presenting information on the front page of the prospectus (and in some suitable part of the annual report) comparing the performance and costs of the fund, over as long a period as feasible, with the corresponding group averages for other load funds, no-load funds, closed-end companies and the overall market performance weighted by the portfolio composition of the fund in question or otherwise adjusted for differences in portfolio risk. However, it is difficult to conceive of Congress enacting this type of disclosure.

While potentially less effective, other measures to facilitate "full disclosure" would still be useful. The SEC's policy toward newspaper advertising by mutual funds could be revised to permit the presentation of standardized comparative performance and cost data, again in an SEC-approved manner, which should help in disseminating relevant information. The SEC itself could, at minimal cost, prepare and make available to the press periodic statistical releases showing comprehensive data on performance (reflecting risk as well as rates of return) and costs of different categories of investment companies. Since the SEC might not be able to make available information for individual companies, it would be more useful still if one or more of the large brokerage houses regularly provided such data to prospective buyers of fund shares.[13]

Mutual fund investors generally know very little about the relative merits of the commodity they are buying. These measures to facilitate disclosure would help to give fund investors reliable (and inexpensive) comparative information on the past performance and current cost of their prospective investment. Thus, they would be in a much better position to appraise the validity of salesmen's claims and make informed judgments. The obvious argument against such disclosure is that the provision of comparable infor-

---

[12] It has been argued that an alternative result might be to stimulate the growth of organizations that act as the sole distributors of the fund shares they sell. However, increased competition by funds sold through brokerage firms and independent dealers should result in lower sales charges for funds generally.

[13] Once this was done by a large brokerage house, the others presumably would be more likely to do so for competitive reasons.

mation is not required in the sale of other commodities. However, for reasons which led to the enactment of the securities acts—including the inability of the average investor to appraise adequately the sales representations made to him and the consequences of misrepresentation to the individual investor and to the economy—Congress has required a higher set of disclosure standards in the sale of securities generally than in most other commodities. Since costs and performance are the only two important elements differentiating one mutual fund from another and since they can be measured objectively, it seems desirable to give the typical small, unsophisticated investor in mutual funds a basis for appraising the sales representations made to him, so far as it is possible to do so.

These two approaches—repeal of the retail price maintenance provisions of Section 22(d) and more complete disclosure—appear to have significant advantages over the SEC's setting a maximum sales load or giving the NASD limited powers over these charges. A third alternative, which would pose fewer problems, is the entry of new competition into the mutual fund field. Large brokerage concerns, and other types of large financial institutions not now in the business, might very well be in a position to sell fund shares aggressively and profitably at a significantly lower cost than the current sales charges. However, the possibility of this without some regulatory stimulus still seems too far off to be useful in the foreseeable future. New competition would be facilitated by the passage of the current SEC-sponsored mutual fund legislation (S. 2224), which would permit other types of financial institutions to enter the mutual fund field.

A concentrated effort to achieve fuller disclosure as cheaply as possible and the amendment of 22(d) should go far toward accomplishing the desired objective of effective price competition in the sale of mutual funds. From an economic viewpoint, either or both of these changes appear to be preferable to the SEC's proposals in this area.

The current SEC proposal either to allow a partial refund of sales charges imposed on front-end load contractual plans or to stretch out the period for collecting these charges represents a substantial modification of their original proposal to prohibit such plans. Again, this seems like the minimal legislative change required to protect the buyers of such plans. The absence of effective price competition is much more serious for contractual plans than for mutual funds generally. There is a greater concentration of low-income, uninformed investors in such plans, a greater prevalence of undesirable and inadequately supervised sales practices, and a much greater potential loss to those investors who are not in a financial position to complete their plans.[14]

[14] U.S. Securities and Exchange Commission, *Special Study of Securities Markets*, part 4, Government Printing Office, Washington, D.C., 1963, pp. 139–212. See also the Dec. 11, 1969, statement by SEC Chairman Budge, *op. cit.*, pp. 27–32, and *Report of the Canadian Committee on Mutual Funds and Investment Contracts, op. cit.*, pp. 363–366.

The front-end load has been associated with significant losses by a sizable fraction of investors—those who could not complete their plans and could probably least afford such losses. Many of these investors had taken on commitments which they were hardly in a position to fulfill. That they did not understand these commitments is suggested by their responses to the Wharton School *Survey of Mutual Fund Investors,* in which four out of ten recent purchasers of contractuals indicated that they were unaware of the disadvantages imposed by the front-end load on those who fail to complete their payments.[15] While the substantial costs of front-end loads to investors who do not complete their plans have been highlighted by the SEC (e.g., a sample survey in 1959 indicated that one out of every six purchasers of front-end load plans paid an effective load of 50 percent), insufficient attention has been paid to the relatively high cost of such plans even if held to maturity. For plans held to maturity, the effective sales charge may amount to 9.9 percent of the offering price, reflecting the fact that the sales charge is concentrated in the early years of the plan whereas the shareholder's equity builds up most rapidly in the later years. This sales charge represents 11 percent of the net amount invested in the fund and is exclusive of custodian fees which might amount to another 2 percent.

Portfolio turnover and the disposition of commission income associated with that turnover are a final area in which there may be significant differences between the interests of management and those of the fund shareholders. Up to this time the SEC has devoted less attention than might have been warranted to the problem of substantially increased fund portfolio turnover rates. Portfolio turnover in mutual funds has increased greatly. In the first quarter of 1969 it amounted to close to three times the nonmember turnover on the New York Stock Exchange as a whole. Such adjusted fund turnover is about 2½ times the corresponding stock turnover rate of pension funds, a group of institutional investors with which the mutual funds might be compared. Fund turnover is roughly five times the turnover rate for small (odd-lot) public investors in NYSE stocks and seven times the redemption rate by purchasers of mutual fund shares.[16]

There is no convincing statistical evidence that high portfolio turnover has either paid off or hurt the mutual fund shareholders. However, in view of the major potential conflicts of interest between shareholder and management over fund turnover, the question may legitimately be raised whether the current trend to higher turnover ratios can be justified.

It is admittedly important to ensure that any action taken by the SEC to curtail excessive turnover does not interfere with legitimate management

[15] U.S. Securities and Exchange Commission, *Special Study of Securities Markets,* part 4, *op. cit.,* pp. 273–349.

[16] Most of the turnover data come directly from sources indicated in Chap. 1. However, the turnover ratio for odd-lot investors is a rough estimate based on comprehensive SEC trading data and sample corporation distributions of share ownership.

prerogatives. As noted in Chapter 1, the dangers inherent in the use of brokerage as compensation for sales of fund shares may be reduced as commission rates become more competitive, but the problem is not likely to disappear. At a minimum, the next step would be to initiate fuller disclosure in this area, so that fund holders are informed of the fund turnover ratio in contrast with selected norms, and perhaps also of the subsequent relative performance of the issues sold and purchased. The absolute and relative (percent of assets) cost of commission expenses might be shown prominently in the income section of the annual report (as well as in the prospectus) as part of the gross management expenses. Thus shareholders in mutual funds will be better able to assess the turnover policies followed by fund management.

Another step, which would be more effective but also more difficult to implement, would be to require that all surplus commission income associated with portfolio turnover (now typically paid to brokers selling the fund's shares) be channeled directly to the mutual fund. This again would not interfere with legitimate management prerogatives and would help ensure that turnover is designed to maximize shareholder rather than management interests.[17] But the most effective step to achieve this objective would be to eliminate surplus commission income through the adoption of a truly competitive commission rate structure.

Several other devices for improving the protection of fund stockholders in conflict-of-interest situations have not been discussed. Of these, probably the most important are strengthening the role played by independent directors and eliminating external investment advisers either by internalization of management or other means. Strengthening the role played by independent directors—by clarification of and greater publicity regarding their responsibilities, by tightening the definition of unaffiliated directors, and perhaps by increasing their proportion—might enhance the position of fund shareholders. This may be desirable as a further protective measure, but, by itself, it is not likely to be as effective as the more direct measures previously considered. Internalization of fund management (or other devices to eliminate the shell between fund shareholders and controlling managers) might be somewhat more effective than simply strengthening the independent directors, since it would provide a closer alignment of power and fiduciary responsibility. Judging from the experience of the few existing internally managed funds, management fees might be considerably reduced. However, this type of action has important limitations: First, it

<hr>

[17] There is some evidence of excessive portfolio turnover in other institutions, including nonprofit organizations. Even universities, perhaps under the prod of the Ford Foundation, have been stepping up their portfolio activity. A substantial question arises about the justification for this development, but in any case disclosure and recapture of surplus commission income might be as desirable here as for mutual funds.

would disrupt existing organizations. Second, its objective, so far as management fees are concerned, might be achieved more easily by increasing stress on the fiduciary responsibility of investment advisers along lines proposed by the SEC. Finally, it would not achieve the other objectives of avoiding the diversion of resources from the funds to selling new fund shares or of protecting new low-income and uninformed investors from some of the less desirable practices in the industry.

So far as institutional investors other than mutual funds are concerned, the absence of external advisers avoids many of the conflict problems found in the typical externally managed mutual fund. There is, however, one important problem characterizing other types of mutual institutions: unlike mutual funds, they can accumulate substantial amounts of surplus funds without distributing them to the owners (for example, the policyholders in mutual life insurance companies or the depositors in savings and loan associations and mutual savings banks). The situation in these mutual organizations is quite different from that in stock corporations, since the owners in the former have no transferable equity in the surplus. This is not the widely publicized problem of ownership without control. It is, rather, a relatively neglected and perhaps more serious problem of nominal ownership without any real equity interest. The problem merits attention, even though it is not a special problem of equity-oriented institutional investors. Among the assets of mutual institutions are billions of dollars of surplus funds that are more likely to enhance the position of the management or of future owners than of the present owners. This is especially true since the control group in the typical large mutual institutional investor, with a great many small policyholders or depositors, is probably even more self-perpetuating than in most public corporations. The solution to this problem is extremely difficult and fortunately is outside the scope of this study.

APPENDIXES

Appendix to Chapter One

Appendix Table 1-1
MARKET VALUE[a] OF STOCKHOLDINGS OF FINANCIAL
INSTITUTIONS AND OTHER INVESTORS, 1964–1968
(Billions of Dollars as of End of Year)

	1964	1965	1966	1967	1968[b]
1. Private noninsured pension funds	33.5	39.7	38.5	49.5	59.6
2. Investment companies, total	34.6	41.2	37.4	51.0	59.6
Mutual funds	26.7	33.5	31.2	42.8	50.9
Other	8.0	7.7	6.2	8.2	8.7
3. Life insurance companies	7.9	9.1	8.8	10.8	12.8
4. Property and casualty insurance companies[c]	11.4	12.0	11.0	13.0	14.7
5. Mutual savings banks	1.6	1.8	1.9	2.1	2.3
6. State and local trust funds	1.7	2.4	2.8	4.2	4.8
7. Common trust funds	3.0	3.5	3.3	3.9	4.4
8. Personal trust funds	65.9	70.4	64.3	75.9	80.1
9. Foundations	12.9	14.1	12.2	14.7	15.8
10. College endowments	5.8	6.4	6.8	8.1	9.0
11. Total institutions (items 1 through 10)[d]	175.9	197.6	183.4	228.6	257.8
12. Foreigners[e]	18.9	19.9	18.1	21.5	25.5
13. Domestic individuals					
(item 14 less item 11 less item 12)	424.4	457.1	385.8	457.7	478.0
14. Total stock outstanding	619.2	674.6	587.3	707.8	761.3

SOURCE: U.S. Securities and Exchange Commission, *Statistical Bulletin*, May, 1969.

[a] Estimated market value of preferred and common stock. Excludes investment company shares but includes foreign issues outstanding in the United States.

[b] Preliminary.

[c] Excludes holdings of insurance company stock.

[d] Excludes holdings of mutual fund shares.

[e] Includes estimate of stock held as direct investment.

Appendix Table 1-2
MARKET VALUE^a OF STOCKHOLDINGS OF SELECTED
CLASSES OF INVESTORS, 1940–1968
(Billions of Dollars as of End of Year)

	1940	1950	1955	1956	1957	1958	1959	1960	1961	1962	1963	1964	1965	1966	1967	1968
1. Private noninsured pension funds	0.1	1.1	6.1	7.1	7.5	11.6	14.5	16.5	22.9	21.9	27.7	33.5	39.7	38.5	49.5	59.6
2. Investment companies, total	0.9	4.3	12.1	13.5	12.2	18.3	20.0	20.5	29.3	26.3	30.8	34.6	41.2	37.4	51.0	59.6
Mutual funds	0.4	1.9	7.2	8.2	7.7	12.2	14.6	15.4	22.2	19.6	23.6	26.7	33.5	31.2	42.8	50.9
Other	0.4	2.3	4.9	5.3	4.5	6.1	5.5	5.1	7.1	6.7	7.2	8.0	7.7	6.2	8.2	8.7
3. Life insurance companies	0.6	2.1	3.6	3.5	3.4	4.1	4.6	5.0	6.3	6.3	7.1	7.9	9.1	8.8	10.8	12.8
4. Property and casualty insurance companies	1.5	3.6	5.4	5.6	5.2	6.7	7.2	7.5	9.3	8.6	9.9	11.4	12.0	11.0	13.0	14.7
5. Mutual savings banks	0.6	0.3	0.8	0.9	0.9	1.1	1.0	1.0	1.1	1.3	1.5	1.6	1.8	1.9	2.1	2.3
6. State and local trust funds	b	b	0.2	0.3	0.3	0.4	0.5	0.6	0.8	1.0	1.3	1.7	2.4	2.8	4.2	4.8
7. Total institutions^c	3.7	11.4	28.3	30.8	29.5	42.0	47.6	51.0	69.4	65.2	78.1	90.3	105.7	99.6	131.6	213.4
8. Foreigners^d	4.6	5.0	9.6	10.2	9.5	12.0	13.4	13.4	16.2	14.9	17.3	18.9	19.9	18.1	21.5	25.5
9. All others^e	69.0	134.2	271.6	281.1	246.2	337.3	372.5	356.8	435.8	380.8	452.0	510.0	549.1	469.7	553.5	522.4
10. Total stock outstanding	77.3	150.6	309.5	322.1	285.2	391.3	433.6	421.2	521.4	461.0	547.3	619.2	674.6	587.3	707.8	761.3

SOURCE: U.S. Securities and Exchange Commission, *Statistical Bulletin*, May, 1969.
^{a} Estimated market value of preferred and common stock. Excludes investment company shares but includes foreign issues outstanding in the United States.
^{b} Less than $50 million.
^{c} Items 1 through 6, and includes a very small amount of stock held by fraternal organizations.
^{d} Includes estimate of stock held as direct investment.
^{e} Item 10 less items 7 and 8, but includes individuals, personal trust funds, and nonprofit institutions.

NET ACQUISITIONS OF PREFERRED AND COMMON STOCK ISSUES[a] BY SELECTED CLASSES OF INVESTORS, 1950–1968

(Billions of Dollars)

	1950	1960	1961	1962	1963	1964	1965	1966	1967	1968[b]
1. Aggregate stock issues										
a. New stock issues	1.9	2.7	4.5	2.3	1.9	3.7	3.2	4.2	4.7	6.3
b. Retirements	0.4	1.0	1.8	1.6	2.2	2.3	3.2	3.0	2.4	7.0
c. Net change (a less b)[c]	1.5	1.7	2.6	0.7	-0.2	1.4	d	1.2	2.3	-0.7
2. Net foreign stock issues	d	0.1	0.4	0.1	d	-0.2	-0.3	0.3	0.2	0.2
3. Net acquisitions by:										
a. Private noninsured pension funds	0.1	1.9	2.3	2.2	2.2	2.2	3.1	3.7	5.2	6.1
b. Investment companies										
For cash	0.1	1.0	1.6	1.1	0.8	1.0	1.4	1.1	2.4	2.9
Other[e]	d	d	0.5	-0.2	0.1	-0.3	-1.2	0.1	0.4	d
c. Life insurance companies	0.3	0.3	0.4	0.4	0.2	0.5	0.7	0.3	1.1	1.3
d. Property and casualty insurance companies[f]	0.1	0.3	0.3	0.2	0.2	0.2	0.2	0.5	0.4	1.0
e. Other financial institutions[g]	0.1	0.2	0.3	0.4	0.5	0.5	0.7	0.6	1.0	1.3
f. Total (items 3a through 3e)	0.7	3.6	5.2	4.1	3.9	4.0	4.8	6.1	10.4	12.6
4. Net acquisitions by foreigners	d	0.2	0.3	0.1	0.2	-0.4	-0.5	-0.3	0.8	2.3
5. Net acquisitions by others[h] (item 1c plus item 2 less item 3f less item 4)	-0.8	-2.0	-2.6	-3.4	-4.3	-2.4	-4.3	-4.9	-8.7	-15.4

SOURCE: U.S. Securities and Exchange Commission, *Statistical Bulletin*, May, 1969.

[a] Excludes shares issued by investment companies.

[b] Preliminary.

[c] Sale of $340 million General Analine Stock by the Attorney General is not included in net new issues; therefore, in 1965, items 1c and 2 less items 3f and 4 do not add up.

[d] Less than $50 million.

[e] Reflects net effect of such transactions as the acquisition of shares through tax-free exchange, and distribution of stock either through liquidation, e.g., M. A. Hanna Co., or under antitrust order, e.g., G.M.-Christiana securities.

[f] Excludes acquisition of life insurance company stock.

[g] Includes state and local trust funds and mutual savings banks.

[h] Includes individuals, personal trust funds, common trust funds, nonprofit institutions, and fraternal organizations.

Appendix Table 1-4

PURCHASES AND SALES OF COMMON STOCKS BY
SELECTED FINANCIAL INSTITUTIONS,[a] 1955–1968
(Millions of Dollars)[b]

	1955	1960	1961	1962	1963	1964	1965	1966	1967	1968
1. Private noninsured pension funds:										
Purchases	975	2,610	3,440	3,205	3,760	4,375	5,585	6,630	10,060	13,065
Sales	290	670	1,170	995	1,555	2,105	2,560	3,005	5,060	7,340
2. Mutual funds:										
Purchases	1,085	2,785	3,955	3,695	4,010	4,770	6,530	10,345	14,925	20,100
Sales	720	2,000	2,755	2,720	3,235	3,885	5,165	9,310	13,325	18,495
3. Life insurance companies:										
Purchases	230	385	605	555	575	790	970	1,100	1,675	2,980
Sales	175[c]	220	370	240	405	455	585	825	875	1,790
4. Property and casualty insurance companies	n.a.	n.a.	n.a.	675	710	765	760	885	1,040	2,025
	n.a.	n.a.	n.a.	475	600	660	700	600	770	1,175
5. Total (item 1 less item 4):										
Purchases	2,290	5,780	8,000	8,135	9,060	10,700	13,845	18,960	27,700	38,170
Sales	1,430	2,890	4,295	4,430	5,795	7,100	9,010	13,740	20,030	28,800

SOURCE: U.S. Securities and Exchange Commission, *Statistical Bulletin*, May, 1969.

[a] Includes only cash transaction; figures do not reflect stock dividends or splits and exclude exchanges of one security for another pursuant to conversion rights, mergers, or plans of reorganization.

[b] Figures have been rounded to nearest $5 million.

[c] n.a. = not available.

NOTE: It should be noted that the differences between purchases and sales of common stocks in this table are not the same as the net acquisitions of preferred and common stocks in Appendix Table 1-3. Partly, of course, this is because preferred stocks are excluded from this table. However, the mutual fund figures in this table differ from the investment company figures in Appendix Table 1-3, not only because of the inclusion of other investment companies and of preferred stocks in Appendix Table 1-3, but to a more important extent because of mutual fund data in this table are obtained by the SEC from the Investment Company Institute and do not include new funds or other nonmembers of the Investment Company Institute. The differences in asset coverage between the SEC and ICI data for mutual funds suggest that mutual fund purchases and sales combined in this table may be understated by about 10% in 1968, with purchases more understated than sales.

Appendix Table 1-5
PERCENTAGE DISTRIBUTION OF MUTUAL
FUND ASSETS,[a] 1955–1968

Calendar year	Net cash and equivalent	Corporate bonds	Preferred stocks	Common stocks
1955	5.6	6.0	6.3	82.1
1956	5.4	7.4	5.6	81.6
1957	6.0	9.0	5.7	79.3
1958	4.8	7.1	4.9	83.2
1959	5.4	6.9	4.5	83.2
1960	5.7	7.3	4.2	82.8
1961	4.3	6.9	3.4	85.4
1962	6.2	7.6	3.5	82.7
1963	5.3	7.1	2.9	84.7
1964	4.6	7.4	2.4	85.6
1965	5.1	7.3	1.7	85.9
1966	8.5	8.4	1.4	81.7
1967	5.7	6.6	1.7	86.0
1968	6.0	6.5	3.2	84.3

SOURCE: Investment Company Institute, *Mutual Fund Fact Book*, 1969.

[a] Market value.

Appendix Table 1-6
PERCENTAGE DISTRIBUTION OF PENSION FUND ASSETS,[a]
1955–1968

Calendar year	Cash and deposits	U.S. government securities	Corporate bonds[b]	Preferred stock	Common stock	Mortgages	Other assets
1955	2.3	16.3	42.7	3.5	30.2	1.8	3.3
1956	2.1	13.3	42.9	3.1	32.1	2.2	4.2
1957	2.1	11.1	47.1	2.9	30.1	2.6	4.2
1958	1.8	8.7	42.2	2.6	38.5	2.6	3.7
1959	1.7	8.1	38.7	2.2	42.7	3.0	3.7
1960	1.5	7.1	39.5	1.9	42.7	3.5	3.8
1961	1.5	5.9	35.1	1.6	48.9	3.5	3.5
1962	1.5	6.2	37.5	1.6	45.3	4.0	3.9
1963	1.4	5.5	34.4	1.3	49.4	4.1	4.0
1964	1.4	4.8	32.4	1.1	51.9	4.4	4.1
1965	1.3	4.2	30.2	1.1	54.5	4.7	4.1
1966	1.3	3.6	30.8	1.1	53.2	5.2	4.8
1967	1.5	2.5	26.5	1.2	58.6	4.7	5.0
1968	1.7	2.6	23.4	1.4	62.6	3.7	4.5

SOURCE: U.S. Securities and Exchange Commission and Social Security Administration.

[a] Market value for private noninsured pension funds.

[b] Includes non-U.S. government bonds.

Appendix Table 1-7
NET NEW MONEY INFLOW—MUTUAL
AND PENSION FUNDS, 1951–1968

| | Net new money inflow— | | | |
| | Mutual funds | | Pension funds | |
	Billions	Assets at beginning of year, %	Billions	Assets at beginning of year, %
1951	$0.4	16.0	$1.6	24.6
1952	0.6	19.4	1.8	22.5
1953	0.4	10.3	2.1	21.9
1954	0.5	12.2	2.2	19.0
1955	0.8	13.1	2.5	18.1
1956	0.9	11.5	2.8	15.5
1957	1.0	11.1	3.1	15.5
1958	1.1	12.6	3.3	14.5
1959	1.5	11.4	3.7	13.1
1960	1.3	8.2	4.0	12.3
1961	1.8	10.6	4.3	11.6
1962	1.6	7.0	4.4	9.7
1963	1.0	4.7	4.6	9.8
1964	1.5	6.0	5.4	9.9
1965	2.4	8.2	6.3	9.9
1966	2.7	7.7	6.6	9.2
1967	1.9	5.4	7.7	10.8
1968	3.0	6.7	8.6	10.4

SOURCE: For mutual funds data, net inflow and assets from Investment Company Institute, *Mutual Fund Fact Book*, 1969. For pension funds data, net inflow and assets for private noninsured pension funds from SEC *Statistical Bulletin* for period 1959–1968; for 1951–1958, estimated from inflow data for corporate pension funds and asset data for private noninsured pension funds and corporate pension funds from SEC data sheets. Total assets for 1951–1954 valued at book; for 1955–1968, valued at market.

Appendix Table 1-8
COMMON STOCK ACTIVITY RATE[a] FOR SELECTED
FINANCIAL INSTITUTIONS, 1960–1968

	1960	1961	1962	1963	1964	1965	1966	1967	1968	1969[b]
Private noninsured pension funds	11.1	12.1	9.7	11.0	10.8	11.3	12.6	17.5	19.1	23.1
Mutual funds	17.6	20.1	17.3	18.6	18.7	21.2	33.5	42.3	46.6	55.6
Life insurance companies	10.1	13.5	9.8	11.2	11.9	13.6	16.0	18.7	27.6	28.1
Property and casualty insurance companies	n.a.[c]	n.a.[c]	7.0	7.8	7.3	6.9	7.2	8.4	12.8	21.0
New York Stock Exchange	12.4	15.2	12.9	14.5	13.6	14.5	19.3	23.0	22.3	20.6

SOURCE: U.S. Securities and Exchange Commission *Statistical Bulletin*, May, 1969, and *Statistical Series Release No. 2391*, Sept. 25, 1969.

[a] Activity rate defined as the average of purchases and sales divided by the average market value of stockholdings at the beginning and at the end of the period.

[b] Annual rate in second quarter of 1969.

[c] n.a.=not available.

Appendix to Chapter Two

We define the intrinsic value of stock at the beginning period 0 to be

$$S_0^N = \frac{Y_0^N}{\rho_0} + G_0 \tag{1}$$

where Y_0^N is the level of future earnings on equity which existing assets may be expected to generate (after allowance for replacement), ρ_0 is the rate at which the market capitalizes equity earnings, and G_0 is the contribution to current stock value of market expectations as to profitable real investment opportunities in the future. If b is the percentage of normalized earnings which is retained and reinvested and r_0 is the average rate of return on this new investment, then $(1 - b)Y_0^N$ is the value of dividends paid, and intrinsic value at the end of the period is

$$S_1^N = \frac{Y_0^N}{\rho_1} + \frac{br_0Y_0^N}{\rho_1} + G_1$$

If the risk premium required on equity investment is declining over time at a decreasing rate, we may write

$$\rho_1 = \rho_0(1 - g) \tag{2}$$

where g is a decreasing function of time. The capital gain which arises from growth in intrinsic value is then a composite of the effects of asset growth due to earnings retention, the excess of the rate of return on new investment over the capitalization rate for equity earnings, and the change in the capitalization rate. Approximating $1/(1 - g)$ by the first two terms of the infinite series $(1 + g + g^2 + \cdots)$ and ignoring changes in G due to the changing capitalization rate, as well as changes due to other factors (which we assume to have an expected value of zero)

$$S_1^N - S_0^N = \frac{bY_0^N r_0}{\rho_0}(1 + g) + \frac{Y_0^N g}{\rho_0}$$

$$= bY_0^N + \frac{b(r_0 - \rho_0)}{\rho_0}Y_0^N + g\left(\frac{br_0 + 1}{\rho_0}\right)Y_0^N$$

Adding dividends and expressing the sum as a percentage of initial intrinsic value, we obtain

$$\frac{(1 - b)Y_0^N + (S_1^N - S_0^N)}{S_0^N} = [1 + \frac{b(r_0 - \rho_0)}{\rho_0} + g\frac{1 + br_0}{\rho_0}]\frac{Y_0^N}{S_0^N} \tag{3}$$

If the retention ratio (relative to normalized earnings) and the ratio of average return on new investment to the capitalization rate remain constant over time, the factor by which the earnings yield is multiplied will vary as the ratio of g to the capitalization rate and will fall over time if the rate of decline in g is large in relation to g itself. The normalized earnings yield will then rise in relation to the single-period return based on equilibrium stock values at both the beginning and end of the period.

To the extent that actual stock values differ from intrinsic values or current earnings from normalized earnings, the single-period realized return will fluctuate about the value on the left of Eq. (3), while the earnings-price ratio will fluctuate about the value implied by solving Eq. (3) for the normalized earnings yield. In the second case, however, the range of fluctuation is much smaller.

If changes in expectations cause the value of Y_0^N or of G to change between periods 0 and 1, then the observed value of the single-period return will presumably reflect this shift, but its expected value (which we have identified with the required return on equity) should not be affected so long as the expected value of such shifts in Y_0^N or G is zero.

Appendix Table 2-1

PERCENTAGE DISTRIBUTION OF TOTAL FINANCIAL ASSETS BY TYPE OF ASSET, 1950–1967

(Percent of Total Wealth)

Year	Demand deposits plus currency	Time deposits at commercial banks	Time deposits at other savings institutions	U.S. government securities	State and local obligations	Corporate and foreign bonds	Corporate stocks	Mortgages	Other financial assets
1950	11.8	3.7	3.5	21.2	2.5	3.9	14.7	6.3	32.4
1951	11.5	3.6	3.5	20.2	2.5	4.0	15.8	6.7	32.1
1952	11.3	3.6	3.8	19.3	2.6	4.2	16.2	7.0	32.0
1953	10.8	3.8	4.1	19.2	2.9	4.4	15.0	7.4	32.4
1954	10.0	3.7	4.2	17.5	3.0	4.3	19.4	7.5	30.4
1955	9.2	3.4	4.3	15.8	3.1	4.2	21.6	7.9	30.5
1956	8.8	3.4	4.5	14.6	3.2	4.3	21.8	8.4	31.0
1957	8.7	3.7	4.9	14.4	3.4	4.7	19.0	8.9	32.3
1958	8.0	3.7	4.8	13.2	3.3	4.5	23.6	8.7	30.2
1959	7.5	3.6	5.0	12.8	3.4	4.5	23.9	9.1	30.2
1960	7.1	3.7	5.3	12.2	3.5	4.6	22.9	9.4	31.3
1961	6.6	3.8	5.2	11.3	3.4	4.4	26.1	9.2	30.0
1962	6.7	4.4	5.7	11.4	3.7	4.5	22.5	9.9	31.2
1963	6.3	4.5	5.8	10.6	3.6	4.4	24.1	10.0	30.7
1964	6.0	4.7	5.9	9.9	3.5	4.3	25.2	10.1	30.4
1965	5.6	5.0	5.8	9.2	3.4	4.2	26.2	10.1	30.5
1966	5.6	5.3	5.9	9.2	3.5	4.5	23.2	10.6	32.2
1967	5.4	5.4	5.8	8.7	3.5	4.5	25.7	10.1	30.9

Appendix Table 2-2
PERCENTAGE DISTRIBUTION OF FINANCIAL
ASSETS OF HOUSEHOLDS, 1950–1967

Year	Corporate stocks	U.S. government securities	Demand deposits plus currency	Time and savings accounts at commercial banks	Time and savings accts. in other savings institutions	State and local obligations	Other assets
1950	33.2	15.4	12.9	7.5	8.1	2.2	20.7
1951	33.2	14.0	12.6	7.2	8.1	2.2	22.7
1952	33.7	13.1	12.2	7.3	8.6	2.3	22.8
1953	31.4	12.8	12.0	7.6	9.5	2.6	24.1
1954	38.6	10.6	10.4	6.8	9.1	2.5	22.0
1955	41.7	9.8	9.3	6.3	9.1	2.7	21.1
1956	41.7	9.3	8.9	6.2	9.6	3.0	21.3
1957	37.2	9.5	8.9	7.1	10.7	3.3	23.3
1958	43.8	7.7	7.7	6.6	10.0	2.8	21.4
1959	44.0	7.7	7.3	6.5	10.3	2.8	21.4
1960	42.3	7.5	7.1	6.7	11.1	3.1	22.2
1961	46.6	6.4	6.2	6.4	10.6	2.9	20.9
1962	41.6	6.6	6.6	7.5	12.1	3.3	22.3
1963	43.7	6.2	6.3	7.4	12.2	2.9	21.3
1964	45.1	5.7	6.1	7.3	12.2	2.8	20.8
1965	46.3	5.4	6.0	7.5	11.9	2.7	20.2
1966	42.2	6.1	6.3	8.4	12.6	2.9	21.5
1967	44.9	5.4	6.0	8.3	12.1	2.5	20.8

Appendix Table 2-3
PERCENTAGE DISTRIBUTION OF FINANCIAL ASSETS
OF PRIVATE PENSION FUNDS, 1950–1967[a]

Year	Corporate stocks	Corporate and foreign bonds	U.S. government securities	Mortgages	Other assets
1950	17.5	44.4	31.7		6.4
1951	18.9	47.3	28.4	1.3	4.1
1952	19.8	49.5	25.3	1.1	4.3
1953	21.6	50.5	22.5	1.8	3.6
1954	24.1	51.9	19.5	1.5	3.0
1955	34.6	44.9	16.5	1.7	2.3
1956	35.3	47.3	13.4	2.0	2.0
1957	33.5	50.4	11.2	2.7	2.2
1958	41.1	45.4	9.2	2.5	1.8
1959	43.9	42.7	8.5	3.0	1.9
1960	44.8	42.6	7.3	3.5	1.8
1961	51.1	37.7	6.2	3.6	1.4
1962	47.9	39.6	6.8	4.2	1.5
1963	51.6	36.5	6.3	4.1	1.5
1964	53.9	34.1	6.1	4.3	1.6
1965	56.6	32.3	5.0	4.7	1.4
1966	53.8	34.4	5.2	5.3	1.3
1967	61.0	29.4	3.7	4.6	1.3

[a]This percentage distribution differs slightly from that shown in Appendix Table 1-6 due to the difference in data sources.

Appendix Table 2-4
PERCENTAGE DISTRIBUTION OF FINANCIAL ASSETS
OF LIFE INSURANCE COMPANIES, 1950–1967

Year	Mortgages	Corporate and foreign bonds	U.S. government securities	State and local obligations	Corporate stocks	Other assets
1950	25.7	39.6	21.6	1.9	3.3	7.9
1951	28.9	41.2	16.5	1.8	3.3	8.3
1952	29.8	42.9	14.4	1.5	3.4	8.0
1953	30.4	43.5	12.9	1.7	3.4	8.1
1954	31.7	43.0	11.1	2.2	4.0	8.0
1955	33.6	42.1	9.8	2.3	4.1	8.1
1956	35.4	42.1	8.2	2.4	3.8	8.1
1957	35.8	42.5	7.2	2.4	3.5	8.6
1958	35.6	42.5	7.0	2.6	3.9	8.4
1959	35.6	42.2	6.4	2.9	4.2	8.7
1960	36.1	41.6	5.6	3.1	4.3	9.3
1961	36.0	41.3	5.0	3.2	5.1	9.4
1962	36.3	41.2	4.8	3.1	4.9	9.7
1963	36.9	40.9	4.3	2.8	5.2	9.9
1964	38.0	40.2	3.9	2.6	5.5	9.8
1965	38.9	39.6	3.3	2.3	5.9	10.0
1966	40.0	39.1	3.0	1.9	5.4	10.6
1967	39.1	38.7	1.7	1.7	6.8	12.0

Appendix Table 2-5
PERCENTAGE DISTRIBUTION OF FINANCIAL ASSETS
OF INSURANCE COMPANIES OTHER THAN LIFE
INSURANCE COMPANIES, 1950–1967

Year	Corporate stocks	State and local obligations	U.S. government securities	Demand deposits plus currency	Corporate and foreign bonds	Other assets
1950	27.0	8.7	42.1	9.5	5.6	7.1
1951	28.3	10.1	39.9	8.7	5.8	7.2
1952	27.9	12.3	37.7	8.4	6.5	7.2
1953	26.8	15.5	36.3	8.3	6.5	6.6
1954	30.7	17.7	32.3	6.8	5.7	6.8
1955	32.9	20.0	29.0	6.2	5.7	6.2
1956	33.0	22.5	26.1	6.0	5.5	6.9
1957	30.3	25.3	25.3	5.9	6.3	6.9
1958	33.9	25.0	22.2	5.2	6.0	7.7
1959	33.6	26.6	21.4	4.8	5.9	7.7
1960	33.3	28.7	19.9	4.6	6.0	7.5
1961	37.3	28.8	17.7	4.4	5.4	6.4
1962	34.6	30.5	17.8	4.4	5.6	7.1
1963	36.9	30.1	16.8	4.0	5.7	6.5
1964	38.9	26.2	15.7	3.7	6.3	9.2
1965	38.0	28.1	14.9	3.2	8.5	7.3
1966	34.5	31.8	14.0	3.2	9.0	7.5
1967	39.3	30.4	11.1	2.9	8.7	7.6

Appendix Table 2-6
PERCENTAGE DISTRIBUTION OF FINANCIAL ASSETS
OF MUTUAL FUNDS, 1950–1967[a]

Year	Corporate and foreign bonds	Corporate stocks	Other assets
1950	8.3	83.3	8.4
1951	10.0	83.3	6.7
1952	7.7	84.6	7.7
1953	7.3	85.4	7.3
1954	6.6	88.5	4.9
1955	6.4	88.5	5.1
1956	7.8	87.8	4.4
1957	9.2	85.0	5.8
1958	6.8	88.6	4.6
1959	7.0	88.0	5.0
1960	7.1	87.0	5.9
1961	7.0	89.0	4.0
1962	7.5	85.9	6.6
1963	7.1	87.7	5.2
1964	7.2	88.0	4.8
1965	7.4	87.8	4.8
1966	8.5	82.8	8.7
1967	6.7	87.5	5.8

[a]This percentage distribution differs slightly from that shown in Appendix Table 1-5 due to the difference in data sources. See Chap. 2, footnote 7.

Appendix Table 2-7
PERCENTAGE DISTRIBUTION OF FINANCIAL
ASSETS OF COMMERCIAL BANKS, 1950–1967

Year	U.S. government securities	State and local obligations	Mortgages	Consumer loans	Bank loans, n.e.c.	Other assets
1950	43.0	5.5	9.2	5.0	18.5	18.8
1951	40.1	5.9	9.3	4.8	20.3	19.6
1952	39.3	6.1	9.5	5.7	21.1	18.3
1953	39.3	6.3	9.8	6.4	19.9	18.3
1954	40.4	7.0	10.2	6.1	19.0	17.3
1955	34.9	6.9	11.2	7.1	22.9	17.0
1956	32.3	6.7	11.8	7.6	25.1	16.5
1957	31.3	7.1	11.7	8.0	25.6	16.3
1958	33.2	7.8	11.9	7.5	24.3	15.3
1959	28.5	7.8	12.9	8.7	27.2	14.9
1960	28.5	7.8	12.7	9.1	27.4	14.5
1961	28.8	8.3	12.5	8.8	26.6	15.0
1962	27.0	9.4	13.0	9.0	26.9	14.7
1963	24.3	10.6	13.8	9.6	27.8	13.9
1964	22.5	10.9	14.2	10.1	28.5	13.8
1965	19.8	11.4	14.6	10.6	30.7	12.9
1966	17.8	11.3	15.1	10.9	31.4	13.5
1967	18.3	12.6	14.7	10.5	30.2	13.7

Appendix Table 2-8
PERCENTAGE DISTRIBUTION OF FINANCIAL ASSETS OF
SAVINGS AND LOAN ASSOCIATIONS, 1950–1967

Year	Mortgages	U.S. government securities	Demand deposits plus currency	Other assets
1950	80.5	8.9	4.1	6.5
1951	80.7	8.3	4.2	6.8
1952	81.1	7.9	4.0	7.0
1953	82.4	7.1	3.4	7.1
1954	82.6	6.3	3.8	7.3
1955	83.3	6.6	3.7	6.4
1956	83.2	6.8	3.3	6.7
1957	83.2	7.5	3.1	6.2
1958	82.8	7.6	3.3	6.3
1959	83.8	7.7	2.5	6.0
1960	84.1	7.3	2.4	6.2
1961	83.8	6.9	2.6	6.7
1962	84.2	6.4	2.9	6.5
1963	84.6	6.5	2.6	6.3
1964	84.8	6.4	2.3	6.5
1965	85.1	6.3	2.2	6.4
1966	85.4	6.5	1.7	6.4
1967	84.8	7.3	1.4	6.5

Appendix Table 2-9
PERCENTAGE DISTRIBUTION OF FINANCIAL ASSETS
OF MUTUAL SAVINGS BANKS, 1950–1967

Year	Mortgages	U.S. government securities	Corporate and foreign bonds	Other assets
1950	37.1	48.7	9.4	4.8
1951	42.1	42.1	9.4	6.4
1952	45.1	37.5	9.9	7.5
1953	47.8	34.2	10.3	7.7
1954	51.0	29.9	9.9	9.2
1955	55.9	27.5	8.3	8.3
1956	59.3	24.6	8.1	8.0
1957	60.2	22.4	9.1	8.3
1958	61.4	20.1	10.1	8.4
1959	64.3	18.8	9.3	7.6
1960	66.5	16.5	9.4	7.6
1961	68.0	15.4	8.4	8.2
1962	70.1	14.5	7.6	7.8
1963	72.8	13.1	6.4	7.7
1964	74.9	12.0	5.7	7.4
1965	76.8	10.7	5.0	7.5
1966	77.7	9.3	5.2	7.8
1967	75.9	8.1	7.8	8.2

Appendix Table 2-10

PERCENTAGE DISTRIBUTION OF FINANCIAL ASSETS OF
STATE AND LOCAL GOVERNMENTS, 1950–1967

Year	U.S. government securities	Corporate and foreign bonds and corporate stocks	Demand deposits plus currency	Time deposits	State and local obligations	Mortgages	Other assets
1950	38.6	6.1	29.8	6.1	15.8	–	3.6
1951	39.1	7.3	28.6	6.0	15.3	–	3.7
1952	40.9	7.7	27.4	5.8	14.6	–	3.6
1953	42.0	8.8	26.1	6.5	14.0	–	2.6
1954	43.3	10.4	22.5	7.1	13.9	0.3	2.5
1955	43.4	11.5	20.7	6.7	14.3	0.6	2.8
1956	44.0	12.8	18.7	6.4	14.9	0.8	2.4
1957	42.1	14.7	18.0	7.0	15.2	1.0	2.0
1958	39.7	16.7	16.7	8.4	15.5	1.2	1.8
1959	40.3	17.9	15.8	7.0	15.3	1.8	1.9
1960	39.0	20.6	12.3	9.3	14.5	2.4	1.9
1961	36.4	23.3	11.8	10.2	13.5	3.1	1.7
1962	34.9	25.5	12.2	10.8	11.3	3.5	1.8
1963	32.1	27.3	14.4	12.0	8.9	3.6	1.7
1964	29.5	29.0	14.8	13.1	7.1	3.9	2.6
1965	29.5	30.0	14.5	14.8	5.8	4.2	1.2
1966	28.2	32.0	12.8	14.8	4.9	4.7	2.6
1967	26.4	35.7	12.8	15.5	4.1	5.2	0.3

Appendix Table 2-11
DISTRIBUTION OF CORPORATE
STOCK, BY HOLDER, 1950–1967
(Percent of Total Corporate Stock)

Year	Households[a]	Life insurance companies	Pension funds	Other insurance companies	Open-end investment companies	Other holders
1950	91.3	1.4	0.8	2.3	1.4	2.8
1951	91.4	1.3	0.8	2.3	1.5	2.7
1952	90.9	1.3	1.0	2.3	1.8	2.7
1953	89.9	1.5	1.3	2.5	2.0	2.8
1954	90.4	1.3	1.2	2.3	2.1	2.7
1955	89.9	1.1	1.9	2.2	2.2	2.7
1956	89.8	1.0	2.1	2.1	2.3	2.7
1957	89.0	1.1	2.5	2.2	2.5	2.7
1958	89.1	1.0	2.8	2.0	2.8	2.3
1959	88.3	1.0	3.2	2.0	3.1	2.4
1960	87.4	1.1	3.7	2.1	3.3	2.4
1961	87.0	1.1	4.0	2.1	3.5	2.3
1962	86.2	1.2	4.3	2.2	3.6	2.5
1963	85.9	1.2	4.6	2.2	3.7	2.4
1964	85.6	1.2	4.9	2.1	3.7	2.4
1965	85.6	1.2	5.1	2.0	4.0	2.1
1966	85.1	1.3	5.5	2.0	4.1	2.0
1967	83.9	1.4	6.1	2.0	4.5	2.1

[a]Including personal trusts and nonprofit institutions.

Appendix Table 2-12

DISTRIBUTION OF CORPORATE AND FOREIGN
BONDS, BY HOLDER, 1950–1967

(Percent of Total Corporate and Foreign Bonds)

Year	Households	State and local governments	Commercial banks	Mutual savings banks	Life insurance companies	Pension funds	Other insurance companies	Other holders
1950	10.0	3.6	5.6	5.4	63.3	7.1	1.8	3.2
1951	8.4	4.2	5.1	5.1	64.0	8.1	1.9	3.2
1952	7.7	4.4	4.4	5.2	63.6	9.4	2.1	3.2
1953	7.0	5.1	4.0	5.3	62.8	10.6	2.1	3.1
1954	6.5	6.1	3.3	5.1	61.7	12.1	1.9	3.3
1955	7.8	6.7	2.8	4.2	60.3	12.9	2.0	3.3
1956	8.3	7.3	2.0	4.1	59.3	14.4	1.8	2.8
1957	8.4	8.0	1.9	4.4	56.9	15.4	1.9	3.1
1958	8.6	8.9	1.6	4.7	55.3	16.0	1.9	3.0
1959	7.9	9.7	1.4	4.3	55.0	16.7	1.9	2.9
1960	7.4	11.3	1.1	4.2	53.5	17.4	1.9	3.2
1961	6.8	13.2	0.9	3.8	52.9	17.7	1.8	2.9
1962	5.7	15.0	0.8	3.4	52.3	17.8	1.8	3.2
1963	4.4	17.0	0.7	3.0	51.8	18.1	1.9	3.1
1964	3.8	18.8	0.8	2.7	50.4	18.3	2.1	3.1
1965	3.7	19.9	0.6	2.3	49.0	18.2	2.7	3.6
1966	4.2	21.5	0.7	2.4	46.5	18.1	2.6	4.0
1967	4.5	23.7	1.1	3.4	44.1	16.8	2.6	3.8

Appendix Table 2-13
DISTRIBUTION OF STATE AND LOCAL
OBLIGATIONS, BY HOLDER, 1950–1967
(Percent of Total State and Local Obligations)

Year	Households	State and local governments	Commercial banks	Life insurance companies	Other insurance companies	Other holders
1950	38.8	14.6	32.8	4.9	4.5	4.4
1951	38.3	14.0	33.8	4.4	5.1	4.4
1952	38.5	13.4	34.1	3.7	6.4	3.9
1953	39.5	12.6	31.6	3.8	7.6	4.9
1954	38.3	11.8	31.7	4.5	8.6	5.1
1955	41.5	11.4	28.3	4.5	9.4	4.9
1956	43.7	11.3	26.1	4.5	9.9	4.5
1957	43.8	11.3	25.8	4.5	10.4	4.2
1958	40.4	11.2	28.1	4.6	10.5	5.2
1959	40.4	11.0	26.7	5.0	11.3	5.6
1960	41.8	10.5	25.6	5.2	11.8	5.1
1961	41.8	9.7	26.9	5.2	12.1	4.3
1962	41.4	8.2	30.1	4.8	11.9	3.6
1963	38.4	6.8	34.1	4.4	12.1	4.1
1964	39.0	5.6	35.4	4.0	11.6	4.4
1965	37.9	4.7	38.2	3.5	11.2	4.5
1966	37.9	4.2	38.3	2.9	11.8	4.9
1967	35.2	3.5	42.1	2.5	11.6	5.0

Appendix Table 2-14
DISTRIBUTION OF U.S. GOVERNMENT
SECURITIES, BY HOLDER, 1950–1967
(Percent of Total Government Securities)

Year	Households	Corporate nonfinancial business	State and local governments	Commercial banks	Savings and loan associations	Mutual savings banks	Life insurance companies	Other insurance companies	Other[a] holders
1950	30.6	9.0	4.0	29.2	0.7	5.0	6.2	2.4	12.9
1951	30.2	9.4	4.5	28.9	0.7	4.5	5.1	2.5	14.2
1952	29.4	8.9	5.0	29.3	0.8	4.3	4.6	2.6	15.1
1953	28.6	9.3	5.6	29.2	0.8	4.1	4.3	2.7	15.4
1954	27.8	8.2	6.3	31.4	0.9	3.8	3.9	2.7	15.0
1955	28.8	10.1	6.7	27.9	1.1	3.7	3.7	2.6	15.4
1956	30.0	8.3	7.3	27.3	1.3	3.6	3.4	2.5	16.3
1957	30.2	8.2	7.6	27.4	1.6	3.5	3.1	2.5	15.9
1958	27.9	7.9	7.2	30.0	1.8	3.2	3.1	2.3	16.6
1959	29.0	10.3	7.6	25.6	2.0	3.0	2.9	2.4	17.1
1960	28.9	8.1	8.0	26.7	2.2	2.8	2.7	2.3	18.3
1961	27.8	7.7	7.9	28.2	2.3	2.6	2.5	2.3	18.2
1962	26.9	7.6	8.1	27.8	2.3	2.6	2.4	2.2	20.1
1963	27.8	7.7	8.3	26.3	2.7	2.5	2.3	2.3	20.1
1964	27.8	6.9	8.2	25.7	2.8	2.4	2.1	2.2	21.9
1965	28.5	6.1	9.0	24.5	3.0	2.3	1.9	2.2	22.5
1966	30.7	5.5	9.2	22.7	3.1	2.0	1.7	2.0	23.1
1967	29.8	4.4	8.5	24.8	3.6	1.9	1.5	1.7	23.8

[a] For U.S. government securities the most important of the other holders is the Federal Reserve System.

Appendix Table 2-15
DISTRIBUTION OF MORTGAGES,
BY HOLDER, 1950–1967
(Percent of Total Mortgages)

Year	Households	Commercial banks	Savings and loan associations	Mutual savings banks	Life insurance companies	Other holders
1950	12.3	21.5	21.6	13.2	25.6	5.8
1951	11.2	20.4	21.6	13.8	26.9	6.1
1952	10.4	19.6	23.0	14.2	26.6	6.2
1953	9.8	18.7	24.6	14.5	26.1	6.3
1954	9.0	18.2	25.9	14.9	25.8	6.2
1955	8.0	17.9	27.0	15.1	25.4	6.6
1956	7.6	17.4	27.6	15.3	25.5	6.6
1957	7.7	16.5	28.5	15.1	25.1	7.1
1958	7.5	16.4	29.6	15.1	24.1	7.3
1959	6.8	16.4	31.1	14.6	22.9	8.2
1960	6.4	15.5	32.5	14.6	22.6	8.4
1961	5.7	15.0	34.0	14.4	21.9	9.0
1962	5.2	15.3	35.2	14.4	21.0	8.9
1963	4.6	15.7	36.6	14.6	20.3	8.2
1964	4.1	16.0	37.0	14.8	20.1	8.0
1965	3.4	16.5	36.9	14.9	20.0	8.3
1966	3.1	16.9	35.9	14.8	20.2	9.1
1967	2.7	17.0	35.8	14.8	19.9	9.8

Appendix Table 2-16
ASSET YIELD REGRESSIONS[a]

Asset class	Regression number	Ratio of money supply to GNP[b]	Elasticity with respect to		Time trend	Constant term	Adjusted R^2[c]	Durbin-Watson statistic	First-order autocorrelation
			Relative supply	Relative financial wealth of major holder					
Corporate stock	1	−3.355 (−2.4)		0.507[d] (−3.2)		2.35	.751	1.69	.60
	2		0.778[e] (1.6)	−0.368[d] (−3.9)		0.04	.816	2.02	.20
	3		0.520[e] (1.7)	−2.900[f] (−3.9)	1.507[g] (3.3)	−1.94	.908	2.07	−.02
Government bonds (10 or more years to maturity)	1	−1.981 (−2.1)		−1.311[h] (−2.1)	0.034 (7.8)	4.30	.937	1.63	.24
Corporate AAA bonds	1	−2.265 (−3.3)	1.092 (3.4)		0.029 (6.5)	−0.60	.942	1.80	.25
Municipal bonds (high grade, 20 years to maturity)	1		1.123 (3.9)			−0.25	.738	1.77	.40
Mortgages	1		3.128[i] (4.2)	−1.754[j] (−3.7)	0.030 (2.5)	−3.44	.825	1.99	−.13
Time deposits in commercial banks	1				0.088 (11.5)	−0.09	.977	1.68	.64
Time deposits in savings institutions other than commercial and mutual savings banks	1		0.292[k] (2.4)		0.040 (8.7)	0.11	.989	1.77	.004

134

a Based on annual data, 1950–1967, and corrected for first-order autocorrelation. All variables in logarithmic form except time. *t* tests shown in parentheses, below regression coefficients to which they refer. Some variables have been scaled for statistical convenience.

b Deviation of the ratio of the money supply to GNP from its time trend.

c Percentage of variation explained by the independent variables only. Excludes that explained by the autoregressive scheme.

d Financial assets of pension funds plus mutual funds as a fraction of all financial assets, lagged one year.

e In computing this variable, the quantity of stock is so defined as to be independent of current price. See text.

f Financial assets of pension funds as a fraction of all financial assets, lagged one year.

g Logarithm of time.

h Financial assets of commercial banks as a fraction of all financial assets.

i Relative supply of mortgages lagged one year.

j Financial assets of savings and loan associations as a fraction of all financial assets, lagged one year.

k The relative supply of mortgages. For any given level of time deposit yield, this is assumed to determine the relative supply of time deposits in savings institutions other than commercial banks.

Appendix Table 2-17

PORTFOLIO WEIGHT REGRESSIONS FOR CORPORATE STOCK, 1950–1967, BY TYPE OF HOLDER[a]

| Proportion of portfolio invested in | Regression number | Elasticity with respect to | | | | | | Constant term | Adjusted R^{2c} | Durbin-Watson statistic | Correction for first-order autocorrelation |
		Relative supply	Yield ratio	Cyclical variable[b]	Variance of earnings yield	Other variable	Time trend				
Households	1	0.432[d] (7.8)	−0.033[e] (−2.7)	0.563 (12.3)	−0.035 (−5.4)			0.03	.885	1.67	.32
	2	0.425[d] (7.5)	−0.030[f] (−2.4)	0.562 (12.0)	−0.033 (−4.9)			0.05	.894	1.71	.30
Pension funds	1	0.866[d] (6.8)		0.474 (4.4)			0.037 (6.2)	−1.66	.955	2.51	−.32
	2			0.271 (2.2)		0.800[g] (22.2)		0.75	.955	2.20	−.19
	3			0.147 (1.7)	−0.072 (−2.9)		0.482[h] (6.3)	0.30	.954	1.99	.37
Life insurance companies	1		−0.276[i] (−3.3)				0.059 (9.2)	−1.50	.929	1.87	.16
	2		−0.216[i] (−2.8)	0.131 (1.8)	−0.044 (−1.9)		0.043 (4.7)	−1.32	.943	1.81	.11
Non-life insurance companies	1		−0.064[e] (−2.8)	0.202 (3.0)		0.327[g] (10.3)		0.86	.891	2.25	−.18
	2		−0.066[f] (−3.5)	0.200 (3.3)		0.316[g] (12.9)		0.86	.900	2.42	−.31
	3			0.307 (5.2)	−0.040 (−3.3)	0.150[g] (3.3)		1.08	.909	1.90	.11

Proportion of portfolio invested in	Regression number	Elasticity with respect to					Time trend	Constant term	Adjusted R^{2c}	Durbin-Watson statistic	Correction for first-order autocorrelation
		Relative supply	Yield ratio	Cyclical[b] variable	Variance of earnings yield	Other variable					
Mutual funds	1	0.049^d (1.6)		0.108 (4.2)			−0.001 (−1.0)	2.03	.457	2.06	−.17
	2		-0.020^j (−2.3)	0.085 (3.5)		0.030^g (2.5)		2.11	.600	1.95	.02
	3		-0.021^k (−2.3)	0.083 (3.4)		0.031^g (2.4)		2.11	.591	1.95	.02

[a] Corrected for first-order autocorrelation. All variables are logarithmic except time. t tests appear in parentheses below the regression coefficients to which they refer. Some variables have been scaled for statistical convenience.

[b] Deviation of the ratio of money supply to GNP from its time trend.

[c] Percentage of variation explained by the independent variables only. Excludes that explained by the autoregressive scheme.

[d] Lagged one year. The quantity of stock is measured in terms of market value.

[e] Ratio of yield on U.S. government securities to three-year average of dividend yield plus percentage capital gain on stock.

[f] Ratio of yield on municipal securities to three-year average of dividend yield plus percentage capital gain on stock.

[g] Financial assets of pension funds plus mutual funds as a fraction of all financial assets, lagged one year.

[h] Logarithm of time.

[i]

[j] Ratio of the yield on mortgages to the earnings yield on stock.

[k] Ratio of yield on corporate bonds to three-year average of dividend yield plus percentage capital gain on stock.

[k] Ratio of yield on U.S. government securities to three-year average of dividend yield plus percentage capital gain on stock.

Appendix Table 2-18

PORTFOLIO WEIGHT REGRESSIONS
FOR HOUSEHOLDS,[a] 1950–1967

Proportion of portfolio invested in	Regression number	Elasticity with respect to					Constant term	Adjusted R^2[c]	Durbin-Watson statistic	Correction for first-order autocorrelation
		Relative supply	Yield ratio	Cyclical variable[b]	Other variable	Time trend				
Corporate stock	1	0.432[d] (7.8)	−0.033[e] (−2.7)	0.563 (12.3)	−0.035[f] (−5.4)		0.03	.885	1.67	.32
	2	0.425[d] (7.5)	−0.030[g] (−2.4)	0.562 (12.0)	−0.033[f] (−4.9)		0.05	.894	1.71	.30
U.S. government securities	1	1.175 (7.8)					−3.30	.907	2.34	.45
	2	0.631 (2.5)	−0.579[h] (−2.7)				−2.14	.947	2.15	.25
	3		−0.729[i] (−2.8)		1.617[j] (3.2)	−0.052 (−12.1)	−3.84	.966	2.25	−.09
Municipal securities	1	1.014 (6.6)				−0.018 (−3.6)	−2.35	.636	2.18	−.33
	2	0.712 (2.9)	−0.227[k] (−1.7)			−0.020 (−3.7)	−1.50	.695	1.99	−.17
Demand deposits	1	1.429[l] (3.2)				−0.030 (−4.2)	−3.62	.949	2.08	.08
	2	1.523[l] (3.7)	−0.312[m] (−4.4)				−3.91	.952	2.16	−.21
	3	1.600[l] (4.5)	−0.736[n] (−5.1)				−3.43	.956	2.29	−.30

| Proportion of portfolio invested in | Regression number | Elasticity with respect to | | | | Time trend | Constant term | Adjusted R^{2c} | Durbin-Watson statistic | Correction for first-order autocorrelation |
		Relative supply	Yield ratio	Cyclical variable[b]	Other variable					
Time deposits in commercial banks	1	1.724[l] (4.2)				0.033 (5.0)	−5.12	.556	2.45	−.08
Time deposits in other savings institutions	1	0.283[o] (2.0)				0.016 (2.9)	−0.74	.911	2.05	−.24
	2	0.415[o,p] (2.5)			0.009[q] (1.4)	0.032 (8.8)	−0.29	.914	2.08	−.29

[a] Corrected for first-order autocorrelation. All variables are logarithmic except time. *t* tests appear in parentheses below the regression coefficients to which they refer.

[b] Deviation of the ratio of money supply to GNP from its time trend.

[c] Percentage of variation explained by the independent variables only. Excludes that explained by the autoregressive scheme.

[d] Lagged one period. The quantity of stock is measured in terms of market value.

[e] Ratio of yield on U.S. government securities to three-year average of dividend yield plus percentage capital gain on stock.

[f] Five-year variance of earnings yield on stock.

[g] Ratio of yield on municipals to three-year average of dividend yield plus percentage capital gain on stock.

[h] Ratio of yield on time deposits in commercial banks to yield on governments.

[i] Ratio of yield on time deposits in other savings institutions to yield on government securities.

[j] Relative financial wealth of commercial banks.

[k] Earnings yield on stock.

[l] The volume of these deposits is assumed to be proportional to total commercial bank deposits, which are largely determined by bank reserves and the required reserve ratios.

[m] Yield on time deposits in commercial banks.

[n] Yield on time deposits in savings institutions other than commercial and mutual savings banks.

[o] Relative supply is assumed to depend ultimately on the relative supply of mortgages and is taken to be proportional to the latter.

[p] Deviation of relative supply from its time trend.

[q] Five-year variance in the earnings yield on stock.

Appendix Table 2-19
PORTFOLIO WEIGHT REGRESSIONS FOR
PENSION FUNDS,[a] 1950–1967

Proportion of portfolio invested in	Regression number	Elasticity with respect to				Constant term	Adjusted R^2[c]	Durbin-Watson statistic	Adjustment for first-order autocorrelation
		Relative supply[b]	Cyclical variable[b]	Other variable	Time trend				
Corporate stock	1	0.866[d] (6.8)	0.474 (4.4)		0.037 (6.2)	−1.66	.955	2.51	−.32
	2		0.271 (2.2)	−0.800[e] (22.2)		0.75	.955	2.20	−.19
	3		0.147 (1.7)	−0.072[f] (−2.9)	0.482[g] (6.3)	0.30	.954	1.99	.37
Corporate bonds	1	0.915 (4.7)			−0.042 (−13.6)	0.45	.919	2.04	−.20
U.S. government securities	1			−1.011[h] (−1.4)	−0.118 (−8.6)	1.24	.958	2.20	.67

[a] Corrected for first-order autocorrelation. All variables are logarithmic except time. t tests appear in parentheses below the regression coefficients to which they refer. Some variables have been scaled for statistical convenience.
[b] Deviation of the ratio of money supply to GNP from its time trend.
[c] Percentage of variation explained by the independent variables only. Excludes that explained by the autoregressive scheme.
[d] Lagged one year. The quantity of stock is measured in terms of market value.
[e] Financial assets of pension funds plus mutual funds as a fraction of all financial assets, lagged one year.
[f] Five-year variance of the earnings yield on stock.
[g] Logarithm of time.
[h] Ratio of yield on corporate securities to yield on government securities.

140

Appendix Table 2-20
PORTFOLIO WEIGHT REGRESSIONS FOR LIFE INSURANCE COMPANIES,[a] 1950–1967

| Proportion of portfolio invested in | Regression number | Elasticity with respect to | | | | | Constant term | Adjusted R^2[c] | Durbin-Watson statistic | Adjustment for first-order autocorrelation |
		Relative supply	Yield ratio	Cyclical variable[b]	Other variable	Time trend				
Corporate stock	1		−0.276[d] (−3.3)			0.059 (9.2)	−1.50	.929	1.87	.16
	2		−0.216[d] (−2.8)	0.131 (1.8)	−0.044[e] (−1.9)	0.043 (4.7)	−1.32	.943	1.81	.11
Corporate bonds	1	0.152 (2.6)				−0.010 (−10.5)	1.29	.684	1.53	.55
Mortgages	1	0.403 (4.8)					0.37	.871	1.17	.59
	2	0.321 (2.5)			−0.682[f] (−3.1)	0.007 (1.6)	2.66	.925	1.55	.41
U.S. government securities	1	2.555 (16.3)					−7.17	.956	1.49	.14
	2	2.658 (22.7)	−2.592[g] (−2.8)				−7.19	.970	1.91	−.02
Municipal securities	1	2.924 (5.6)				−0.059 (−4.1)	−4.50	.691	1.50	.48

[a] Corrected for first-order autocorrelation. All variables are logarithmic except time. t tests appear in parentheses below the regression coefficients to which they refer. Some variables have been scaled for statistical convenience.

[b] Deviation of the ratio of money supply to GNP from its time trend.

[c] Percentage of variation explained by the independent variables only. Excludes that explained by the autoregressive scheme.

[d] Ratio of the yield on mortgages to the earnings yield on stock.

[e] Five-year variance of the earnings yield on stock.

[f] Relative financial wealth of savings and loan associations, life insurance companies, commercial banks, and mutual savings banks.

[g] Ratio of yield on corporate securities to yield on government securities.

141

Appendix Table 2-21
PORTFOLIO WEIGHT REGRESSIONS FOR NON-LIFE
INSURANCE COMPANIES,[a] 1950–1967

Proportion of portfolio invested in	Regression number	Elasticity with respect to				Time trend	Constant term	Adjusted R^2 [c]	Durbin-Watson statistic	Adjustment for first-order autocorrelation
		Relative supply	Yield ratio	Cyclical variable[b]	Other variables					
Corporate stock	1		−0.064[d] (−2.8)	0.202 (3.0)	0.327[e] (10.3)		0.86	.891	2.25	−.18
	2		−0.066[f] (−3.5)	0.200 (3.3)	0.316[e] (12.9)		0.86	.900	2.42	−.31
	3			0.307 (5.2)	0.150[e] (3.3) −0.040[g] (−3.3)		1.08	.909	1.90	.11
Municipal securities	1	2.091 (17.3)					−1.73	.961	2.00	.11
	2	1.519 (5.4)	−0.472[h] (−2.2)			0.021 (2.2)	−1.18	.968	2.19	−.05
	3	1.321 (4.3)	−0.698[i] (−2.6)			0.027 (2.7)	−0.90	.972	2.05	.11
U.S. government securities	1	1.576 (16.0)					−3.35	.967	1.75	.30
	2	1.629 (18.3)	−0.226[j] (−1.2)				−3.51	.970	1.70	.17
	3	1.315 (12.9)			−0.481[k] (−3.3)		−2.07	.978	1.56	−.11

| Proportion of portfolio invested in | Regression number | Elasticity with respect to | | | | | Constant term | Adjusted R^{2c} | Durbin-Watson statistic | Adjustment for first-order autocorrelation |
		Relative supply	Yield ratio	Cyclical variable[b]	Other variables	Time trend				
Corporate bonds	1	1.477 (2.1)			-2.658[k] (-4.3)	0.065 (5.3)	-0.08	.592	2.08	.58
Demand deposits	1					-0.068 (-24.0)	-0.01	.983	1.87	.23
	2	1.565 (17.0)	-0.180[l] (-2.0)				-3.87	.972	2.39	-.19

[a] Corrected for first-order autocorrelation. All variables are logarithmic except time. t tests appear in parentheses below the regression coefficients to which they refer. Some variables have been scaled for statistical convenience.
[b] Deviation of thr ratio of money supply to GNP from its time trend.
[c] Percentage of variation explained by the independent variables only. Excludes that explained by the autoregressive scheme.
[d] Ratio of yield on U.S. government securities to three-year average of dividend yield plus percentage capital gain on stock.
[e] Financial assets of pension funds plus mutual funds as a percentage of all financial assets, lagged one year.
[f] Ratio of yield on municipal securities to three-year average of dividend yield plus percentage capital gain on stock.
[g] Five-year variance of earnings yield on stock.
[h] Ratio of yield on government securities to that on municipal securities.
[i] Ratio of yield on corporate securities to that on municipal securities.
[j] Ratio of yield on municipal securities to that on government securities.
[k] Relative supply of municipal securities.
[l] Yield on municipal securities.

143

Appendix Table 2-22
PORTFOLIO WEIGHT REGRESSIONS
FOR MUTUAL FUNDS,[a] 1950–1967

| Proportion of portfolio invested in | Regression number | Elasticity with respect to | | | | | Constant term | Adjusted R^{2c} | Durbin-Watson statistic | Adjustment for first-order autocorrelation |
		Relative supply	Yield ratio	Cyclical variable[b]	Other variable	Time trend				
Corporate stock	1	0.049[d] (1.6)		0.108 (4.2)		−0.001 (−1.0)	2.03	.457	2.06	−.17
	2		−0.020[e] (−2.3)	0.085 (3.5)	0.030[f] (2.5)		2.11	.600	1.95	.02
	3		−0.021[g] (−2.3)	0.083 (3.4)	0.031[f] (2.4)		2.11	.591	1.95	.02
Corporate bonds	1		−0.351[h] (−3.0)		−3.149[i] (−3.6)		7.26	.376	1.93	−.15

[a] Corrected for first-order autocorrelation. All variables are logarithmic except time. t tests appear in parentheses below the regression coefficients to which they refer. Some variables have been scaled for statistical convenience.

[b] Deviation of the ratio of money supply to GNP from its time trend.

[c] Percentage of variation explained by the independent variables only. Excludes that explained by the autoregressive scheme.

[d] Lagged one year. The quantity of stock is measured in terms of market value.

[e] Ratio of yield on corporate bonds to three-year average of dividend yield plus percentage capital gain on stock.

[f] Financial assets of pension funds plus mutual funds as a fraction of all financial assets lagged one year.

[g] Ratio of yield on U.S. government securities to three-year average of dividend yield plus percentage capital gain on stock.

[h] Ratio of the earnings yield on stock to the yield on corporate securities.

[i] Relative financial wealth of life insurance companies, state and local government securities, and pension funds.

Appendix Table 2-28

PORTFOLIO WEIGHT REGRESSIONS FOR COMMERCIAL BANKS,[a] 1950–1967

Proportion of portfolio invested in	Regression number	Elasticity with respect to		Time trend	Constant term	Adjusted R^2[b]	Durbin-Watson statistic	Adjustment for first-order autocorrelation
		Relative supply	Relative financial wealth of major holders					
U.S. government securities	1	1.275 (26.8)	-2.624^c (−4.3)		8.43	.987	1.45	.10
	2	1.001 (2.6)	-2.994^c (−3.6)	−0.014 (−0.7)	10.80	.987	1.69	.04
Mortgages	1	0.488 (4.9)	-1.311^d (−5.8)	0.017 (4.9)	3.14	.989	1.82	.26
Municipal securities	1			0.049 (8.8)	−0.69	.945	1.60	.59

[a] Corrected for first-order autocorrelation. All variables are logarithmic except time. *t* tests appear in parentheses below the regression coefficients to which they refer. Some variables have been scaled for statistical convenience.

[b] Percentage of variation explained by the independent variables only. Excludes that explained by the autoregressive scheme.

[c] Proportion of total financial wealth of commercial banks, households, and state and local government securities.

[d] Proportion of total financial wealth accounted for by savings and loan associations, life insurance companies, mutual savings banks, and commercial banks.

145

Appendix Table 2-24

PORTFOLIO WEIGHT REGRESSIONS FOR
MUTUAL SAVINGS BANKS,[a] 1950–1967

Proportion of portfolio invested in	Regression number	Elasticity with respect to					Time trend	Constant term	Adjusted R^{2}[b]	Durbin-Watson statistic	Adjustment for first-order autocorrelation
		Relative supply	Yield ratio	Relative financial wealth of major holders	Other variable						
Mortgages	1	0.951 (9.3)						−0.29	.976	1.69	.63
	2	0.743 (8.6)		−0.848[c] (−6.7)			0.011 (4.0)	2.79	.986	1.31	.49
U.S. government securities	1	2.035 (21.3)						−4.72	.981	1.65	.39
	2			−0.394[d] (−2.2)			−0.100 (−28.3)	2.62	.995	1.26	.68
	3		−0.610[e] (−4.2)				−0.099 (−76.6)	1.67	.998	1.31	.34
Corporate bonds	1	4.174 (8.6)			−2.300[f] (−11.3)			−1.47	.921	1.80	.26

[a] Corrected for first-order autocorrelation. All variables are logarithmic except time. *t* tests appear in parentheses below the regression coefficients to which they refer. Some variables have been scaled for statistical convenience.

[b] Percentage of variation explained by the independent variables only. Excludes that explained by the autoregressive scheme.

[c] Relative financial wealth of savings and loan associations, life insurance companies, commercial banks, and mutual savings banks.

[d] Relative financial wealth of commercial banks.

[e] Ratio of yield on corporate securities to that on government securities.

[f] Relative supply of mortgages.

Appendix Table 2-25

PORTFOLIO WEIGHT REGRESSIONS FOR STATE AND LOCAL GOVERNMENT SECURITIES,[a] 1950–1967

Proportion of portfolio invested in	Elasticity with respect to		Time trend	Constant term	Adjusted R^2[b]	Durbin-Watson statistic	Adjustment for first-order autocorrelation
	Relative supply	Other variable					
Corporate bonds	0.350 (1.4)		0.077 (5.8)	−0.62	.861	1.82	.87
U.S. government securities	0.886 (7.4)	−0.954[c] (−3.1)		1.46	.771	2.20	.69
Municipal securities	1.678 (4.5)		−0.006[d] (−13.9)	−1.31	.932	1.30	.60
Demand deposits		2.604[e] (8.4)	0.001[d] (2.3)	−6.51	.928	1.81	−.01
Time deposits	1.817[f] (3.5)		0.093 (10.9)	−5.73	.958	2.11	.23

[a] Corrected for first-order autocorrelation. All variables are logarithmic except time. t tests appear in parentheses below the regression coefficients to which they refer. Some variables have been scaled for statistical convenience.

[b] Percentage of variation explained by the independent variables only. Excludes that explained by the autoregressive scheme.

[c] Relative financial wealth of commercial banks.

[d] Second-degree time trend.

[e] Ratio of money supply to GNP.

[f] The volume of these deposits is assumed to be proportional to the volume of total bank deposits, which is largely determined by bank reserves and the required reserve ratios.

Appendix to Chapter Three

Aberdeen Fund	deVegh Mutual Fund
Affiliated Fund	Dividend Shares
American Business Shares	Dow Theory Investment Fund[a]
American Investors Fund	Dreyfus Fund
American Mutual Fund	Eaton and Howard Balanced Fund
Anchor Growth Stock Fund	Eaton and Howard Stock Fund
Anchor Income Fund	Energy Fund
Associated Fund Trust	Enterprise Fund
Axe-Houghton Fund A	Equity Fund
Axe-Houghton Fund B	Fidelity Capital Fund
Axe-Houghton Stock Fund	Fidelity Fund
Axe Science Corporation	Fidelity Trend Fund[a]
Blue Ridge Mutual Fund	Financial Industrial Fund
Boston Common Stock Fund	First Investors Fund
Boston Foundation Fund	Founders Mutual Fund
Boston Fund	Franklin Common Stock Series
Broad Street Investing Corporation	Franklin Utilities Series
Bullock Fund	Fundamental Investors
Canadian Fund	Fund of America[a]
Capital Shares[a]	Group Securities Aerospace-Science Fund
Century Shares Trust	Group Securities Common Stock Fund
Channing Balanced Fund	Group Securities Fully Administered Fund
Channing Common Stock Fund	Growth Industry Shares
Channing Growth Fund	Guardian Mutual Fund
Channing Income Fund	Hamilton Funds—Series H-DA
Channing Special Fund	Harbor Fund
Chase Fund of Boston	Imperial Capital Fund
Chemical Fund	Income Fund of Boston
Colonial Fund	Investment Company of America
Colonial Growth Shares	Investment Trust of Boston
Commerce Fund	Investors Mutual[a]
Commonwealth Capital Fund[a]	Investors Stock Fund[a]
Commonwealth Income Fund	Investors Variable Payment Fund[a]
Commonwealth Investment Company	Istel Fund
Commonwealth Stock Fund	Johnston Mutual Fund
Composite Fund	Keystone B-1 (investment bond)
Corporate Leaders Trust Fund Certificates, Series "B"	Keystone B-2 (medium growth bond)
	Keystone B-4 (discount bond)
Decatur Income Fund	Keystone K-1 (income fund)
Delaware Fund	Keystone K-2 (growth fund)

Appendix Table 3-1
MUTUAL FUNDS INDICATED IN ANALYSIS OF
INVESTMENT PERFORMANCE
(January, 1960–June, 1968)   *(Continued)*

Keystone S-1 (high grade)	Price, T. Rowe, Growth Stock Fund
Keystone S-2 (income)	Price, Rowe, New Horizons Fund[a]
Keystone S-3 (growth)	Provident Fund for Income[a]
Keystone S-4 (lower-priced)	Puritan Fund
Lexington Research Investing Corporation	Putnam, George, Fund of Boston
Life Insurance Investors	Putnam Growth Fund
Loomis-Sayles Mutual Fund	Putnam Income Fund
Massachusetts Fund	Putnam Investors Fund
Massachusetts Investors Growth Stock Fund	Scudder Stevens & Clark Balanced Fund
Massachusetts Investors Trust	Scudder Stevens & Clark Common Stock F
Moody's Capital Fund	Selected American Shares
Morton, B. C.,—Growth Series[a]	Shareholders' Trust of Boston
Morton, B. C., Fund—Insurance Series[a]	State Street Investment Corporation
Mutual Investing Foundation	Steadman Science and Growth Fund
National Investors Corporation	Stein Roe and Farnham Balanced Fund
Nation-Wide Securities Company	Stein Roe and Farnham Stock Fund
National Securities Dividend Series	Technology Fund
National Securities Income Series	United Accumulative Fund
National Securities Stock Series	United Income Fund
National Securities Growth Stocks Series	United Science Fund
New England Fund	United Funds Canada—International
Northeast Investors Trust[a]	Value Line Income Fund
One William Street Fund	Value Line Fund
Oppenheimer Fund	Value Line Special Situations Fund
Penn Square Mutual Fund	Washington Mutual Investors Fund
Philadelphia Fund	Wellington Fund
Pine Street Fund	Wellington Fund
Pioneer Fund	Windsor Fund
Polaris Fund	Wisconsin Fund

[a] Funds included only for period from April, 1964, through June, 1968.

Appendix Table 3-2
COMPARISON OF INVESTMENT PERFORMANCE
OF MUTUAL FUNDS AND RANDOM PORTFOLIOS
(January, 1960–June, 1968)

Risk class (beta coefficient)	Number in sample		Mean beta coefficient		Mean variance		Mean return			
	Mutual funds	Equally weighted random portfolios[a]	Mutual funds	Equally weighted random portfolios[a]	Mutual funds	Equally weighted random portfolios[a]	Mutual funds	Equally weighted random portfolios[a]	Proportionally weighted random portfolios, variant 1[b,d]	Proportionally weighted random portfolios, variant 2[c,d]
Low risk ($\beta = .5-.7$)	28	17	.614	.642	0.000877	0.000872	0.091	0.128	0.116	0.101
Medium risk ($\beta = .7-.9$)	53	59	.786	.800	0.001543	0.001293	0.106	0.131	0.097	0.084
High risk ($\beta = .9-1.1$)	22	60	.992	.992	0.002304	0.001948	0.135	0.137	0.103	0.092

[a] NYSE stocks only, assuming an equal investment as of beginning of period in each stock included. Number in sample and mean beta coefficients within each of the three risk classes are approximately the same for equally weighted and proportionally weighted random portfolios. Mean variance was not computed for proportionally weighted random portfolios.

[b] Variant 1: NYSE stocks only, assuming probability of investment in each stock proportional to amount outstanding as of beginning of period and equal amount invested in each stock included.

[c] Variant 2: NYSE stocks only, assuming equal probability of security inclusion, and amount invested in included stock proportional to amount outstanding as of beginning of period.

[d] Portfolios selected by either variant 1 or 2 would have the same expected return. The differences in the mean returns between these two variants suggest that there is a wide variability in the returns realized by particular random portfolios.

Appendix Table 3-3
COMPARISON OF INVESTMENT PERFORMANCE
OF MUTUAL FUNDS AND RANDOM PORTFOLIOS
(January, 1960–March, 1964)

Risk class (beta coefficient)	Number in sample		Mean beta coefficient		Mean variance		Mean return			
	Mutual funds	Equally weighted random portfolios	Mutual funds	Equally weighted random portfolios	Mutual funds	Equally weighted random portfolios	Mutual funds	Equally weighted random portfolios	Proportionally weighted random portfolios, variant 1	Proportionally weighted random portfolios, variant 2
Low risk ($\beta = .5-.7$)	31	22	.593	.637	0.000851	0.000950	0.085	0.100	0.105	0.129
Medium risk ($\beta = .7-.9$)	40	57	.801	.803	0.001428	0.001328	0.093	0.111	0.091	0.088
High risk ($\beta = .9-1.1$)	33	51	.998	.993	0.002334	0.002022	0.091	0.099	0.086	0.082

Appendix Table 3-4

COMPARISON OF INVESTMENT PERFORMANCE
OF MUTUAL FUNDS AND RANDOM PORTFOLIOS
(April, 1964-June, 1968)

Risk class (beta coefficient)	Number in sample		Mean beta coefficient		Mean variance		Mean return			
	Mutual funds	Equally weighted random portfolios	Mutual funds	Equally weighted random portfolios	Mutual funds	Equally weighted random portfolios	Mutual funds	Equally weighted random portfolios	Proportionally weighted random portfolios, variant 1	Proportionally weighted random portfolios, variant 2
Low risk ($\beta = .5-.7$)	45	27	.631	.619	0.001065	0.000790	0.096	0.153	0.126	0.128
Medium risk ($\beta = .7-.9$)	49	41	.784	.803	0.001469	0.001194	0.124	0.173	0.122	0.104
High risk ($\beta = .9-1.1$)	15	46	.958	.995	0.002501	0.001831	0.195	0.191	0.131	0.125

Appendix Table 3-5
CHARACTERISTICS OF INVESTMENT PERFORMANCE
OF MUTUAL FUNDS AND RANDOM PORTFOLIOS WITH
VARIANCE MEASURE OF RISK
(January, 1960–June, 1968)

Risk class (variance)	Number in sample		Mean variance		Mean beta coefficient		Mean return	
	Mutual funds	Equally weighted random portfolios[a]	Mutual funds	Equally weighted random portfolios[a]	Mutual funds	Equally weighted random portfolios[a]	Mutual funds	Equally weighted random portfolios[a]
Low risk ($\sigma^2 = 0.0009$–0.0015)	48	62	0.00120	0.00118	.731	.760	0.102	0.128
Medium risk ($\sigma^2 = 0.0015$–0.0022)	25	51	0.00182	0.00184	.883	.974	0.118	0.142
High risk ($\sigma^2 = 0.0022$–0.0036)	18	50	0.00280	0.00279	1.018	1.206	0.138	0.162

[a] NYSE stocks only, assuming an equal investment as of beginning of period in each stock included.

Appendix Table 3-6
CHARACTERISTICS OF INVESTMENT PERFORMANCE
OF MUTUAL FUNDS AND RANDOM PORTFOLIOS WITH
VARIANCE MEASURE OF RISK
(January, 1960–March, 1964)

Risk class (variance)	Number in sample		Mean variance		Mean beta coefficient		Mean return	
	Mutual funds	Equally weighted random portfolios	Mutual funds	Equally weighted random portfolios	Mutual funds	Equally weighted random portfolios	Mutual funds	Equally weighted random portfolios
Low risk ($\sigma^2 = 0.0009$–0.0015)	36	75	0.00122	0.00119	.736	.753	.091	.119
Medium risk ($\sigma^2 = 0.0015$–0.0022)	29	51	0.00178	0.00181	.885	.941	.083	.100
High risk ($\sigma^2 = 0.0022$–0.0036)	26	53	0.00274	0.00288	1.060	1.197	.100	.092

Appendix Table 3-7
CHARACTERISTICS OF INVESTMENT PERFORMANCE
OF MUTUAL FUNDS AND RANDOM PORTFOLIOS
WITH VARIANCE MEASURE OF RISK
(April, 1964–June, 1968)

Risk class (variance)	Number in sample		Mean variance		Mean beta coefficient		Mean return	
	Mutual funds	Equally weighted random portfolios	Mutual funds	Equally weighted random portfolios	Mutual funds	Equally weighted random portfolios	Mutual funds	Equally weighted random portfolios
Low risk ($\sigma^2 = 0.0009$–0.0015)	58	48	0.00116	0.00119	.724	.791	.122	.148
Medium risk ($\sigma^2 = 0.0015$–0.0022)	15	75	0.00182	0.00184	.866	1.003	.142	.191
High risk ($\sigma^2 = 0.0022$–0.0036)	20	44	0.00281	0.00271	.984	1.211	.166	.240

Appendix Table 3-8
COMPARISON OF INVESTMENT PERFORMANCE OF
MUTUAL FUNDS IN DIFFERENT ASSET SIZE GROUPS
(January, 1960–June, 1968)

Risk class (beta coefficient)	Number in sample				Mean return			
	$10 to 50[a]	$50 to 100	$100 to 500	$500 and over	$10 to 50[a]	$50 to 100	$100 to 500	$500 and over
Low risk ($\beta = .5-.7$)	8	5	14	1	0.088	0.093	0.092	0.105
Medium risk ($\beta = .7-.9$)	11	12	18	12	0.101	0.111	0.105	0.110
High risk ($\beta = .9-1.1$)	3	3	13	3	0.125	0.153	0.131	0.146

[a] Asset size in millions of dollars as of the end of 1967.

Appendix Table 3-9
COMPARISON OF INVESTMENT PERFORMANCE OF
MUTUAL FUNDS IN DIFFERENT ASSET SIZE GROUPS
(April, 1964–June, 1968)

Risk class (beta coefficient)	Number in sample				Mean return			
	$10 to 50[a]	$50 to 100	$100 to 500	$500 and over	$10 to 50[a]	$50 to 100	$100 to 500	$500 and over
Low risk ($\beta = .5-.7$)	13	8	19	5	0.097	0.088	0.101	0.092
Medium risk ($\beta = .7-.9$)	7	10	20	11	0.147	0.102	0.129	0.133
High risk ($\beta = .9-1.1$)	3	2	7	3	0.193	0.178	0.206	0.182

[a] Asset size in millions of dollars as of the end of 1967.

Appendix Table 3-10
COMPARISON OF INVESTMENT PERFORMANCE OF
MUTUAL FUNDS WITH DIFFERENT SALES CHARGES
(January, 1960–June, 1968)

Risk class (beta coefficient)	Number in sample			Mean return		
	Below 8.25%[a]	8.25 to 8.5%	Over 8.5%	Below 8.25%[a]	8.25 to 8.5%	Over 8.5%
Low risk $(\beta = .5–.7)$	9	15	3	0.090	0.091	0.099
Medium risk $(\beta = .7–.9)$	20	28	4	0.112	0.104	0.094
High risk $(\beta = .9–1.1)$	6	13	3	0.151	0.129	0.135

[a] Sales charges at end of 1967 as percent of sales price. No-load funds are included in the below-8.25% group.

Appendix Table 3-11
COMPARISON OF INVESTMENT PERFORMANCE OF
MUTUAL FUNDS WITH DIFFERENT SALES CHARGES
(April, 1964–June, 1968)

Risk class (beta coefficient)	Number in sample			Mean return		
	Below 8.25%[a]	8.25 to 8.5%	Over 8.5%	Below 8.25%[a]	8.25 to 8.5%	Over 8.5%
Low risk $(\beta = .5–.7)$	16	24	4	0.096	0.097	0.093
Medium risk $(\beta = .7–.9)$	16	26	6	0.142	0.125	0.073
High risk $(\beta = .9–1.1)$	4	8	2	0.188	0.179	0.206

[a] Sales charges at end of 1967 as percent of sales price. No-load funds are included in the below-8.25% group.

Appendix Table 3-12
COMPARISON OF INVESTMENT PERFORMANCE OF
MUTUAL FUNDS WITH DIFFERENT MANAGEMENT
EXPENSE RATIOS
(January, 1960–June, 1968)

Risk class (beta coefficient)	Number in sample			Mean return		
	Below 0.60%[a]	0.60 to 0.75%	Over 0.75%	Below 0.60%[a]	0.60 to 0.75%	Over 0.75%
Low risk ($\beta = .5-.7$)	7	9	7	0.093	0.085	0.093
Medium risk ($\beta = .7-.9$)	14	17	19	0.103	0.102	0.114
High risk ($\beta = .9-1.1$)	0	11	10	. . . . .	0.126	0.140

[a] Management expenses in 1960 as percent of average assets during year.

Appendix Table 3-13
COMPARISON OF INVESTMENT PERFORMANCE OF
MUTUAL FUNDS WITH DIFFERENT MANAGEMENT
EXPENSE RATIOS
(April, 1964–June, 1968)

Risk class (beta coefficient)	Number in sample			Mean return		
	Below 0.60%[a]	0.60 to 0.75%	Over 0.75%	Below 0.60%[a]	0.60 to 0.75%	Over 0.75%
Low risk ($\beta = .5-.7$)	22	18	4	0.089	0.103	0.108
Medium risk ($\beta = .7-.9$)	19	23	7	0.120	0.133	0.108
High risk ($\beta = .9-1.1$)	5	6	4	0.172	0.221	0.185

[a] Management expenses in 1967 as percent of average assets during year.

Appendix Table 3-14
COMPARISON OF INVESTMENT PERFORMANCE OF
MUTUAL FUNDS WITH DIFFERENT STOCK
PORTFOLIO TURNOVER RATIOS
(January, 1960–June, 1968)

Risk class (beta coefficient)	Number in sample			Mean return		
	Below 25%[a]	25 to 50%	Over 50%	Below 25%[a]	25 to 50%	Over 50%
Low risk ($\beta = .5-.7$)	10	11	6	0.087	0.094	0.094
Medium risk ($\beta = .7-.9$)	18	16	9	0.106	0.105	0.111
High risk ($\beta = .9-1.1$)	1	6	10	0.092	0.112	0.148

[a] These are averages of turnover ratios for the years 1966–1968, inclusive. The turnover ratio in each year is defined as the lesser of purchases or sales of portfolio stock divided by the average market value of stockholdings at the beginning and end of the year.

Appendix Table 3-15
COMPARISON OF INVESTMENT PERFORMANCE
OF MUTUAL FUNDS WITH DIFFERENT STOCK
PORTFOLIO TURNOVER RATIOS
(April, 1964–June, 1968)

Risk class (beta coefficient)	Number in sample			Mean return		
	Below 25%[a]	25 to 50%	Over 50%	Below 25%[a]	25 to 50%	Over 50%
Low risk ($\beta = .5-.7$)	16	15	5	0.093	0.099	0.096
Medium risk ($\beta = .7-.9$)	12	16	16	0.117	0.134	0.135
High risk ($\beta = .9-1.1$)	2	2	9	0.263	0.169	0.187

[a] These are averages of turnover ratios for the years 1966–1968, inclusive. The turnover ratio in each year is defined as the lesser of purchases or sales of portfolio stock divided by the average market value of stockholdings at the beginning and end of the year.

Appendix Table 3-16
COMPARISON OF INVESTMENT PERFORMANCE OF
MUTUAL FUNDS WITH DIFFERENT INVESTMENT
OBJECTIVES
(January, 1960–June, 1968)

Risk class (beta coefficient)	Number in sample					Mean return				
	Growth funds[a]	Growth-income funds	Income-growth funds	Income-growth-stability funds		Growth funds[a]	Growth-income funds	Income-growth funds	Income-growth-stability funds
Low risk ($\beta = .5-.7$)	3	5	4	16		0.069	0.101	0.097	0.091
Medium risk ($\beta = .7-.9$)	15	24	7	7		0.112	0.100	0.100	0.122
High risk ($\beta = .9-1.1$)	20	1	0	1		0.138	0.095	. . . . .	0.135

[a] Investment objectives for 1967 as classified by Arthur Wiesenberger Services.

Appendix Table 3-17
COMPARISON OF INVESTMENT PERFORMANCE
OF MUTUAL FUNDS WITH DIFFERENT
INVESTMENT OBJECTIVES
(April, 1964–June, 1968)

Risk class (beta coefficient)	Number in sample				Mean return			
	Growth funds[a]	Growth-income funds	Income-growth funds	Income-growth-stability funds	Growth funds[a]	Growth-income funds	Income-growth funds	Income-growth-stability funds
Low risk ($\beta = .5–.7$)	8	17	6	14	0.095	0.106	0.093	0.088
Medium risk ($\beta = .7–.9$)	20	14	6	9	0.122	0.110	0.123	0.152
High risk ($\beta = .9–1.1$)	13	0	0	2	0.195	......	......	0.193

[a] Investment objectives for 1967 as classified by Arthur Wiesenberger Services.

Appendix Table 3-18
QUARTERLY AND MONTHLY REGRESSIONS RELATING
NET PURCHASES OF ALL COMMON STOCKS BY
MUTUAL FUNDS TO MOVEMENT AND LEVEL OF
NYSE COMMON STOCK PRICES[a]

Quarterly: First Quarter, 1953–First Quarter, 1969

1) $\dfrac{M}{M_{-1}} = \underset{(64.48)}{1.019} + \underset{(0.55)}{0.006} \dfrac{(NP)}{A}$

$\bar{R}^2 = 0$
$DW = 1.95$
$\rho = 0.124$

2) $\dfrac{M}{M_{-1}} = \underset{(81.78)}{1.034} + \underset{(0.93)}{0.010} \dfrac{(NP)'}{A}$

$\bar{R}^2 = .002$
$DW = 1.95$
$\rho = 0.117$

3) $\dfrac{M}{M_{-1}} = \underset{(62.47)}{1.033} - \underset{(-0.47)}{0.005} \dfrac{(NP)_{-1}}{A_{-1}}$

$\bar{R}^2 = 0$
$DW = 1.96$
$\rho = 0.135$

4) $\dfrac{M}{M_{-1}} = \underset{(79.94)}{1.027} + \underset{(0.15)}{0.002} \dfrac{(NP)'_{-1}}{A_{-1}}$

$\bar{R}^2 = 0$
$DW = 1.95$
$\rho = 0.131$

5) $\dfrac{M}{M_{-1}} = \underset{(15.87)}{0.970} + \underset{(0.48)}{0.002} \dfrac{P'}{A} + \underset{(0.89)}{0.014} \dfrac{S}{A}$

$\bar{R}^2 = 0$
$DW = 1.95$
$\rho = 0.116$

6) $\dfrac{M}{M_{-1}} = \underset{(16.95)}{1.074} - \underset{(-0.85)}{0.003} \dfrac{P'_{-1}}{A_{-1}} - \underset{(-0.63)}{0.010} \dfrac{S_{-1}}{A_{-1}}$

$\bar{R}^2 = 0$
$DW = 1.96$
$\rho = 0.154$

7) $\dfrac{M}{M_{-1}} = \underset{(44.10)}{1.031} + \underset{(0.64)}{0.007} \dfrac{(NP)}{A} - \underset{(-0.45)}{0.005} \dfrac{(NP)_{-1}}{A_{-1}} - \underset{(-0.51)}{0.006} \dfrac{(NP)_{-2}}{A_{-2}}$

$\bar{R}^2 = 0$
$DW = 1.96$
$\rho = 0.123$

8) $\dfrac{M}{M_{-1}} = \underset{(53.23)}{1.038} + \underset{(0.95)}{0.011} \dfrac{(NP)'}{A} + \underset{(0.31)}{0.004} \dfrac{(NP)'_{-1}}{A_{-1}} + \underset{(0.05)}{0.001} \dfrac{(NP)'_{-2}}{A_{-2}}$

$\bar{R}^2 = 0$
$DW = 1.95$
$\rho = 0.115$

9) $\dfrac{NP}{A} = \underset{(-1.64)}{-5.016} + \underset{(0.65)}{1.06} \dfrac{M}{M_{-1}} + \underset{(1.49)}{2.41} \dfrac{M_{-1}}{M_{-2}} + \underset{(1.65)}{2.66} \dfrac{M_{-2}}{M_{-3}}$

$\bar{R}^2 = .020$
$DW = 2.07$
$\rho = 0.211$

10) $\dfrac{NP}{A} = \underset{(4.63)}{2.190} + \underset{(0.40)}{0.010} M - \underset{(-1.02)}{0.026} M_{-1} + \underset{(0.30)}{0.043} \dfrac{(NP)_{-2}}{A_{-2}}$

$\bar{R}^2 = .140$
$DW = 1.98$
$\rho = 0.012$

11) $\dfrac{(NP)'}{A} = \underset{(-1.85)}{-4.459} + \underset{(0.98)}{1.485} \dfrac{M}{M_{-1}} + \underset{(0.68)}{1.036} \dfrac{M_{-1}}{M_{-2}} + \underset{(0.70)}{1.043} \dfrac{M_{-2}}{M_{-3}}$

$\bar{R}^2 = 0$
$DW = 1.94$
$\rho = -0.031$

Appendix Table 3-18
QUARTERLY AND MONTHLY REGRESSIONS RELATING
NET PURCHASES OF ALL COMMON STOCKS BY
MUTUAL FUNDS TO MOVEMENT AND LEVEL OF
NYSE COMMON STOCK PRICES[a] *(Continued)*

Quarterly: First Quarter, 1953–First Quarter, 1969 *(Continued)*

12) $\dfrac{(NP)'}{A} = -1.095 + 0.051\,M - 0.048\,M_{-1} - 0.056\,\dfrac{(NP)'_{-2}}{A_{-2}}$
   $\quad\quad\quad (-3.65)\quad (2.17)\quad\quad (-2.05)\quad\quad (-0.42)$

$\bar{R}^2 = .016$
$DW = 1.95$
$\rho = -0.118$

13) $M = 13.160 + 1.109\,\dfrac{(NP)'}{A} + 1.385\,\dfrac{(NP)'_{-1}}{A_{-1}} + 0.865\,M_{-2}$
   $\quad\quad\;\; (3.10)\quad\; (1.35)\quad\quad\quad (1.61)\quad\quad\quad (14.35)$

$\bar{R}^2 = .924$
$DW = 1.63$
$\rho = 0.532$

14) $\dfrac{M}{\overline{M}} = 0.943 + 0.005\,\dfrac{NP}{A}$
   $\quad\;\; (36.99)\quad (0.51)$

$\bar{R}^2 = 0$
$DW = 1.58$
$\rho = 0.648$

15) $\dfrac{M}{\overline{M}} = 0.948 - 0.002\,\dfrac{(NP)'}{A}$
   $\quad\;\; (39.58)\;\; (-0.22)$

$\bar{R}^2 = 0$
$DW = 1.53$
$\rho = 0.649$

Monthly: June, 1966–June, 1969

16) $\dfrac{M}{M_{-1}} = 1.006 + 0.006\,\dfrac{(NP)}{A}$
   $\quad\quad\;\; (160.20)\;\; (0.49)$

$\bar{R}^2 = 0$
$DW = 2.02$
$\rho = -0.130$

17) $\dfrac{M}{M_{-1}} = 1.007 - 0.004\,\dfrac{(NP)'}{A}$
   $\quad\quad\;\; (161.88)\;\; (-0.35)$

$\bar{R}^2 = 0$
$DW = 2.01$
$\rho = -0.040$

18) $\dfrac{M}{M_{-1}} = 1.008 - 0.002\,\dfrac{(NP)_{-1}}{A_{-1}}$
   $\quad\quad\;\; (156.81)\;\; (-0.19)$

$\bar{R}^2 = 0$
$DW = 2.02$
$\rho = -0.083$

19) $\dfrac{M}{M_{-1}} = 1.007 - 0.001\,\dfrac{(NP)'_{-1}}{A_{-1}}$
   $\quad\quad\;\; (163.80)\;\; (-0.06)$

$\bar{R}^2 = 0$
$DW = 2.02$
$\rho = -0.081$

20) $\dfrac{M}{M_{-1}} = 0.976 - 0.002\,\dfrac{P'}{A} + 0.034\,\dfrac{S}{A}$
   $\quad\quad\;\; (23.91)\;\; (-0.23)\quad\quad (1.07)$

$\bar{R}^2 = 0$
$DW = 1.97$
$\rho = 0.015$

21) $\dfrac{M}{M_{-1}} = 1.076 - 0.018\,\dfrac{P'_{-1}}{A_{-1}} - 0.019\,\dfrac{S_{-1}}{A_{-1}}$
   $\quad\quad\;\; (29.26)\;\; (-1.95)\quad\quad (-0.62)$

$\bar{R}^2 = .087$
$DW = 2.11$
$\rho = -0.038$

Appendix Table 3-18

QUARTERLY AND MONTHLY REGRESSIONS RELATING
NET PURCHASES OF ALL COMMON STOCKS BY
MUTUAL FUNDS TO MOVEMENT AND LEVEL OF
NYSE COMMON STOCK PRICES[a] *(Continued)*

Monthly: June, 1966–June, 1969 *(Continued)*

22) $\dfrac{M}{M_{-1}} = 1.009 + 0.006 \dfrac{NP}{A} - 0.001 \dfrac{(NP)_{-1}}{A_{-1}} - 0.012 \dfrac{(NP)_{-2}}{A_{-2}}$
   (142.64) (0.48)   (−0.04)   (−0.90)

$\bar{R}^2 = 0$
$DW = 2.02$
$\rho = -0.110$

23) $\dfrac{M}{M_{-1}} = 1.005 - 0.006 \dfrac{(NP)'}{A} + 0.004 \dfrac{(NP)'_{-1}}{A_{-1}} - 0.008 \dfrac{(NP)'_{-2}}{A_{-2}}$
   (137.44) (−0.52)   (0.32)   (−0.72)

$\bar{R}^2 = 0$
$DW = 1.99$
$\rho = 0.005$

24) $\dfrac{NP}{A} = -14.710 + 1.572 \dfrac{M}{M_{-1}} + 9.314 \dfrac{M_{-1}}{M_{-2}} + 3.997 \dfrac{M_{-2}}{M_{-3}}$
   (−4.18)   (0.86)   (5.35)   (2.28)

$\bar{R}^2 = .473$
$DW = 1.84$
$\rho = 0.035$

25) $\dfrac{NP}{A} = -1.326 - 0.024\,M + 0.041\,M_{-1} - 0.012 \dfrac{(NP)_{-2}}{A_{-2}}$
   (−0.75) (−0.90)   (1.70)   (−0.07)

$\bar{R}^2 = 0$
$DW = 1.90$
$\rho = 0.440$

26) $\dfrac{(NP)'}{A} = -16.479 + 0.104 \dfrac{M}{M_{-1}} + 10.944 \dfrac{M_{-1}}{M_{-2}} + 5.120 \dfrac{M_{-2}}{M_{-3}}$
   (−3.86)   (0.05)   (5.40)   (2.54)

$\bar{R}^2 = .504$
$DW = 1.89$
$\rho = 0.134$

27) $\dfrac{(NP)'}{A} = -2.398 - 0.050\,M + 0.074\,M_{-1} - 0.059 \dfrac{(NP)'_{-2}}{A_{-2}}$
   (−0.97) (−1.70)   (2.77)   (−0.34)

$\bar{R}^2 = 0$
$DW = 1.92$
$\rho = 0.559$

28) $M = 132.919 - 0.553 \dfrac{(NP)'}{A} + 1.300 \dfrac{(NP)'_{-1}}{A_{-1}} - 0.326\,M_{-2}$
   (6.38) (−0.62)   (1.29)   (−1.61)

$\bar{R}^2 = 0$
$DW = 2.01$
$\rho = 0.911$

---

[a] M/M_{-1} represents the ratio (in percent) of the end of period value to the beginning of period value of the Standard and Poor's Composite Price Index for NYSE stocks; *(NP)*, net purchases of portfolio stock in billions of dollars; $(NP)'$, net purchases of portfolio stock less net sales of fund shares; A, the total fund assets at the beginning of the period in billions of dollars; P, gross purchases, and S, gross sales, of portfolio stock; P', gross purchases of portfolio stock less net sales of fund shares; the ratios of NP and related variables to A are expressed in percent; the subscripts −1, −2, and −3 represent one, two and three periods earlier; $\bar{R}^2$ is the coefficient of determination adjusted for degrees of freedom, ρ is the first-order autoregressive coefficient, and DW is the Durbin-Watson statistic. $\bar{M}$ is the mean value of the Standard and Poor's index for the following year. All variables in the relationships presented in the table have been adjusted for first-order serial correlation. They have also been estimated without adjustment for serial correlation. The $\bar{R}^2$ presented is the ratio of the explained variance of the dependent variable, after the coefficients of the regression have been adjusted for serial correlation, to the total variance of the dependent variable.

Appendix Table 3-19
INVESTMENT PERFORMANCE OF MUTUAL FUNDS
(July, 1968–September, 1969)

Risk class (beta coefficient)	Number in sample	Mean beta coefficient	Mean return
Low risk ($\beta = .5-.7$)	28	.614	-0.016
Medium risk ($\beta = .7-.9$)	53	.786	-0.028
High risk ($\beta = .9-1.1$)	22	.992	-0.077

Appendix Table 3-20
COMPARISON OF INVESTMENT PERFORMANCE OF
MUTUAL FUNDS WITH DIFFERENT MANAGEMENT
EXPENSE RATIOS
(July, 1968–September, 1969)

Risk class (beta coefficient)	Number in sample			Mean return		
	Below 0.60%[a]	0.60 to 0.75%	Over 0.75%	Below 0.60%[a]	0.60 to 0.75%	Over 0.75%
Low risk ($\beta = .5-.7$)	13	12	3	-0.014	0.000	-0.084
Medium risk ($\beta = .7-.9$)	32	19	2	-0.018	-0.042	-0.063
High risk $\beta = .9-1.1$)	8	9	5	-0.073	-0.069	-0.097

[a] Management expenses in 1968 as percent of average assets during year.

Appendix to Chapter Four

Appendix Table 4-1

ANNUAL REGRESSIONS RELATING NET PURCHASES
OF INDIVIDUAL NYSE STOCKS BY MUTUAL FUNDS
TO SUBSEQUENT RELATIVE STOCK EARNINGS [a]

(Selected Years, 1954–1967)

	Year of stock purchase	Year of subsequent earnings [b]	Regression
1)	1954	1965	$\frac{NP}{H} = -0.0000 - 0.0002 \left(\frac{E_{11}}{P_0}\right)' + 0.0001 \overline{\left(\frac{D}{E}\right)} + 0.0007\beta$ $\quad$ (-0.04) $\quad$ (-1.14) $\quad$ (0.09) $\quad$ (1.82) $\quad$ $\overline{R}^2 = .002$
2)	1954	1962	$\frac{NP}{H} = -0.0001 - 0.0001 \left(\frac{E_8}{P_0}\right)' + 0.0003 \overline{\left(\frac{D}{E}\right)} + 0.0006\beta$ $\quad$ (-0.11) $\quad$ (-0.71) $\quad$ (0.34) $\quad$ (1.59) $\quad$ $\overline{R}^2 = 0$
3)	1954	1959	$\frac{NP}{H} = -0.0002 + 0.0000 \left(\frac{E_5}{P_0}\right)' + 0.0003 \overline{\left(\frac{D}{E}\right)} + 0.0005\beta$ $\quad$ (-0.28) $\quad$ (0.09) $\quad$ (0.40) $\quad$ (1.49) $\quad$ $\overline{R}^2 = 0$
4)	1954	1957	$\frac{NP}{H} = -0.0004 + 0.0004 \left(\frac{E_3}{P_0}\right)' + 0.0002 \overline{\left(\frac{D}{E}\right)} + 0.0004\beta$ $\quad$ (-0.56) $\quad$ (1.56) $\quad$ (0.25) $\quad$ (1.19) $\quad$ $\overline{R}^2 = .003$
5)	1954	1955	$\frac{NP}{H} = -0.0002 + 0.0004 \left(\frac{E_1}{P_0}\right)' + 0.0001 \overline{\left(\frac{D}{E}\right)} + 0.0002\beta$ $\quad$ (-0.48) $\quad$ (1.48) $\quad$ (0.46) $\quad$ (0.65) $\quad$ $\overline{R}^2 = .003$
6)	1954	1954	$\frac{NP}{H} = -0.0003 + 0.0004 \left(\frac{E_0}{P_0}\right)' + 0.0000 \overline{\left(\frac{D}{E}\right)} + 0.0004\beta$ $\quad$ (-0.56) $\quad$ (1.24) $\quad$ (0.06) $\quad$ (1.25) $\quad$ $\overline{R}^2 = .002$

7)   1954   1965

$$\frac{NP}{H} = \begin{array}{llll} 0.0000 & - 0.0001 \left(\dfrac{E_{11}}{P_0}\right)' & - 0.0004 \overline{\left(\dfrac{D}{E}\right)} & + 0.0016\beta \\ (0.01) & (-0.62) & (-0.46) & (2.89) \end{array}$$
$$-0.2645\sigma^2 + 0.0088\,(IQ) + 0.0032\,(SK)$$
$$(-1.81) \qquad\quad (0.37) \qquad\quad (0.95)$$

$\overline{R}^2 = .009$

8)   1957   1965

$$\frac{NP}{H} = \begin{array}{llll} -0.0000 & - 0.0004 \left(\dfrac{E_8}{P_0}\right)' & + 0.0003 \overline{\left(\dfrac{D}{E}\right)} & + 0.0007\beta \\ (-0.00) & (-0.82) & (0.39) & (0.70) \end{array}$$

$\overline{R}^2 = 0$

9)   1957   1962

$$\frac{NP}{H} = \begin{array}{llll} -0.0002 & - 0.0001 \left(\dfrac{E_5}{P_0}\right)' & + 0.0003 \overline{\left(\dfrac{D}{E}\right)} & + 0.0006\beta \\ (-0.13) & (-0.35) & (0.40) & (0.67) \end{array}$$

$\overline{R}^2 = 0$

10)   1957   1960

$$\frac{NP}{H} = \begin{array}{llll} -0.0001 & - 0.0002 \left(\dfrac{E_3}{P_0}\right)' & + 0.0003 \overline{\left(\dfrac{D}{E}\right)} & + 0.0006\beta \\ (-0.06) & (-0.43) & (0.41) & (0.60) \end{array}$$

$\overline{R}^2 = 0$

11)   1957   1958

$$\frac{NP}{H} = \begin{array}{llll} 0.0002 & - 0.0004 \left(\dfrac{E_1}{P_0}\right)' & + 0.0003 \overline{\left(\dfrac{D}{E}\right)} & + 0.0005\beta \\ (0.17) & (-0.80) & (0.39) & (0.55) \end{array}$$

$\overline{R}^2 = 0$

12)   1957   1957

$$\frac{NP}{H} = \begin{array}{llll} 0.0005 & - 0.0007 \left(\dfrac{E_0}{P_0}\right)' & + 0.0004 \overline{\left(\dfrac{D}{E}\right)} & + 0.0005\beta \\ (0.38) & (-1.00) & (0.46) & (0.51) \end{array}$$

$\overline{R}^2 = 0$

13)   1957   1965

$$\frac{NP}{H} = \begin{array}{llll} 0.0005 & - 0.0004 \left(\dfrac{E_8}{P_0}\right)' & + 0.0003 \overline{\left(\dfrac{D}{E}\right)} & + 0.0012\beta \\ (0.27) & (-0.86) & (0.33) & (0.89) \end{array}$$
$$-0.0020\sigma^2 - 0.0235\,(IQ) + 0.0011\,(SK)$$
$$(-0.01) \qquad\quad (-0.43) \qquad\quad (0.13)$$

$\overline{R}^2 = 0$

14)   1958   1966

$$\frac{NP}{H} = \begin{array}{llll} 0.0007 & - 0.0001 \left(\dfrac{E_8}{P_0}\right)' & + 0.0001 \overline{\left(\dfrac{D}{E}\right)} & - 0.0002\beta \\ (2.41) & (-0.72) & (0.32) & (-0.85) \end{array}$$

$\overline{R}^2 = 0$

15)   1958   1963

$$\frac{NP}{H} = \begin{array}{llll} 0.0007 & - 0.0001 \left(\dfrac{E_5}{P_0}\right)' & + 0.0000 \overline{\left(\dfrac{D}{E}\right)} & - 0.0002\beta \\ (2.28) & (-0.38) & (0.26) & (-0.94) \end{array}$$

$\overline{R}^2 = 0$

Appendix Table 4-1

ANNUAL REGRESSIONS RELATING NET PURCHASES
OF INDIVIDUAL NYSE STOCKS BY MUTUAL FUNDS
TO SUBSEQUENT RELATIVE STOCK EARNINGS [a]
(Selected Years, 1954–1967) *(Continued)*

	Year of stock purchase	Year of subsequent earnings [b]	Regression
16)	1958	1961	$\dfrac{NP}{H} = 0.0008 - 0.0001 \left(\dfrac{E_3}{P_0}\right)' + 0.0000 \left(\overline{\dfrac{D}{E}}\right) - 0.0002\beta$ $\quad\ \ (2.43)\quad (-0.83)\qquad\quad (0.23)\qquad\quad (-0.93)$ $\qquad \overline{R}^2 = 0$
17)	1958	1959	$\dfrac{NP}{H} = 0.0007 - 0.0001 \left(\dfrac{E_1}{P_0}\right)' + 0.0001 \left(\overline{\dfrac{D}{E}}\right) - 0.0002\beta$ $\quad\ \ (2.50)\quad (-0.80)\qquad\quad (0.31)\qquad\quad (-0.93)$ $\qquad \overline{R}^2 = 0$
18)	1958	1958	$\dfrac{NP}{H} = 0.0007 - 0.0000 \left(\dfrac{E_0}{P_0}\right)' + 0.0000 \left(\overline{\dfrac{D}{E}}\right) - 0.0003\beta$ $\quad\ \ (2.33)\quad (-0.32)\qquad\quad (0.22)\qquad\quad (-1.14)$ $\qquad \overline{R}^2 = 0$
19)	1958	1966	$\dfrac{NP}{H} = 0.0007 - 0.0001 \left(\dfrac{E_8}{P_0}\right)' + 0.0000 \left(\overline{\dfrac{D}{E}}\right) + 0.0004\beta$ $\quad\ \ (1.49)\quad (-0.86)\qquad\quad (0.19)\qquad\quad (1.02)$ $\qquad\quad - 0.0999\sigma^2 - 0.0043\,(IQ) + 0.0034\,(SK)$ $\qquad\qquad (-1.27)\qquad\ (-0.31)\qquad\quad (1.61)$ $\qquad \overline{R}^2 = .004$
20)	1959	1967	$\dfrac{NP}{H} = 0.0004 - 0.0002 \left(\dfrac{E_8}{P_0}\right)' + 0.0002 \left(\overline{\dfrac{D}{E}}\right) - 0.0000\beta$ $\quad\ \ (1.42)\quad (-1.62)\qquad\quad (1.62)\qquad\quad (-0.20)$ $\qquad \overline{R}^2 = .003$
21)	1959	1964	$\dfrac{NP}{H} = 0.0003 - 0.0001 \left(\dfrac{E_5}{P_0}\right)' + 0.0002 \left(\overline{\dfrac{D}{E}}\right) - 0.0000\beta$ $\quad\ \ (1.13)\quad (-0.86)\qquad\quad (1.74)\qquad\quad (-0.06)$ $\qquad \overline{R}^2 = .001$
22)	1959	1962	$\dfrac{NP}{H} = 0.0002 - 0.0000 \left(\dfrac{E_3}{P_0}\right)' + 0.0002 \left(\overline{\dfrac{D}{E}}\right) - 0.0000\beta$ $\quad\ \ (0.85)\quad (-0.18)\qquad\quad (1.74)\qquad\quad (-0.12)$ $\qquad \overline{R}^2 = 0$
23)	1959	1960	$\dfrac{NP}{H} = 0.0002 + 0.0000 \left(\dfrac{E_1}{P_0}\right)' + 0.0002 \left(\overline{\dfrac{D}{E}}\right) - 0.0000\beta$ $\quad\ \ (0.80)\quad (0.20)\qquad\quad (1.75)\qquad\quad (-0.16)$ $\qquad \overline{R}^2 = 0$

24) 1959 | 1959

$$\frac{NP}{H} = 0.0003 - 0.0001 \left(\frac{E_0}{P_0}\right)' + 0.0002 \overline{\left(\frac{D}{E}\right)} - 0.0000\beta$$
$$(1.20) \quad (-0.78) \qquad (1.77) \qquad (-0.24)$$

$\overline{R}^2 = .001$

25) 1959 | 1959

$$\frac{NP}{H} = 0.0014 - 0.0002 \left(\frac{E_8}{P_0}\right)' + 0.0002 \overline{\left(\frac{D}{E}\right)} + 0.0002\beta$$
$$(3.51) \quad (-1.75) \qquad (1.72) \qquad (0.53)$$
$$+ 0.0913\sigma^2 - 0.0296 (IQ) - 0.0083 (SK)$$
$$(1.43) \qquad (-2.48) \qquad (-4.16)$$

$\overline{R}^2 = .032$

26) 1964 | 1967

$$\frac{NP}{H} = 0.0003 - 0.0001 \left(\frac{E_3}{P_0}\right)' + 0.0001 \overline{\left(\frac{D}{E}\right)} - 0.0001\beta$$
$$(0.87) \quad (-0.90) \qquad (0.42) \qquad (-0.44)$$

$\overline{R}^2 = 0$

27) 1964 | 1965

$$\frac{NP}{H} = 0.0003 - 0.0003 \left(\frac{E_1}{P_0}\right)' + 0.0001 \overline{\left(\frac{D}{E}\right)} + 0.0000\beta$$
$$(1.13) \quad (-2.30) \qquad (0.48) \qquad (0.22)$$

$\overline{R}^2 = .002$

28) 1964 | 1964

$$\frac{NP}{H} = 0.0005 - 0.0005 \left(\frac{E_0}{P_0}\right)' + 0.0001 \overline{\left(\frac{D}{E}\right)} + 0.0000\beta$$
$$(1.89) \quad (-3.34) \qquad (0.53) \qquad (0.11)$$

$\overline{R}^2 = .007$

29) 1964 | 1967

$$\frac{NP}{H} = 0.0003 - 0.0001 \left(\frac{E_3}{P_0}\right)' + 0.0005 \overline{\left(\frac{D}{E}\right)} - 0.0007\beta$$
$$(0.84) \quad (-0.54) \qquad (1.52) \qquad (-2.09)$$
$$+ 0.0930\sigma^2 - 0.0033 (IQ) - 0.0026 (SK)$$
$$(3.63) \qquad (-0.40) \qquad (-2.76)$$

$\overline{R}^2 = .014$

30) 1965 | 1966

$$\frac{NP}{H} = 0.0000 + 0.0000 \left(\frac{E_1}{P_0}\right)' - 0.0003 \overline{\left(\frac{D}{E}\right)} + 0.0002\beta$$
$$(0.18) \quad (0.07) \qquad (-1.16) \qquad (1.26)$$

$\overline{R}^2 = .001$

31) 1965 | 1965

$$\frac{NP}{H} = -0.0001 + 0.0002 \left(\frac{E_0}{P_0}\right)' - 0.0002 \overline{\left(\frac{D}{E}\right)} + 0.0002\beta$$
$$(-0.30) \quad (1.28) \qquad (-1.13) \qquad (1.08)$$

$\overline{R}^2 = .002$

32) 1965 | 1966

$$\frac{NP}{H} = -0.0005 - 0.0000 \left(\frac{E_1}{P_0}\right)' - 0.0002 \overline{\left(\frac{D}{E}\right)} + 0.0002\beta$$
$$(-1.64) \quad (-0.25) \qquad (-0.99) \qquad (0.75)$$
$$- 0.0682\sigma^2 + 0.0200 (IQ) + 0.0009 (SK)$$
$$(-2.49) \qquad (2.92) \qquad (1.16)$$

$\overline{R}^2 = .007$

Appendix Table 4-1
ANNUAL REGRESSIONS RELATING NET PURCHASES
OF INDIVIDUAL NYSE STOCKS BY MUTUAL FUNDS
TO SUBSEQUENT RELATIVE STOCK EARNINGS [a]
(Selected Years, 1954–1967)   *(Continued)*

	Year of stock purchase	Year of subsequent earnings [b]	Regression
33)	1966	1967	$\frac{NP}{H} = -0.0054 + 0.0019 \left(\frac{E_1}{P_0}\right)' + 0.0005 \overline{\left(\frac{D}{E}\right)} + 0.0012\beta$ $\quad\ (-6.40)\quad (4.88)\qquad\quad (0.61)\qquad\quad (2.18)$ $\overline{R}^2 = .026$
34)	1966	1966	$\frac{NP}{H} = -0.0050 + 0.0021 \left(\frac{E_0}{P_0}\right)' + 0.0004 \overline{\left(\frac{D}{E}\right)} + 0.0009\beta$ $\quad\ (-7.60)\quad (5.55)\qquad\quad (0.74)\qquad\quad (1.90)$ $\overline{R}^2 = .026$
35)	1966	1967	$\frac{NP}{H} = -0.0054 + 0.0019 \left(\frac{E_1}{P_0}\right)' + 0.0006 \overline{\left(\frac{D}{E}\right)} + 0.0005\beta$ $\quad\ (-5.55)\quad (5.02)\qquad\quad (0.78)\qquad\quad (0.61)$ $\quad + 0.0917\sigma^2 - 0.0011\,(IQ) - 0.0003\,(SK)$ $\quad\ (1.43)\qquad\quad (-0.05)\qquad\quad (-0.12)$ $\overline{R}^2 = .026$
36)	1967	1967	$\frac{NP}{H} = 0.0003 - 0.0000 \left(\frac{E_0}{P_0}\right)' - 0.0003 \overline{\left(\frac{D}{E}\right)} + 0.0003\beta$ $\quad\ (1.11)\quad (-0.14)\qquad\quad (-1.29)\qquad\quad (1.55)$ $\overline{R}^2 = .002$
37)	1967	1967	$\frac{NP}{H} = 0.0003 + 0.0000 \left(\frac{E_0}{P_0}\right)' - 0.0001 \overline{\left(\frac{D}{E}\right)} - 0.0009\beta$ $\quad\ (0.87)\quad (0.26)\qquad\quad (-0.59)\qquad\quad (-2.88)$ $\quad + 0.1030\sigma^2 + 0.0070\,(IQ) + 0.0004\,(SK)$ $\quad\ (3.37)\qquad\quad (0.90)\qquad\quad (0.42)$ $\overline{R}^2 = .023$

[a] The variables in the equations are defined in the text except for σ^2, which is the variance, (IQ) which is one-half the interquartile range, and (SK) a measure of skewness. The prime on the E_n/P_0 ratios indicates deflation by the corresponding market ratio.

[b] Terminal year of earnings covered by regression.

Appendix Table 4-2
POOLED QUARTERLY REGRESSIONS RELATING PRICE
BEHAVIOR OF INDIVIDUAL NYSE STOCKS TO MUTUAL
FUND NET PURCHASES
(1958–1959, 1964–1965, and 1966–1967[a])

1958–1959

1) $$\frac{R}{M} = \underset{(9.78)}{0.7145} + \underset{(3.42)}{0.1172} \left(\frac{NP}{H}\right) - \underset{(-1.56)}{0.0189} \left(\frac{NP}{H}\right)_{-1} + \underset{(0.37)}{0.0046} \left(\frac{NP}{H}\right)_{-2} + \underset{(2.42)}{0.0618} \beta$$

$$+ \underset{(3.06)}{0.2280} \left(\frac{R}{M}\right)_{-3} \qquad \qquad \bar{R}^2 = .09$$

1964–1965

2) $$\frac{R}{M} = \underset{(6.48)}{0.8616} + \underset{(1.14)}{0.0492} \left(\frac{NP}{H}\right) - \underset{(-0.83)}{0.0202} \left(\frac{NP}{H}\right)_{-1} + \underset{(0.08)}{0.0010} \left(\frac{NP}{H}\right)_{-2} - \underset{(-0.55)}{0.0223} \beta$$

$$+ \underset{(1.30)}{0.1678} \left(\frac{R}{M}\right)_{-3} \qquad \qquad \bar{R}^2 = 0$$

1966–1967

3) $$\frac{R}{M} = \underset{(16.97)}{0.8659} + \underset{(2.75)}{0.0151} \left(\frac{NP}{H}\right) + \underset{(2.76)}{0.0137} \left(\frac{NP}{H}\right)_{-1} + \underset{(0.71)}{0.0037} \left(\frac{NP}{H}\right)_{-2} + \underset{(3.01)}{0.0661} \beta$$

$$+ \underset{(0.99)}{0.0460} \left(\frac{R}{M}\right)_{-3} \qquad \qquad \bar{R}^2 = .06$$

---

[a] R_i is the ratio of the price of the ith issue at the end of a quarter plus dividends during the quarter to its price at the beginning of the quarter; M is the corresponding value of Fisher combination link relatives covering all NYSE stock; and NP_i represents the net purchases, and H_i the end-of-period dollar holdings, of the stock in the quarter by all funds covered. The subscripts −1, −2, and −3 refer to the preceding three quarters respectively. $\bar{R}^2$ is the coefficient of determination adjusted for degrees of freedom, and the numbers in parentheses under the regression coefficients represent t values. To avoid undue complexity, the i subscripts are deleted in the table.

Appendix Table 4-3

QUARTERLY REGRESSIONS RELATING PRICE BEHAVIOR
OF INDIVIDUAL STOCKS TO MANAGEMENT INVESTMENT
COMPANY PURCHASES AND SALES

(Fourth Quarter, 1967–First Quarter, 1968^{a})

Part A: All Stocks Combined

1) $\left(\dfrac{R}{M}\right)_4 = 1.004 + 3.077 \left(\dfrac{P}{O}\right)_4 - 1.631 \left(\dfrac{S}{O}\right)_4$ 　　　　$\bar{R}^2 = .090$
　　　　　(130.53)　(9.54)　　　　　(−4.16)

2) $\left(\dfrac{R}{M}\right)_4 = 1.019 + 3.458 \left(\dfrac{P}{O}\right)_4 - 1.300 \left(\dfrac{S}{O}\right)_4 - 0.316 \left(\dfrac{H}{O}\right)_4$ 　$\bar{R}^2 = .098$
　　　　　(112.32)　(10.03)　　　　　(−3.21)　　　　　(−3.04)

3) $\left(\dfrac{R}{M}\right)_1 = 0.992 + 1.432 \left(\dfrac{P}{O}\right)_1 - 2.252 \left(\dfrac{S}{O}\right)_1$ 　　　　$\bar{R}^2 = .083$
　　　　　(154.55)　(5.74)　　　　　(−8.48)

4) $\left(\dfrac{R}{M}\right)_1 = 0.997 + 1.544 \left(\dfrac{P}{O}\right)_1 - 2.201 \left(\dfrac{S}{O}\right)_1 - 0.089 \left(\dfrac{H}{O}\right)_1$ 　$\bar{R}^2 = .083$
　　　　　(129.75)　(5.65)　　　　　(−8.15)　　　　　(−1.06)

5) $\left(\dfrac{R}{M}\right)_1 = 0.998 - 0.591 \left(\dfrac{P}{O}\right)_4 - 0.615 \left(\dfrac{S}{O}\right)_4 + 1.338 \left(\dfrac{P}{O}\right)_1 - 2.583 \left(\dfrac{S}{O}\right)_1$ 　$\bar{R}^2 = .151$
　　　　　(146.65)(−1.97)　　　(−1.76)　　　　　(4.91)　　　　　(−8.33)

Part B: NYSE Stocks

6) $\left(\dfrac{R}{M}\right)_4 = 0.988 + 3.293 \left(\dfrac{P}{O}\right)_4 - 1.819 \left(\dfrac{S}{O}\right)_4$ 　　　　$\bar{R}^2 = .125$
　　　　　(139.90)　(10.60)　　　　　(−4.93)

7) $\left(\dfrac{R}{M}\right)_1 = 0.989 + 1.667 \left(\dfrac{P}{O}\right)_1 - 1.955 \left(\dfrac{S}{O}\right)_1$ 　　　　$\bar{R}^2 = .092$
　　　　　(159.60)　(6.42)　　　　　(−7.78)

Part C: American Stock Exchange Stocks

8) $\left(\dfrac{R}{M}\right)_4 = 1.110 + 1.348 \left(\dfrac{P}{O}\right)_4 - 0.531 \left(\dfrac{S}{O}\right)_4$ 　　　　$\bar{R}^2 = 0$
　　　　　(33.69)　(1.21)　　　　　(−0.35)

9) $\left(\dfrac{R}{M}\right)_1 = 1.010 + 1.342 \left(\dfrac{P}{O}\right)_1 - 5.078 \left(\dfrac{S}{O}\right)_1$ 　　　　$\bar{R}^2 = .113$
　　　　　(40.72)　(1.83)　　　　　(−4.33)

^{a} R_i is the ratio of the price of the ith issue at the end of the quarter to its price at the beginning; M is the corresponding value of the Fisher combination link relatives covering all NYSE stock; P_i represents the gross purchases, S_i the gross sales, and H_i the end-of-period dollar holdings of the stock in the quarter by all funds covered; and O_i is the amount of the stock outstanding as of the end of the quarter. The subscripts 4 and 1 represent, respectively, the fourth quarter of 1967 and the first quarter of 1968. $\bar{R}^2$ is the coefficient of determination adjusted for degrees of freedom, and the numbers in parentheses under the regression coefficients represent t values. Regressions (2) and (4), using initial rather than terminal holdings, would be respectively,

$$\left(\dfrac{R}{M}\right)_4 = 1.019 + 3.142 \left(\dfrac{P}{O}\right)_4 - 0.984 \left(\dfrac{S}{O}\right)_4 - 0.316 \left(\dfrac{H}{O}\right)_4$$

and 　　$$\left(\dfrac{R}{M}\right)_1 = 0.997 + 1.455 \left(\dfrac{P}{O}\right)_1 - 2.112 \left(\dfrac{S}{O}\right)_1 - 0.089 \left(\dfrac{H}{O}\right)_1$$

To avoid undue complexity, the i subscripts are deleted in the table.

Appendix Table 4-4

QUARTERLY REGRESSIONS RELATING MANAGEMENT
INVESTMENT COMPANY PURCHASES AND SALES OF
INDIVIDUAL STOCKS TO PREVIOUS TRADING AND
TO PRICE BEHAVIOR OF ISSUE
(Fourth Quarter, 1967–First Quarter, 1968^a)

All Stocks Combined	

1) $\left(\dfrac{P}{O}\right)_1 = 0.007 + 0.511 \left(\dfrac{P}{O}\right)_4 - 0.025 \left(\dfrac{S}{O}\right)_4$
   $\qquad\;\; (7.61)\quad(12.94)\qquad\qquad(-0.52)$
   $\bar{R}^2 = .228$

2) $\left(\dfrac{P}{O}\right)_1 = -0.032 + 0.425 \left(\dfrac{P}{O}\right)_4 + 0.034 \left(\dfrac{S}{O}\right)_4 + 0.021 \left(\dfrac{R}{M}\right)_4$
   $\qquad\;\; (-4.47)\quad(9.60)\qquad\qquad(0.68)\qquad\qquad(5.29)$

   $\qquad\quad + 0.018 \left(\dfrac{R}{M}\right)_1 + 0.016 \left(\dfrac{H}{O}\right)_1$
   $\qquad\qquad (3.30)\qquad\qquad(1.24)$
   $\bar{R}^2 = .263$

3) $\left(\dfrac{S}{O}\right)_1 = 0.006 + 0.208 \left(\dfrac{P}{O}\right)_4 + 0.406 \left(\dfrac{S}{O}\right)_4$
   $\qquad\;\; (6.85)\quad(5.99)\qquad\qquad(9.67)$
   $\bar{R}^2 = .248$

4) $\left(\dfrac{S}{O}\right)_1 = 0.039 + 0.141 \left(\dfrac{P}{O}\right)_4 + 0.287 \left(\dfrac{S}{O}\right)_4 - 0.002 \left(\dfrac{R}{M}\right)_4$
   $\qquad\;\; (6.33)\quad(3.72)\qquad\qquad(6.69)\qquad\qquad(-0.65)$

   $\qquad\quad - 0.034 \left(\dfrac{R}{M}\right)_1 + 0.051 \left(\dfrac{H}{O}\right)_1$
   $\qquad\qquad (-7.42)\qquad\qquad(4.80)$
   $\bar{R}^2 = .323$

^{a} R_i is the ratio of the price of the ith issue at the end of the quarter to its price at the beginning; M is the corresponding value of the Fisher combination link relatives covering all NYSE stock; P_i represents the gross purchases, S_i the gross sales, and H_i the end-of-period holdings of the stock in the quarter by all funds; and O_i is the amount of the stock outstanding as of the end of the quarter. The subscripts 4 and 1 represent, respectively, the fourth quarter of 1967 and the first quarter of 1968. $\bar{R}^2$ is the coefficient of determination adjusted for degrees of freedom, and the numbers in parentheses under the regression coefficients represent t values. To avoid undue complexity, the i subscripts are deleted in the table.

Appendix Table 4-5

SELECTED REGRESSIONS BETWEEN TRADING BEHAVIOR
OF PACE-SETTING MANAGEMENT INVESTMENT
COMPANIES IN FIRST QUARTER OF 1968 AND OTHER
COMPANIES IN SECOND QUARTER[a]

1) $\dfrac{(FP)_{i2}}{D_i} = 0.013 + 0.555 \dfrac{(LP)_{i1}}{O_i}$
$\quad\quad\quad\;\;$ (7.22)$\;\;$ (3.04)
$\bar{R}^2 = .047$
$N = 167$

2) $\dfrac{(FP)_{i2}}{O_i} = 0.007 + 0.590 \dfrac{(LP)_{i1}}{O_i} + 0.556 \dfrac{(FP)_{i1}}{O_i}$
$\quad\quad\quad\;\;$ (3.69)$\;\;$ (3.59)$\quad\quad$ (6.27)
$\bar{R}^2 = .227$
$N = 167$

3) $\dfrac{(LP)_{i2}}{O_i} = 0.001 - 0.002 \dfrac{(FP)_{i1}}{O_i}$
$\quad\quad\quad\;\;$ (5.18)$\;\;$ (−0.45)
$\bar{R}^2 = 0$
$N = 927$

4) $\dfrac{(LP)_{i2}}{O_i} = 0.001 - 0.002 \dfrac{(FP)_{i1}}{O_i} + 0.050 \dfrac{(LP)_{i1}}{O_i}$
$\quad\quad\quad\;\;$ (4.95)$\;\;$ (−0.45)$\quad\quad$ (2.09)
$\bar{R}^2 = .003$
$N = 927$

5) $\dfrac{(FS)_{i2}}{O_i} = 0.010 - 0.201 \dfrac{(LS)_{i1}}{O_i}$
$\quad\quad\quad\;\;$ (8.47)$\;\;$ (−0.97)
$\bar{R}^2 = 0$
$N = 167$

6) $\dfrac{(FP)'_{i2}}{O_i} = 0.009 + 0.795 \dfrac{(LP)'_{i1}}{O_i}$
$\quad\quad\quad\;\;$ (4.53)$\;\;$ (4.56)
$\bar{R}^2 = .156$
$N = 108$

7) $\dfrac{(FP)'_{i2}}{O_i} = 0.008 + 0.770 \dfrac{(LP)'_{i1}}{O_i} + 0.195 \dfrac{(FP)'_{i1}}{O_i}$
$\quad\quad\quad\;\;$ (3.45)$\;\;$ (4.46)$\quad\quad$ (1.94)
$\bar{R}^2 = .178$
$N = 108$

8) $\dfrac{(LP)'_{i2}}{O_i} = 0.0004 + 0.007 \dfrac{(FP)'_{i1}}{O_i}$
$\quad\quad\quad\;\;$ (4.28)$\;\;$ (1.56)
$\bar{R}^2 = .002$
$N = 934$

9) $\dfrac{(LP)'_{i2}}{O_i} = 0.0004 + 0.007 \dfrac{(FP)'_{i1}}{O_i} + 0.017 \dfrac{(LP)'_{i1}}{O_i}$
$\quad\quad\quad\;\;$ (4.20)$\;\;$ (1.54)$\quad\quad$ (0.71)
$\bar{R}^2 = .001$
$N = 934$

10) $\dfrac{(FS)'_{i2}}{O_i} = 0.0004 + 0.001 \dfrac{(LS)'_{i1}}{O_i}$
$\quad\quad\quad\;\;$ (2.73)$\;\;$ (0.32)
$\bar{R}^2 = 0$
$N = 934$

[a] In Eqs. 1 to 5, the pacesetters, or leaders, are defined as the twenty-five investment companies with highest growth rates in the first quarter of 1968 of those companies with a market value of common stock over $15 million; in Eqs. 6 to 10 they are the ten investment companies with highest growth rates of companies with a market value of common stock over $50 million. $(FP)_i$ and $(LP)_i$ are the gross volume of purchases of the ith stock by the followers and leaders; $(FS)_i$ and $(LS)_i$ are the corresponding gross volume of sales; O_i is the number of outstanding shares; and the subscripts 1 and 2 represent the first and second quarters of 1968. $\bar{R}^2$ is the coefficient of determination adjusted for degrees of freedom; N is the number of stock issues used as observations; and the numbers in parentheses under the regression coefficients represent t values. Only stock issues for which the first independent variable in an equation had a nonzero value were included in that regression.

Appendix to Chapter Five

Appendix Table 5-1
CUMULATIVE ABNORMAL RETURN OF PURCHASES
AND SALES BY MUTUAL FUNDS, 1958–1967

Risk class (beta coefficient) and period	Months subsequent to purchase									
	1–3		1–6		1–12		1–18		1–24	
	Purchase	Sales	Purchase	Sales	Purchase	Sales	Purchase	Sales	Purchase	Sales
					A. Performance Measures					
1958–1959										
.4–.8	5.1	6.5	1.2	4.4	5.3	3.1	0.8	−0.7	−0.0	−1.1
.8–1.2	2.1	2.4	2.8	−1.1	−1.0	−1.1	−1.6	−1.3	−3.1	−2.2
1.2–1.6	6.1	−1.0	4.4	−2.9	−0.2	−3.4	−1.8	−2.9	−2.5	−4.3
1.6–2.0	17.1	15.8	11.1	4.5	8.0	3.2	2.3	5.0	−1.6	−1.6
1964–1965										
.4–.8	4.5	−6.8	6.6	0.7	5.2	−1.5	2.9	−3.6	1.7	−4.4
.8–1.2	−17.5	−6.1	−7.0	−0.4	−1.7	−2.0	−5.1	−3.0	−5.2	−3.0
1.2–1.6	2.2	−7.7	2.1	4.2	4.4	−0.2	1.9	0.7	0.5	0.8
1.6–2.0	36.5	−2.6	23.2	15.4	17.1	4.1	6.6	15.4	8.0	16.9
1966–1967										
.4–.8	−6.3	−10.9	−5.4	−3.2	−6.8	−5.4				
.8–1.2	−1.6	−17.1	1.2	−12.5	−7.2	−12.5				
1.2–1.6	5.5	−27.1	1.7	−20.2	−8.1	−18.6				
1.6–2.0	23.2	−13.7	8.3	−19.0	−7.3	−38.4				

Appendix Table 5-1

CUMULATIVE ABNORMAL RETURN OF PURCHASES
AND SALES BY MUTUAL FUNDS, 1958–1967 *(Continued)*

B. Number in Sample

Risk class (beta coefficient) and period	1–3		1–6		1–12		1–18		1–24	
	Purchase	Sales	Purchase	Sales	Purchase	Sales	Purchase	Sales	Purchase	Sales
1958–1959										
.4–.8	563	470	563	470	563	470	563	470	563	470
.8–1.2	1,499	1,019	1,497	1,018	1,495	1,018	1,495	1,018	1,495	1,018
1.2–1.6	812	592	812	591	811	591	811	591	811	591
1.6–2.0	205	118	205	118	205	118	205	118	205	118
1964–1965										
.4–.8	1,150	1,174	1,150	1,174	1,150	1,174	1,150	1,174	1,150	1,173
.8–1.2	2,256	1,901	2,256	1,899	2,256	1,899	2,255	1,898	2,253	1,897
1.2–1.6	1,247	1,033	1,246	1,033	1,244	1,026	1,239	1,021	1,239	1,021
1.6–2.0	323	238	323	238	323	238	323	238	323	238
1966–1967										
.4–.8	1,096	1,417	1,094	1,410	662	940				
.8–1.2	1,966	2,347	1,964	2,346	1,208	1,554				
1.2–1.6	1,048	1,215	1,041	1,208	748	894				
1.6–2.0	357	372	357	370	234	278				

Appendix Table 5-2

CUMULATIVE ABNORMAL RETURN OF PURCHASES
OF MUTUAL FUNDS BY HOLDING PERIOD, 1958–1967

Risk class (beta coefficient) and period	Holding period (months)	Months subsequent to purchase				
		1–3	1–6	1–12	1–18	1–24
1958–1959						
.4–.8	4–6	13.6	12.8	5.1	4.8	—0.1
	7 or more	4.5	0.4	5.3	0.6	—0.0
.8–1.2	4–6	0.4	0.3	1.3	—0.8	—1.1
	7 or more	2.2	2.9	—1.1	—1.7	—3.2
1.2–1.6	4–6	—8.5	—9.2	—7.9	—9.0	—7.8
	7 or more	7.1	5.4	0.3	—1.3	—2.2
1.6–2.0	4–6	36.4	11.2	12.2	1.7	—2.8
	7 or more	16.6	11.1	7.9	2.3	—1.6
1964–1965						
.4–.8	4–6	1.3	8.8	2.6	1.1	1.0
	7 or more	5.9	5.7	6.3	3.6	2.0
.8–1.2	4–6	—14.2	—0.8	1.1	—5.4	—4.9
	7 or more	—18.7	—9.2	—2.6	—4.9	—5.4
1.2–1.6	4–6	—7.1	—13.8	—5.4	—4.1	—0.4
	7 or more	5.8	8.2	8.0	4.1	0.9
1.6–2.0	4–6	52.8	12.4	25.8	13.5	23.3
	7 or more	28.0	28.5	12.3	2.8	—2.0
1966–1967						
.4–.8	4–6	—9.0	—12.7	—12.1		
	7 or more	—6.1	—4.7	—5.9		
.8–1.2	4–6	—11.6	—13.9	—18.0		
	7 or more	—0.5	2.7	—5.5		
1.2–1.6	4–6	7.9	—15.1	—21.3		
	7 or more	5.3	3.8	—5.9		
1.6–2.0	4–6	6.7	8.7	—8.3		
	7 or more	24.2	8.3	—7.2		

Appendix Table 5-3

INCREMENTAL ABNORMAL RETURN OF PURCHASES
OF MUTUAL FUNDS BY HOLDING PERIOD, 1958–1967

Risk class (beta coefficient) and period	Holding period (months)	Months subsequent to purchase				
		1–3	4–6	7–12	13–18	19–24
1958–1959						
.4–.8	4–6	13.6	12.1	−3.1	2.5	−10.4
	7 or more	4.5	−4.2	11.2	−8.8	−4.0
.8–1.2	4–6	0.4	−0.7	1.7	−5.3	0.6
	7 or more	2.2	3.1	−5.6	−2.8	−6.5
1.2–1.6	4–6	−8.5	−10.5	−6.6	−11.0	−5.3
	7 or more	7.1	4.1	−3.8	−4.7	−4.7
1.6–2.0	4–6	36.4	−13.1	13.0	−18.7	−13.5
	7 or more	16.6	6.2	4.5	−7.8	−10.4
1964–1965						
.4–.8	4–6	1.3	16.1	−3.0	−2.7	0.5
	7 or more	5.9	5.8	5.7	−2.4	−3.7
.8–1.2	4–6	−14.2	13.4	7.7	−13.8	−2.3
	7 or more	−18.7	3.7	7.5	−5.1	−5.2
1.2–1.6	4–6	−7.1	−19.1	1.7	−0.9	14.5
	7 or more	5.8	11.5	7.8	−4.1	−5.9
1.6–2.0	4–6	52.8	−22.0	38.4	−8.0	58.4
	7 or more	28.0	29.7	−2.8	−6.1	−13.8
1966–1967						
.4–.8	4–6	−9.0	−16.3	−11.5		
	7 or more	−6.1	−2.4	−8.2		
.8–1.2	4–6	−11.6	−17.2	−19.5		
	7 or more	−0.5	7.7	−11.5		
1.2–1.6	4–6	7.9	−34.9	−27.4		
	7 or more	5.3	0.7	−29.7		
1.6–2.0	4–6	6.7	11.5	−22.8		
	7 or more	24.2	−10.1	−29.7		

Appendix Table 5-4
NUMBER OF QUARTERLY PURCHASES ANALYZED
IN APPENDIX TABLES 5-2 AND 5-3

Risk class (beta coefficient) and period	Holding period (months)	Months subsequent to purchase				
		1–3	1–6, 4–6	1–12, 7–12	1–18, 13–18	1–24, 19–24
1958–1959						
.4–.8	4–6	38	38	38	38	38
	7 or more	525	525	525	525	525
.8–1.2	4–6	75	75	74	74	74
	7 or more	1,424	1,422	1,421	1,421	1,421
1.2–1.6	4–6	54	54	54	54	54
	7 or more	758	758	757	757	757
1.6–2.0	4–6	14	14	14	14	14
	7 or more	191	191	191	191	191
1964–1965						
.4–.8	4–6	227	227	227	227	227
	7 or more	923	923	923	923	923
.8–1.2	4–.6	459	459	459	459	459
	7 or more	1,797	1,797	1,797	1,796	1,794
1.2–1.6	4–6	263	263	261	259	259
	7 or more	984	983	983	980	980
1.6–2.0	4–6	68	68	68	68	68
	7 or more	255	255	255	255	255
1966–1967						
.4–.8	4–6	111	111	109		
	7 or more	995	983	553		
.8–1.2	4–6	222	222	213		
	7 or more	1,744	1,742	995		
1.2–1.6	4–6	150	150	148		
	7 or more	898	891	600		
1.6–2.0	4–6	36	36	35		
	7 or more	321	321	199		

Appendix to Chapter Six

Appendix Table 6-1
COEFFICIENTS OF DETERMINATION DERIVED FROM
QUARTERLY REGRESSIONS RELATING RELATIVE STOCK
EARNINGS[a] ON INDIVIDUAL NYSE STOCKS TO DIVIDEND
PAYOUT AND RISK
(Selected Quarters, March, 1958–March, 1968)

Quarter of stock purchase	Year of subsequent earnings				
	Current	1 year	3 years	5 years	8 years
3/1958	.008	.026	.005	.006	.101
6/1958	.008	.037	.004	.007	.106
9/1958	.010	.019	.002	.004	.085
12/1958	.020	.002	.007	.002	.062
3/1959	.008	.006	.002	.007	.013
6/1959	.012	.016	.008	.002	.005
9/1959	.011	.019	.010	.003	.004
12/1959	.007	.013	.011	.004	.004
3/1960	.009	.011	.001	.019	.018
3/1964	0	.035	.058		
6/1964	.002	.034	.057		
9/1964	.003	.041	.042		
12/1964	.002	.042	.027		
3/1965	.014	.053	.041		
6/1965	.012	.050			
9/1965	.014	.045			
12/1965	.002	.012			
3/1966	.002	.006			
6/1966	0	.003			
9/1966	.003	0			
12/1966	.005	0			
3/1967	.006	0			
6/1967	.014				
9/1967	.023				
12/1967	.020				
3/1968	.001				

[a] The ratio of subsequent earnings to initial price for individual stocks divided by the corresponding market ratio.

Appendix Table 6-2
STANDARD ERRORS OF ESTIMATE DERIVED FROM
QUARTERLY REGRESSIONS RELATING RELATIVE STOCK
EARNINGS[a] ON INDIVIDUAL NYSE STOCKS TO DIVIDEND
PAYOUT AND RISK
(Selected Quarters, March, 1958–March, 1968)

Quarter of stock purchase	Year of subsequent earnings				
	Current	1 year	3 years	5 years	8 years
3/1958	.66	.73	.86	.71	.80
6/1958	.62	.64	.83	.69	.79
9/1958	.60	.61	.80	.69	.76
12/1958	.60	.69	.70	.68	.74
3/1959	.52	.84	.76	.68	.79
6/1959	.47	.84	.78	.68	.77
9/1959	.49	.90	.78	.67	.80
12/1959	.66	1.02	.79	.68	.84
3/1960	.94	1.10	.71	.78	.76
3/1964	.55	.59	.71		
6/1964	.47	.58	.70		
9/1964	.46	.57	.66		
12/1964	.50	.55	.65		
3/1965	.53	.59	.62		
6/1965	.51	.54			
9/1965	.52	.53			
12/1965	.50	.56			
3/1966	.48	.60			
6/1966	.48	.60			
9/1966	.49	.60			
12/1966	.58	.58			
3/1967	.58	.64			
6/1967	.58	.59			
9/1967	.58				
12/1967	.58				
3/1968	.74				

[a] The ratio of subsequent earnings to initial price for individual stocks divided by the corresponding market ratio.

INDEX

INDEX